PRIVATE ENVIRONMENTAL GOVERNANCE

MICHAEL P. VANDENBERGH
Professor and David Daniels Allen Distinguished Chair in Law
Vanderbilt University Law School

SARAH E. LIGHT
Mitchell J. Blutt and Margo Krody Blutt Presidential Professor
Professor of Legal Studies & Business Ethics
The Wharton School, University of Pennsylvania

JAMES SALZMAN
Donald Bren Distinguished Professor of Environmental Law
Bren School of Environmental Science & Management, UCSB
School of Law, UCLA

CONCEPTS AND INSIGHTS SERIES®

FOUNDATION PRESS

860 Blue Gentian Road, Suite 350
Eagan, MN 55121
1-877-888-1330

Published in the United States of America

ISBN: 978-1-63659-694-5

To Linda and Patrick

M.P.V.

To Chris, Max, and Mori

S.E.L.

To Ray and Patty

J.E.S.

PREFACE

The field of environmental law and policy is evolving and growing in importance as climate change, toxics, biodiversity, environmental justice, and other topics become increasingly central to public debates, classrooms, and careers. All three co-authors learned environmental law as a subfield of administrative law, with the central focus on the adoption of environmental statutes by Congress and their implementation through the courts and executive branch at the state and federal levels. We continue to believe that government has a critical—and in some cases the only—role to play in achieving national and international environmental goals.

But when working in government, in private practice, and in the academy, we have repeatedly encountered forms of environmental governance that do not fit within the traditional government-focused conception of environmental law. For each of us, our experiences taught us that many of the important forms of environmental protection were occurring outside of the standard government-focused model. These other forms of governance were not always successful, but they were a central, and largely overlooked, aspect of the daily practice of how to address environmental challenges. In short, in an era of partisan gridlock in Congress, when new federal pollution control statutes are difficult to adopt and the Supreme Court has narrowed agencies' ability to adapt their existing statutory authorities to new problems, the public environmental law model is especially incomplete. It does not explain what lawyers, managers, and advocates have actually been doing to address climate change and many other important environmental problems.

This book reflects our view that understanding environmental law and policy today requires a focus on governance, not just government, and an expanded view of the available actors, actions, and conceptual frameworks needed to address environmental challenges. Consider that a private certification standard addresses the sustainable harvesting of 20% of the fish caught for human consumption around the world. Environmental, social, and governance (ESG) investing has become a widely adopted and hotly contested approach. Environmental supply chain contracting requirements are used by 80% of the largest companies in seven of the major global sectors. More than 300 of the largest companies in the world have committed to using 100% renewable power. Private conservation organizations in the United States have protected an area the size of Utah from development. Environmental lawyers, business managers, and advocates are heavily engaged in each of these private environmental governance (PEG) initiatives. Put simply, environmental protection in the 21st century cannot be understood (or taught) without these stories.

To be sure, PEG is not always effective or a substitute for public governance. But it is clear that many environmental practitioners are using PEG tools in their everyday practice. This book is designed to help them succeed by providing an introduction to the tools, actors, and theory of PEG.

The book is divided into three parts. Part I introduces PEG. It wrestles both with the ways that PEG reflects the major themes and issues of environmental law and policy, and its different interactions with existing barriers to public governance. Part I also addresses many of the risks of PEG, including greenwashing and the potential for undermining support for public governance. Part II addresses a cluster of climate-related subject-matter areas in which PEG has played a central role: climate change, the energy transition, climate change adaptation, and climate change justice. Part III examines the application of PEG to a set of broader environmental challenges, such as toxic chemicals, waste, water, land conservation, and natural resource management.

We wrote this book to be as user friendly as possible. It is not intended to be a treatise or casebook but, rather, a text that can be read with interest from cover to cover. Depending on teaching needs, each chapter is written as largely stand-alone so that it can be assigned on its own or in a different order than is presented in the book.

To ensure the text reads easily, we have minimized the use of footnotes. There is little worse than reading legal scholarship where your eyes have to bounce back and forth between text and citations like watching competitive pickleball. As a result, we have only provided footnotes for references in the text that cannot easily be found through an internet search. If you cannot find a particular source, feel free to reach out to the authors through Professor Sarah E. Light at Wharton (lightsa@wharton.upenn.edu) or Professor Michael Vandenbergh at Vanderbilt (michael.vandenbergh@vanderbilt.edu). To make the book as teacher-friendly as possible, we have also written an Instructor's Manual, available through Foundation Press. We also have provided a supplemental reading list at the end of the text. The reading list includes many of the sources that we relied on for the text as well as additional sources for readers who want to take a deeper dive into PEG.

We are grateful for the review of chapters and concepts by Linda Breggin, Mark Cohen, Jonathan Gilligan, and Will Martin. We are thankful for the student research assistance of Michael Alessandro, Jennifer Cole, Carrigan English, Ash Gillis, Molly Gray, Jackson

Ferrell, Jackie Lewis, Faith Lowery, Aaron Megar, Patti Moore, Kate Richardson, Paul Schwartzentraub, Ethan Thorpe, and Dan Vickers. Some of the text was adapted from material published in earlier sources by the authors, and those sources are included in the list of Supplemental Readings at the end of the book.

Professor Light's work was supported by the Legal Studies and Business Ethics Department of the Wharton School and the Climate Center of Wharton's ESG Initiative. Professor Salzman's work was supported by the UCSB Bren School of Environmental Science & Management. Professor Vandenbergh's work was supported by the Vanderbilt Dean's Fund, the Sally Shallenberger Brown EELU Program Fund, and his 2022 Andrew Carnegie Fellowship from the Carnegie Corporation of New York. The statements made and views expressed in this text are solely the responsibility of the authors.

M.P.V.
S.E.L.
J.E.S.

October 2023

SUMMARY OF CONTENTS

PART III. PEG IN ACTION: TOXICS, WASTE, WATER, AND NATURAL RESOURCES

TABLE OF CONTENTS

PART II. PEG IN ACTION: CLIMATE AND ENERGY

PRIVATE ENVIRONMENTAL GOVERNANCE

Part I
TOOLS AND CONCEPTS

Chapter 1

AN INTRODUCTION TO PRIVATE ENVIRONMENTAL GOVERNANCE

I. Why Study Private Environmental Governance?

Just over 50 years ago, a flurry of laws launched the modern era of environmental protection. The Clean Air Act, Clean Water Act, Endangered Species Act, and other innovative statutes created a powerful set of tools to clean up and protect the nation's environment. This dynamic period, though, was brief. By the 1990s, increased partisanship had set in; environmental initiatives in Congress had slowed to a dribble. Yet public concern over environmental protection remained strong as new kinds of environmental threats took center stage—from climate change and microplastics pollution to agricultural runoff and toxic chemicals.

As government efforts slowed, other groups stepped forward. It turned out that when it came to environmental protection, Washington, D.C., and state capitals were not the only places that mattered. Around the country and the globe, managers of civic and advocacy groups, corporations, investors, universities, and other organizations began to develop new ways that they could address environmental problems. The result was an explosion of *private environmental governance* (PEG).

PEG complements, spurs, and even competes with government environmental laws, policies, and programs. In many respects, PEG has become one of the most effective and exciting aspects of environmental protection in the 21st century. To put it bluntly, you cannot understand the range of environmental protection efforts that really matter today unless you understand PEG.

If this seems an exaggeration, consider the following. When you eat some fish, perhaps a Filet-o-Fish at McDonalds or a filet bought at a Whole Foods grocery store, the fish was probably from a fishery regulated by a private certification organization such as the Marine Stewardship Council. If you bought some furniture at IKEA or lumber at Home Depot, the wood likely came from forests certified for sustainable timber management. If you bought an LED light bulb at Walmart, you were part of the store's shift to promoting LED bulbs for households, which has led to annual carbon emissions reductions greater than the reductions from any major industrial sector. If you borrowed money from one of the six largest national banks in the

United States, the bank you borrowed from likely had adopted climate-conscious lending practices that bar lending to some large carbon-emitting projects. If you participated in an effort to preserve a local forest, you may have worked with a private non-profit organization that purchased or placed a conservation easement on the land. In doing so, you were participating in a form of PEG that has protected an area as large as the state of Utah.

These actions, and thousands of others, are shifting behavior and in many cases leading to significant environmental protection. These are all private initiatives, and it is well past time for students and practitioners of environmental law and policy to broaden their understanding of environmental protection strategies. Environmental laws, of course, are important but so too are actions by private actors. Accounting for PEG can not only unlock a more nuanced understanding of the tools available to solve environmental problems, but also identify legal and business risks and opportunities that were unimaginable decades ago.

To be sure, these approaches are controversial. Critiques abound from the left that private action does not go far enough, smacks of "greenwashing," or validates a market system that caused the problem in the first place. And more recently, critiques on the right argue that "woke" firms engaging in PEG (or more broadly, in ESG—environmental, social, and governance initiatives) are straying too far from their profit-maximization mandates. We will explain and address these critiques throughout the book. Whichever side of this debate you support, though, realize that both critiques spring from the common understanding that PEG represents an important development.

This Chapter provides an introduction to the concept of PEG, explains why it is a subject worthy of study, and offers three brief cases to highlight issues that make this young field both exciting and challenging.

II. What Is PEG?

When the authors of this book took introductory environmental law courses in the 1980s and 1990s, the courses were taught as part of administrative law, focusing on the constitutional authority for environmental statutes, the processes, functions, and review of agency regulations, and enforcement of government requirements. International environmental law courses focused on the agreements among nations and the activities of the United Nations and other international governmental organizations. This focus on the role of governments was entirely appropriate at the time—roughly two dozen major U.S. environmental statutes were adopted from 1970 to 1990, and many international environmental agreements were adopted and new bodies created such as the UN Environment Program. If you wanted to understand environmental law and policy, government was the place to look.

Although accurate thirty years ago, this focus presents a huge blind spot today. Government laws, policies, and programs still remain at the core of environmental law and policy—the passage of the Inflation Reduction Act in 2022 puts the federal government back into the climate conversation. But the center of balance has shifted in the United States and around the globe. *Private actors* now perform important traditional environmental protection functions, a shift from purely public governance to governance that includes PEG. At the global level, the growing role of private actors has been described as a type of transnational governance, but sometimes private actors play an important role within the borders of any one country. We focus in this book on both the domestic and international levels and use the term PEG.

Many early PEG innovations began with efforts to protect natural resources and have impressive results to show for it. Today, roughly 60% of all seafood caught for human consumption in U.S. fisheries is certified to a private sustainability standard developed after international processes failed to produce meaningful treaties. Almost 15% of all temperate forests are subject to a similar private certification standard, also developed after unsuccessful international treaty negotiations. Vibrant markets exist in ecosystem services, stream and wetlands mitigation. Project finance lenders that provide more than 70% of the loans used for large power plants and other projects around the world follow the Equator Principles, a private standard requiring environmental investigations and disclosures.

More than 80% of the largest companies in the world require their suppliers to meet environmental standards even though governments typically do not require companies to do so. These supply chains matter—Walmart recently worked with the World Wildlife Fund, the Environmental Defense Fund and other environmental advocacy groups in a commitment to reduce its worldwide supply chain carbon emissions by a billion tons by 2030, an amount comparable to the annual emissions of Germany or Japan, the sixth and seventh largest emitting nations. Roughly half of all residential construction in the U.S. is subject to the U.S. Green Building Council's LEED standard, a private measure designed to reduce energy use and carbon emissions and improve air quality in buildings. Something big has been going on.

A simple definition cannot capture all the forms of PEG that have emerged in the last several decades. For purposes of this book, we view PEG as occurring when private organizations play the standard-setting, implementation, monitoring, enforcement, funding, and/or adjudication roles traditionally played by government actors to address environmental concerns. The subject matter of these actions may include taking steps to reduce pollution and other environmental harms, to conserve common pool resources, or achieve more equitable distributions of environmental harms and benefits. These efforts may take place in the absence of government intervention, or they may take place alongside it.

You may notice that this definition does not consider intent. As we shall see throughout the book, there are many reasons private actors may protect the environment. PEG may arise from efforts at branding ("We are the green company!") or risk management. It may be in response to social media pressure or demands from employees. Or it may stem from the fact that it is no longer sufficient for a company, university, or other organization to have a legal license to operate. These organizations now need a social license to operate. Or it may be a combination of all of these and others. The key question is whether it leads to improved environmental protection.

A simple example regarding a company's actions on climate change makes this clear. At the outset, the company may reduce its carbon emissions because of motivations from within the organization. It may find that reducing its carbon footprint reduces energy costs or reduces the risk it faces from climate change, so it has direct economic incentives to reduce emissions. It may find that recruiting, retaining, and motivating employees requires a good reputation on climate change. An investment firm might face pressure not only from its employees, but also from individual investors and pension funds, or it may own such a broad portfolio of shares in different firms and industries that it sees reducing the systemic risks of climate change as being in its interest (this common owner concept is an interesting one that we will return to in Chapter 8).

In addition to internal drivers, the company may be motivated by outside pressure. In some cases, the pressure may arise from advocacy groups or coalitions of advocacy groups and firms that participate in collaborative initiatives, such as Climate Action 100+, which uses information and investor pressure to induce the largest-emitting firms to make climate commitments. The company may have investors, lenders, or insurers who threaten not to do business with the company or to change the management of the company unless it reduces emissions. It may have corporate or retail buyers of its products or sellers of raw materials that favor emissions reductions. If the company is a retailer, it may respond to customer demand that arises from individual consumer purchases or organized boycotts. A company also may not only be a recipient of pressure for carbon emissions reductions, but it may apply pressure to other companies through supply chain contracting requirements. If the company is in the financial sector, it may use investment screens or engagement, lending policies, insurance policies, or similar steps to put pressure on other companies to disclose and reduce emissions.

Not surprisingly, strong parallels exist between public and private governance on pollution and natural resource management. For most of the areas subject to major federal pollution control statutes—water, air, toxics, hazardous waste management—a parallel private governance program has arisen. The same is true for natural resource management areas, such as biodiversity and ecosystem protection, and the sustainability of forests and fisheries. Similarly, many of the tools or instruments commonly used by governments—prescriptive standards, information disclosure, tradable permits, and others—have PEG parallels. For instance, some governments have adopted carbon taxes; but so have Microsoft and many other global firms, which use an internal cost of carbon emissions when making management decisions. Statutes and regulations rely on prescriptive standards, but PEG initiatives also impose prescriptive standards through collective standard-setting such as the LEED green building standards or through including environmental terms in supply chain contracts, commercial loan agreements, and commercial lease agreements.

A. Why Focus on PEG Now?

Why has PEG emerged in the last few decades? Part of the motivation is due to the longstanding partisanship and stalemate in national politics. It's just hard to pass new environmental laws. This is not to say it is impossible—yet even the Inflation Reduction Act passed by the slimmest of margins and efforts (to date unsuccessfully) have followed to repeal some of its key provisions. Policy advocates looking for new options to achieve environmental protection thus turn to PEG tools in subject matter areas where the environmental problem is difficult for governments to regulate. Examples include global commons issues that make enforcing international agreements on sustainable fisheries or timber harvesting so challenging.

Climate change has been described as the beast of all global commons problems, and much of the growth of PEG has occurred around efforts to accelerate climate change mitigation and adaptation. The rapid expansion of carbon requirements in global supply chain networks may be one way to bypass the inability of nations to reach adequate international agreements through the U.N. Framework Convention on Climate Change—if a company operating in one country is motivated to reduce its supply chain emissions, it can extend an emissions requirement and compliance assistance to its suppliers around the world without regard to national boundaries or the need for international agreements.

In the deeply contested policy environment (a recent poll concluded that climate change is the most polarized issue in the U.S.), PEG potentially offers private sector solutions that bypass partisan gridlock and solution aversion. To take one example, because of powerful agricultural lobbying efforts, most environmental laws contain exemptions for farming activities. This makes it difficult to regulate agricultural nutrient and pesticide runoff. PEG requirements are beginning to emerge, though. These efforts take advantage of the fact that retailers and food processors are sensitive to their reputations among consumers and investors and can play a role in improving the practices of farmers. PEG initiatives also can bypass concerns about government intrusion into households and reduce energy use from the household sector.

B. Is PEG Real?

Environmental groups have often been suspicious of corporate environmental initiatives and, let's be clear, sometimes for good reason. One problem is that PEG cannot reach some companies and some industry sectors. Many companies highly value the social license to operate, but some do not. Chester Bowles, the head of the price administration during the New Deal era, memorably said that 20% of industry will comply with the law no matter what, 5% will only comply if forced to do so, and the companies in the other 75% will comply only if they think that the noncompliant 5% will not get away with violating the law. PEG programs can influence the environmental performance of many companies, but they do not have the coercive ability to use the powerful civil and criminal sanctions that government agencies can use. So, when a company, industry sector or type of environmental problem is dominated by those who refuse to act, we can expect PEG programs to fall short. An example is an effort to develop a certification and standards system to protect tropical fish. The system used a sustainable fish label to harness the environmental concerns of aquarium shop customers and to create pressure on the fishing industry. The fishing industry consisted of many small harvesters around the globe that were immune to pressure and hard to target, so the effort collapsed.

Private "green" standards can fall short if some of the standards are inadequate or counterproductive. For instance, competition between private certification standards for sustainably harvested timber could confuse consumers, who may not be aware that one standard developed by environmental groups is much more protective than the other developed by timber interests. In other words, if a private standard was developed to serve the interests of a particular industry sector or group, the standards could simply be anticompetitive or serve other vested interests rather than promoting sustainability.

A related concern is that relying on companies to provide what government has traditionally provided—protection of the environment and other forms of public welfare—may undermine support for government programs. This is sometimes called negative spillover, and it could happen in two ways. If companies engage in greenwashing—announcing pro-environmental steps that create a positive image but are insufficient or not implemented—they could undermine the perceived need for (and public support for) government action. Similarly, the use of advocacy group resources to stimulate PEG initiatives could leave fewer resources for advocacy efforts with legislatures, government agencies, and courts.

Remember, too, that laws not only steer behavior but also serve an expressive function. They signal which ideas society thinks are important. Critics of PEG worry that relying on the private sector for environmental protection could signal that pursuing private interests through markets is more important than pursuing public interests through democratic processes and government action. If over-consumption induced by the market economy is the key problem, these critics worry that private governance will implicitly validate the market economy in the eyes of the public and undermine the value of collective, government actions.

Finally, can you trust what the companies report? The emission and effluent data that companies provide regulatory agencies must be accurate or they risk civil and even criminal sanctions. But how do we know whether the reported greenhouse gas reductions of BigOil Corp. or supply chain management claims of RetailGiant, Inc. are accurate? Few companies are willing to open their books to the public, much less to skeptical environmental groups.

These concerns are most often voiced by environmental advocates. Business leaders have their own concerns. Some argue that economic efficiency is best achieved by forcing companies to focus only on shareholder profits and that companies should be discouraged or prevented from pursing social or environmental goals beyond compliance with public laws. The famous Milton Friedman quote that "the social responsibility of business is to increase its profits" captures this idea. In this view, if regulation is needed, government should do it. Companies should stick to what they do best: making money for their shareholders.

It is worth noting that many business leaders have begun to take a different approach in recent years—one that focuses on promoting long-term value for all stakeholders (including employees, customers, the local community, and the environment), not just profits for shareholders. We will examine these objections and this debate over corporate purpose in more detail in Chapter 5.

And finally, there is a new critique of PEG grounded in part in a concern about profit maximization, but not necessarily subscribing to the view that governments should regulate to protect the environment either. Beginning in 2021, more than a dozen state governments have adopted laws that prohibit financial institutions (including banks, asset management firms, and in some cases, insurance companies) that engage in environmental, social and governance initiatives (ESG), including PEG initiatives, from doing business with their state or municipal governments.[1] The sponsor of Florida's law argued it was necessary to stand up against a "far left extreme agenda."

Ceres, a non-profit group that focuses on investor climate initiatives, responded by organizing a "Freedom to Invest" campaign designed to counter the 140-plus state anti-ESG bills. Empirical studies of such laws, most notably a study of Texas's law adopted in 2021, have demonstrated that these laws have actually raised the cost of borrowing or otherwise doing business substantially—on the order of between $300–$500 million annually. Many state legislatures have declined to adopt similar anti-ESG/PEG laws after concluding that doing so would be financially costly for their states. So despite the backlash against PEG and ESG—especially in the financial sector—these private governance initiatives are moving forward.

C. The Practice of PEG

Regardless of where you stand on debates about the strengths and weaknesses of PEG, private governance is undoubtedly becoming a common practice of many environmental lawyers, business managers, and advocates. There is no question that managers need to understand the forces that are leading to the adoption of PEG initiatives—both internal and external. Business managers are the

[1] ESG refers to the practice of business firms, particularly investors and financial firms, taking environmental, social, or governance factors into account in their decision making. There is some overlap between ESG and PEG. However, PEG is narrower than ESG both because it focuses only on environmental, rather than social and governance factors, and because it requires that the private actions be some form of governance, rather than encompassing any effort to manage environmental risks.

decisionmakers about how to adopt, implement, and comply with these new private initiatives.

For lawyers, companies increasingly seek legal counsel from law firms on their environmental performance beyond simply regulatory compliance. A recent study found that almost all the largest law firms in the U.S. disclose that their lawyers practice in PEG-related practice areas. The same growth is happening in the non-profit world. Lawyers working for the Environmental Defense Fund, the World Wildlife Fund, the World Resources Institute, Ceres, the U.S. Green Building Council, the Forest Stewardship Council, and other organizations focus much of their time on PEG. Lawyers working as in-house counsel for companies, institutional investors, lenders, and insurers have seen a rapid escalation in interest in environmental, social and governance, socially responsible investing, and corporate social responsibility issues (known as ESG, socially responsible investing (SRI), and corporate social responsibility (CSR)).

If business firm managers are making decisions about whether to engage in PEG, what do lawyers do in the PEG field? A lawyer for an advocacy group might advise the group on the legal risks of naming-and-shaming campaigns directed at companies or products and might provide guidance on designing the procedures and substantive standards for a new certification system. An in-house counsel at an institutional investment firm might review new private standards for disclosing climate risks and develop a policy for corporate disclosures and new investments. An in-house counsel at a bond rating agency might develop policies on how to develop and deploy environmental, social and governance ratings in ways that comply with government securities laws around the world.

A lawyer in a law firm might advise private sector clients on all these issues. A leading environmental lawyer in Seattle describes her practice as consisting largely of private governance. In training sessions for other lawyers, she describes her role as "the 5 C's": commitments, communications, contracts, codes of conduct, and compliance.[2]

- *Commitments* includes counseling clients about whether to commit to emissions reduction goals and other environmental targets (for example, committing to be "net zero" in carbon emissions by a particular date).
- *Communications* includes counseling clients on the information that the company discloses to the public

[2] Lauren A. Hopkins, Beveridge & Diamond, "Private Climate Governance" presented at the American Bar Association Conference Climate Change in the West: Land, People, Markets and Law (June 18, 2021).

and internally to its employees. Many companies are under pressure not only to disclose environmental information to federal, state, and local agencies, but also to private organizations like the Global Reporting Initiative and CDP. A common saying among lawyers who practice in the PEG area is that "disclosure anywhere is disclosure everywhere," so inconsistencies in reporting requirements among multiple reporting platforms can make adequate reporting a challenge.

- *Contracts* includes counseling, drafting, and litigating over the environmental terms in procurement policies, supply chain contracts and other agreements. Large companies increasingly include of pollution disclosure and reduction requirements in their supply chain contracts. The work on this topic also includes environmental investigations and terms in commercial real estate sales and leases, mergers and acquisitions, commercial lending, and insurance agreements.
- *Codes of Conduct* includes counseling clients on the drafting, formation, and implementation of internal firm environmental, health, and safety policies. Well-drafted and implemented policies can improve environmental performance, reduce brand risks, and reduce the risks of civil and criminal penalties if violations occur.
- *Compliance* includes counseling clients on how to meet internal and external private codes of conduct and other standards. It also includes responding to enforcement actions and dispute resolution proceedings arising from private certification standards.

III. Three Examples of Private Environmental Governance

Even though PEG has grown rapidly in the last two decades and many environmental lawyers now engage with PEG issues on a daily basis, PEG remains a less studied area than traditional public environmental law and policy. Thus it is easy to overlook the many ways that private organizations perform the functions of and use similar tools as public governance. We provide three brief examples from the pollution control and natural resource management areas to highlight the complex relationship between private and public governance and the challenges this creates. We will explore all of these issues later in the book.

A. Fisheries: The Marine Stewardship Council's Certification and Labeling System

The story of how a private organization, the Marine Stewardship Council (MSC), emerged to set the standard for almost 20% of all fish caught for human consumption around the world provides insights into the procedures and tools of PEG and the gap-filling role that PEG is playing on natural resource management at a global scale. Over-fishing in international waters is one of the most difficult natural resource governance problems. More than 70% of all major fisheries are over-exploited, and open-ocean fisheries are often used as the classic example of the tragedy of the commons, in which each country or company has an interest in extracting as much of the resource as possible because they get all the benefits of the resource but share the costs with others (see Chapter 2). In the case of wild-caught fish in open ocean fisheries, countries and companies have incentives to catch far more than the sustainable yield from any one fishery. After all, they reason, if they don't catch the fish then another vessel will. Overfishing has important effects on the ability to feed the global population: fish and seafood are a significant source of animal protein for over half of the world's population, and developing countries are particularly reliant on this source of protein.

The governance story begins with extensive negotiations among nations in the 1980s that failed to achieve an international agreement to address overfishing. The World Wildlife Fund (WWF), a global non-governmental conservation group, played a leading role in advocating for laws to promote more sustainable fisheries, but it and other conservation groups were unable to push national governments to reach an adequate international agreement or induce adequate enforcement of national and international standards.

Unilever, a multinational corporation, was the largest seller of fresh fish in Europe in the 1990s, but it was at risk of losing its fish supply and was facing increasing reputational pressure from environmental advocacy groups and consumers about its role in the depletion of global fisheries. In Germany, consumers were threatening to boycott Unilever's fish products, and the environmental campaign slogan was "no fish, no fish sticks."

Once it was clear that the traditional United Nations-sponsored process would not yield an effective international agreement, WWF and other conservation groups turned their attention to promoting sustainable fisheries directly with the seafood industry, recognizing that Unilever and other leading seafood companies and retailers still faced reputational and consumer pressure. In short, although national governments lacked the incentives to engage in a collective process to reduce unsustainable harvests, advocacy groups and industry were motivated to do so. Rather than doubling down on advocacy with national and international governments, WWF and Unilever turned to each other and started a process that ultimately created a new organization with its own private set of sustainable fisheries standards.

The new organization, which emerged in the late 1990s, was the Marine Stewardship Council (MSC), a non-profit, non-governmental standard-setting organization with an office in London, a board of directors with representatives from advocacy groups, industry, and other stakeholders, and initial funding from private philanthropies including the Packard Foundation. As we shall see in Chapter 11, a similar process had occurred with the Forest Stewardship Council (FSC), as well as other collaborative private efforts focused on farmed fish, mining, palm oil, cotton, sugarcane, soy, and beef.

The MSC is the leading standard-setting and standard-promoting organization with the overall goal of sustainable ocean fisheries. MSC allows fisheries that are certified to use an MSC eco-label indicating that the item was produced from a fishery that meets the standards. Fish processors and retailers hope to gain a market advantage by using the MSC label. Once you start to look for it, you will see that the label is used on products ranging from the McDonalds Filet-o-Fish and the wild caught fish sold at Walmart and Sam's Club to fish served at Red Lobster restaurants.

The MSC functions much like a government agency set up to regulate fisheries. Instead of accountability to political officials who in turn are accountable to the public through democratic processes, the board and managers of the MSC are accountable to the stakeholders in the process. These include advocacy organizations, seafood companies, retailers, and others. Each of these stakeholder groups is represented on the MSC board of trustees and on a stakeholder council, and the governance of the organization occurs through resolution of the competing interests of these groups. In the absence of support from the key environmental and industry stakeholders, the effort collapses, but both groups have an interest in seeing it succeed so long as a better government option (for their particular interest) does not exist.

Setting up an organization to certify sustainable fisheries is one thing; determining what counts as sustainable is quite another. Over an 18-month period in the late 1990s, MSC developed a set of criteria to define a sustainable fishery, a process for assessing a fishery's compliance with the criteria and for auditing fishing companies, and a program for certifying the fishery so retailers can use the MSC label for their products. In addition to philanthropic support, ongoing funding for MSC is generated by selling the labeling rights to seafood products. This, of course, creates some additional risk of capture.

The MSC certification process for a fishery relies on transparency and a deliberative process to establish its legitimacy. The process begins with MSC notifying relevant parties that it will assess the fishery and inviting the parties to provide comments and information. The MSC then assembles a scientific team to study the fishery and publish assessment results in reports posted on the MSC website. The standard is then developed and submitted to board of trustees. The process also allows appeals by the fishing industry and conservation groups to contest the score that the scientific team assigned to the fishery. To review the appeals, the MSC has formed a group of independent lawyers who are asked to determine whether the standard is arbitrary or unreasonable. After the fishery has been certified, the fishery is subject to surveillance audits on an annual basis as well as a reassessment every five years.

If the process functions as designed, determinations of sustainable yield are made in a transparent way based on the recommendations of a technical advisory board of scientists and a stakeholder council. A standard is then announced, and a public comment process follows. After the comments are processed and responded to, the MSC board of trustees considers and adopts the standard.

If this sounds like a government regulatory process, it should. MSC's procedural provisions for standards development and certification process closely track the core elements of the federal Administrative Procedure Act's requirements for notice-and-comment rulemaking. The MSC steps include a public notice of a proposed standard, a comment period, responses to comments by the standard-setting organization, transparent deliberations by the decision-making body followed by public announcement of the new standard, and appeal rights, along with a process for future revisions. Enforcement of the standard also tracks government agency processes, with third-party auditors performing the enforcement role, decertification as the sanction, and a dispute resolution process. Thus a first insight for PEG is that private and public governance have strong similarities. Private actors may perform many of the same functions as public agencies and have developed similar procedures and tools.

The MSC process also suggests that accountability can derive not just from the incentives created by government enforcement of public laws in public courts, but from other motivations. Even in the absence of national or international laws, some companies may promote sustainable fisheries out of concerns over brand reputation, the future supply of fish, retail customer preferences, corporate supply chain procurement requirements, and investor pressure.

The MSC story also shows the dynamic between public and private governance. MSC was created to fill a gap in public governance. The failure to adopt an international agreement to limit overfishing created the space for a private governance organization to step up. Seven years after the MSC was founded, its approach was largely followed by the UN Food and Agriculture Organization (FAO) in its guidelines for certification and eco-label programs for wild-caught ocean fish. They establish the minimum procedural and substantive requirements of certification and eco-label programs for wild-caught ocean fish. In short, national governments were unable to act collectively, spurring development of the MSC which, in turn, prompted national governments to respond through a UN organization by setting minimum standards for fisheries certification that were largely modeled on the MSC standards.

MSC has a mixed success rate and its share of critics. For starters, the success of certification depends on the demand for sustainably harvested fish by corporate and retail buyers. They need a business reason to justify the premium paid for certification. Some government officials see MSC as a threat to their prerogative to set fisheries standards. Advocacy groups have argued that the MSC standards may be insufficient, pointing to weaknesses in the standards and in their enforcement. Conversely, some seafood product companies argue that the MSC sets standards that are too stringent and should be relaxed.

The MSC example demonstrates that private certification organizations sometimes emerge to address global commons problems like the harvesting of fish from open-ocean fisheries, and it shows the complex interactions between public and private governance. We turn next to how private governance has played a role in responding to an even more difficult global commons problem—climate change.

B. Fossil Fuels: Bank Policies and the Leasing of Federal Lands in Alaska

The Arctic National Wildlife Refuge (ANWR) has been the subject of political controversy for over four decades. Spanning 19 million acres of northeastern Alaska, ANWR has been praised as America's Eden, one of the last wild places in the country. Although the refuge is home to various species—including polar bears, caribou, and migratory birds—it is also the site of one of the most coveted commodities in the global economy over the last century: a major untapped reservoir of oil.

ANWR has been the center of a fifty-year-long political battle between two competing interests. One side has argued for the development of ANWR's oil fields, citing the importance of oil to the Alaskan economy and the national security implications of relying on imported oil. The other side has argued that ANWR should not be developed, but preserved, noting the refuge's iconic status and support of local wildlife and the subsistence lifestyle of Alaskan Native Tribes.

Initially deemed the Arctic National Wildlife Range, 8.9 million acres of Alaskan wilderness were originally set aside as public land in 1960. Twenty years later, in December 1980, the Alaska National Interest Land Conservation Act (ANILCA) renamed the range to the Arctic National Wildlife *Refuge* (ANWR) and expanded the area to include 19 million total acres. Of this 19 million, most was set aside as wilderness area and was not to be developed. One area particularly promising for oil and gas development, the 1.5-million-acre Coastal Plain, could not be developed without express authorization from Congress. Bills to authorize drilling have been introduced in every Congressional session over the last three decades—an annual test of development and environmental political power in Washington—but all failed. Until 2017.

That year, Congress authorized a leasing program in ANWR's Coastal Plain. The program required the Department of the Interior to sell the rights to at least one lease by 2021. An auction for approximately 1 million acres of the 1.5-million-acre Coastal Plain was held in the last days of the Trump Administration.

This auction, though sought for decades by oil and gas interests, was a failure. No major oil companies participated, and half of the leases went unsold. Most of the private sector had lost interest in developing the ANWR oil fields. What caused this lack of private interest?

Perhaps surprisingly, banks and financial institutions provided a large source of resistance to the private development of the ANWR oil reserves. Environmental advocacy groups began targeting the carbon footprint of major banks' loan portfolios in the early 2000s, using naming-and-shaming campaigns directed at retail customers, employees, and corporate executives in the C-suite (the chief executive officer, chief financial officer, etc.). For instance, Wells Fargo was the subject of a boycott for its role in financing the Dakota Access Pipeline. In addition, BlackRock and other major institutional investors, which own a large percentage of the shares of the major banks, began pushing for the companies they invest in to disclose climate risks and plan for a decarbonized economy. The banks also may have assumed that a carbon tax or other government regulation of fossil fuels was somewhere on the horizon.

Although it is difficult to single out the influence of any one of these drivers, the response of the banks to pressure to reduce the carbon footprint of their lending was prompt and widespread. In the months leading up to the ANWR auction, numerous banks and financial institutions around the globe began to adopt policies against lending to Arctic oil development projects. Between 2017 and 2021, the number of financial institutions with these policies grew from zero to over fifty. Notably, among these were all six major U.S. banks.

The banks' policies were swiftly met with opposition. A group of Republican legislators wrote a letter to President Trump describing the policies as "discriminat[ion] against the American energy sector," and suggesting that federal funding be withheld from any bank implementing an anti-drilling policy. Agreeing with the legislators, the Office of the Comptroller of the Currency issued a proposed rule to prohibit banks from declining to lend to entire sectors or sets of projects like Arctic drilling. Despite these pressures from the government, the banks did not budge, instead sticking to their anti-drilling policies.

Politicians attributed the failure of the ANWR leasing plan to the banks' anti-drilling policies, but what led to the growth of the bank anti-drilling policies in the first place? In large part, the banks were responding to pressure from advocacy groups (such as the Sierra Club) and large financial asset management companies. The banks also faced pressure on behalf of the Gwich'in people, whose way of life could be substantially altered by the development of ANWR. Following the 2017 boycott of Wells Fargo over the Dakota Access Pipeline, banks may have been especially sensitive to criticism from environmental advocacy and indigenous groups.

To be sure, other factors played a role in the banks' decision-making. First, the leases themselves were far from a surefire investment, coming with an array of risks. One such risk was from future government regulation. With the auction occurring days before President Biden took office, companies were unsure of how the new administration would handle these leases. In fact, one of Biden's first acts in office was to issue an executive order halting all development in the Coastal Plain. His administration later withdrew the Office of the Comptroller of the Currency's proposed rule that would have prohibited banks from declining, on a blanket basis, to lend to Arctic drilling projects. Nor was it certain the projected amounts of oil in the oil fields were accurate. The only seismic survey was conducted in the late 1980s. In light of this uncertainty paired with the already-high cost of Arctic drilling, it is possible that some lenders would not have wanted to make this investment even without the pressure felt from advocacy groups and institutional investors. Private governance initiatives thus were used as a tool to push banks away from financing the Alaska projects that would generate large carbon emissions, but it is unclear if these tools will be enough to dissuade banks from pursuing other investments that are more obviously lucrative.

What is clear is that this case turns the standard model of public environmental governance on its head. Polling indicates that substantial majorities of the U.S. population want government to do more to address climate change. The Trump administration favored the position of oil companies in the name of jobs and energy security. Perhaps surprisingly, in the case of ANWR, a range of private sector actors—lenders, investors, and advocacy groups—provided effective environmental protection over the objections of government officials. If the polling is accurate, these private sector actors pursued what the public wanted government to do more than did government officials.

So why should an environmental lawyer or business manager care? The story of ANWR makes clear that it is no longer sufficient for environmental lawyers, business managers, advocacy groups, and policymakers to focus only on the processes of federal, state, and local governments. To succeed in the environmental law and policy field, they need to understand the drivers, vocabulary, and tools of PEG, as well.

C. Energy Efficiency: Advocacy Groups and Retailers Accelerate the Uptake of LED Light Bulbs

We rarely think of households as major polluters, but they account for roughly 39% of all electricity demand in the United States. In total, U.S. households emit as much carbon as all the sources in all the countries of South America combined. Even small changes in household energy use and carbon emissions have globally significant implications. Among all types of sources, the electricity generation sector is the second leading source of carbon emissions in the U.S. (after the transportation sector). So reducing household electricity use can be as important as directly regulating greenhouse gas emissions from entire industry sectors.

For much of the 20th century, electricity consumption closely tracked GDP. As the economy grew, not surprisingly, people used more electricity. But this close relationship changed in the early 2000s. For the first time since the Second World War, per capita household electricity use levelled off. By 2010, it had begun a sustained decline. Electricity consumption had decoupled from economic growth. What caused the major reduction in household electricity use?

Federal legislation surely played an important role. In 2007 Congress adopted the Energy Independence and Security Act, which increased energy-efficiency standards for light bulbs and appliances. The compact fluorescent light (CFL) bulbs that met the early federal standards were not popular with consumers, and CFLs were mostly sold through specialty retailers. Their high cost, unattractive light, and concerns about mercury in the bulbs limited their appeal. Despite limited initial consumer demand, in 2007 Walmart, working with the Environmental Defense Fund and other advocacy groups, began a campaign to market CFLs and place them in prominent locations in their stores. They also worked with suppliers to reduce prices. The campaign was a success. Walmart far exceeded its goal of selling 100 million CFL bulbs. CFLs used only 25% of the electricity of then-standard incandescent light bulbs, so the energy savings and carbon emissions reductions from replacing 100 million incandescent bulbs with CFLs was substantial.

CFLs remained unpopular with many consumers, though, and they got caught up in political partisanship. Congress prevented enforcement of the light-bulb standards in 2011. But, as we saw with the ANWR example, the story was not over. The traditional response would have environmental advocacy groups lobby for government reinstatement of the standards and industry groups lobby against it. Instead, light bulb manufacturers announced that they would continue to improve the efficiency of light bulbs, regardless of whether the government standards changed, and major retailers got on board.

Walmart introduced a program for light-emitting diode (LED) bulbs that mirrored its CFL program—but with an added incentive. Walmart announced that if a light bulb manufacturer could produce an LED bulb that generated attractive light and that Walmart could sell it for under $10, it would make the bulb its house brand and would promote it extensively. Walmart is the largest retailer in America, several times larger than Kroger and Target, its two closest competitors, so this was no small inducement. In 2013, Walmart made LEDs its house brand. Because LED bulbs require only 15% of the electricity of standard incandescent bulbs, Walmart's massive platform contributed to a remarkably fast uptake of LED bulbs by U.S. households. In 2017, LEDs outsold all other bulb types for the first time.

Whether or not you are a fan of Walmart or any other major retailer, the light bulb example demonstrates that public governance and private governance sometimes complement, rather than oppose, one another. Public governance took the early lead in changing consumer purchases of more efficient light bulbs; private governance stepped up when lightbulbs became part of the partisan political debate and public leadership for energy efficiency fell away.

The light bulb example also demonstrates that the effect of PEG on pollution can be indirect but dramatic. Sales of energy-efficient light bulbs helped drive a major decrease in per capita household electricity use. Less electricity demand meant less coal and gas burned to produce energy. The lawyers, business managers, environmental activists, and government policymakers who worked on light bulb efficiency contributed to one of the most important climate mitigation efforts of the last two decades. As with the other examples above, they worked in ways and drew on skills that do not easily fit in the traditional model of environmental law and policy.

IV. The Path Forward

In some respects, these case studies could not be more different—fishery management, oil drilling, and lightbulbs. But they all make clear the same basic point—PEG has become an increasingly important field whose requirements go beyond those imposed by governments. As a result, PEG poses substantial opportunities and challenges for environmental law and policy, as well as for those who practice in the field. When confronting an environmental or natural resource problem, asking the traditional question of environmental law and policy: "What can government do?" is no longer sufficient. The question now must be: "What can any organization do?" The organization best suited to a problem may well be government, but in the increasingly polarized, gridlocked policy world it may instead be an advocacy group, retailer, investor, lender, or some combination of these.

In the chapters that follow, we will explore more deeply what PEG is and how it affects environmental protection. Along the way, we will address the "What," "Who," and "How" of PEG. We will then turn to the "When, Whether, and Why"? By the end of the book, you will be able to answer these fundamental questions about PEG that influence the practice of modern environmental law and policy:

- What are the tools and subject matter areas addressed by PEG?
- What is motivating companies, advocacy groups, and other organizations to adopt PEG?
- What are the legal, social, and economic rules of the road that allow or require firms to engage in PEG, and what constrains their actions?

- What are the effects on environmental protection, natural resource management, and environmental justice?
- What are the interactions between public and private governance?

An old joke tells the story of a someone who comes across a person on their hands and knees searching for keys under a streetlight. The narrator joins in the search and, after a few minutes of failed searching, asks where the keys were lost. The person responds they are in the park across the street. When asked why the person is searching here instead of the nearby park, the person says "well, this is where the light is." Like most current practitioners, we started in the environmental field with the standard assumption that public authority is the only important driver of environmental law and policy. After years of practicing environmental law and managing organizations in government, the private sector, and the academy, though, we have realized that a lot of the action is happening across the street. This book shines the light in that park.

After reading this book, you will not look at environmental law and policy the same way. You will see the regulatory landscape through a broader lens, understanding how some common terms and concepts obscure important aspects of environmental protection and can shut down innovative thinking. And you will understand the emerging new terms used by experts in law, business and advocacy group management, and other fields—terms that can be a barrier to entry if they are not mastered. You also will become familiar with new tools to address pollution and natural resource problems, tools that are particularly useful for problems that have been the most resistant to government solutions over the last half century, including climate change, toxic chemicals, non-point source water pollution, fisheries depletion, deforestation, and others. You also will be better able to take a more informed, critical look at proposed environmental solutions and distinguish valuable PEG initiatives from those that are simply greenwashing. Put on your headlamps, and let's cross the street and get started.

QUESTIONS AND DISCUSSION

1. A common concern with PEG is the lack of accountability or sanction. After all, if Walmart had not met its goal of selling LED bulbs, it is not clear there would have been any consequence. No executives would have gone to jail; nor would the company have to pay any fines. Try saying, "I tried," to the IRS when failing to pay your taxes and see how that works out. Nor can we be certain about achievements. How do we know companies accurately report their environmental impacts? Do you trust companies to be truthful

when announcing environmental initiatives? What are some ways to address such a "credibility gap"?

2. Critics have argued that private standard-setting can undermine the ability of governments to act. In what ways do you think PEG initiatives could undermine government regulation of natural resources and pollution? Supporters of certification standards and other private governance approaches, in turn, reply that they fill gaps when government has been unable to act and actually make government action more likely. In what ways might they promote government action on these issues?

3. A company forces its supplier to reduce carbon emissions, but it only does so because it knows that it will save money. In its industry, reducing carbon emissions will require reducing energy use, and that will allow the company to demand lower prices from its suppliers. Has it engaged in PEG? Why or why not?

4. Should banks be permitted to decline to lend to entire sectors of the economy like fossil-fuel intensive projects on their own? Or should they be required to engage in individualized assessments of borrower and project risk? Is there a difference between declining to lend to fossil-fuel intensive projects and other sectors that might be subject to naming-and-shaming or consumer boycotts like gun manufacturing, or cigarettes?

5. In the press conference announcing passage of the 2023 Florida law targeting financial companies with ESG goals, the sponsor, House Speaker Paul Renner, stated:

> The goal of corporate activism seen in environmental, social, and governance investing is to bypass democracy and transform capitalism to serve an ideological agenda. We will not allow these martini millionaires to push unsafe and unsound investment practices that silence debate in the political process, weaken investment strategies for Florida retirees, and discriminate against any individual's beliefs.[3]

How would you reply to Representative Renner's concerns about companies engaged in PEG initiatives?

6. When are PEG initiatives likely to fill gaps in public environmental laws and government programs?

---

[3] Florida Governor Press Office News Release, *Governor Ron DeSantis Announces Legislation to Protect Floridians from the Woke ESG Financial Scam*, February 13, 2023.

Chapter 2

PERSPECTIVES ON ENVIRONMENTAL GOVERNANCE

In seeking to solve environmental problems, all too often decision makers (whether lawyers, regulators, or business people) look first to the law or other governance approaches rather than to the problem itself. To be sure, the law often creates the framework within which environmental problems can be resolved. But one cannot intelligently apply the law or design a private solution without also understanding the forces that created the problem in the first place.

Consider, for example, the seemingly different environmental threats described in the introduction to Chapter 1—climate change, crashing fisheries, toxics. All of these problems share a similar trait, of course, since they directly relate to environmental protection. But the similarities run far deeper. Regardless of whether the actor trying to solve an environmental problem is government, business, or an environmental group, the *underlying* drivers of the problems are the same. Protecting the environment is hard for everyone. This Chapter explains why.

We will explore the fundamental challenges of environmental governance. What are the basic causes of environmental harms? Why are environmental problems so difficult to manage? And what conceptual frameworks can we use to shape our response?

It is no exaggeration to say that these core questions resonate throughout the entire field of environmental protection, irrespective of whether solutions are coming from the public or private sectors. Just as Neo in the classic movie, *The Matrix,* comes to understand that his world is composed of just 1's and 0's, so, too, must we come to understand that there are just a few discrete drivers of environmental harms. Understanding these key drivers provides the critical first step in effective environmental protection.

I. Why Do We Have Environmental Problems?

Every major human settlement faces environmental challenges. And it has been so throughout history. The ancient cities of Babylon and Egypt, medieval cities of Paris and Beijing, and modern cities of Sydney and Flint have all confronted the challenge of water pollution. Pollution seems an inescapable result of dense populations, major industrial activity, or agricultural production, no matter the historic era. But why has this always been the case, despite best intentions? The simple economics principles described below help explain why.

Misaligned incentives underlie most environmental problems. While protecting the environment often provides a net benefit to *society*, the economic interests of the *individual* parties involved often can encourage harmful activities. Thus a basic challenge for environmental policy lies in understanding the reward structures of the parties and then changing incentives so that environmental protection reinforces rather than collides with the parties' self-interest. In the following examples, consider how costs and benefits are allocated.

- In the case of toxics, a company may choose voluntarily to reformulate its products in favor of more costly organic or more sustainably sourced materials, but it may end up raising its product prices and losing market share to cheaper alternatives if its competitors do not reformulate their products as well.
- A neighbor of a factory may be having constant sore throats because of particulate emissions, but the bother to her isn't worth the cost of bringing a lawsuit.
- All of her neighbors may have sore throats, too, but they can't seem to come together to negotiate with or sue the factory.

On its face, one might think that the market would automatically promote environmental protection. The most basic principle of economics, after all, is supply and demand. As the supply of a valuable good becomes scarce, its price rises. No one doubts that clean air and water are valuable. So shouldn't we expect that as they become scarcer their price should also rise, making it more expensive to pollute?

Yet this clearly does not happen in real life. The market has somehow failed, as it does when the company decides not to reformulate its products and the factory's neighbors can't come together to sue the factory. To correct these market failures and craft an effective response, we first need to understand the distortions at play.

A. Public Goods

Try to buy some clean air. Sure, you can buy real estate in the wilds of Alaska where the air is clean, but you own the land there, not the air. In fact, your neighbor can breathe it right after it blows through. It turns out that many environmental amenities, such as clean air and scenic vistas, are called *public goods*. Their benefits can be shared by everyone, but owned by no one. No one owns the air. No one can sell it or prevent others from using it.

The same is true for *ecosystem services*. Largely taken for granted, healthy ecosystems provide a variety of critical services. Created by the interactions of living organisms with their environment, these ecosystem services provide both the conditions and processes that sustain human life—purifying air and water, detoxifying and decomposing waste, renewing soil fertility, regulating climate, mitigating droughts and floods, controlling pests, and pollinating plants. Not surprisingly, recent research has demonstrated the extremely high costs to replace many of these services if they were to fail. Looking at just one ecosystem service that soil provides, the provision of nitrogen to plants, offers an example. Nitrogen is supplied to plants through both nitrogen-fixing organisms and recycling of nutrients in the soil. If nitrogen were provided by commercial fertilizer rather than natural processes, the lowest cost estimate for crops in the United States would be $45 billion; the figure for all land plants would be $320 billion.

The value of $320 billion is estimated by calculating replacement costs—what we'd have to pay to replace the ecosystem service of nitrogen fixing by other means. But what are these natural goods and services *really* worth? Perhaps surprisingly, in the eyes of the market they are not worth anything. We have no shortage of markets for ecosystem goods (such as clean water and apples), but the services underpinning these goods (such as water purification and pollination) are free.

Make no mistake, these environmental amenities have value—just ask yourself how much it's worth to you to breathe unpolluted air—but they have no *market* value. There is no market to exchange public goods such as ecosystem services and, as a result, they have no price. This explains the riddle of why pollution does not become expensive as clean air is "used up." Because there's no market for clean air or climate stability, there are no direct price mechanisms to signal the scarcity or degradation of these public goods until they fail. Hence, despite their obvious importance to our well being, ecosystem services largely have been ignored in environmental law and policy. Partly as a result, ecosystems are degraded.

B. Externalities

To make this more practical, assume that you own a chemical factory. When you balance your firm's financial books, you notice something odd. In figuring out your bottom line, you subtract your costs to operate (such as labor, materials, utilities, etc.) from the revenue you earn from selling your chemicals. But the pollution from your smokestacks does not reduce your bottom line. Your factory *is* causing real costs in the form of acid rain, smog, and reduced air visibility. But, as described above, because clean air is a public good you do not have to pay as you "use up" the clean air. It acts as a sink for your pollution at no cost. As a result, in seeking to maximize short-term economic gain, you do not consider the cost of your pollution. You can "overuse" the clean air and continue polluting. The costs from damage to forests, increased respiratory ailments, and reduced pleasure in clear vistas from your pollution are very real, but they are *external* to the costs you currently pay to operate. These costs are borne by the public and known as *externalities*.

An economist looking at this problem has a simple solution—"Just get the prices right!" If your factory has to pay for the external harm it causes, then it will pay for its pollution and likely reduce it. The process for forcing the factory to recognize environmental and social costs is known as *internalizing externalities* and reflects a basic lesson of economics—when we have to pay for something, we use less of it than if it is free. By internalizing externalities, we correct the market failure by charging for environmental harms and providing more accurate price signals to buyers.

This works both ways. Assume that you own a wetland beside your factory. The wetland provides a nursery for young fish to spend their first few months in relative safety before entering the adjacent river. The outdoors enthusiasts who fish along the river and the sporting good stores who sell fishing tackle all benefit from the services your wetland provides, but they don't pay you for them. While your factory's pollution generates *negative externalities*, your wetland provides *positive externalities*. The fact that you don't have to pay for the costs caused by your pollution removes any incentive to reduce pollution. Equally the fact that no one pays you for the wetland's benefits removes any incentive to conserve it rather than pave it over for a parking lot.

If all negative externalities were internalized—if all costs imposed on the environment were borne by the polluting party—then environmentally harmful products and processes would be relatively more costly and the market would reinforce environmental protection. Equally, if positive externalities were internalized—if benefits generated by ecosystem services such as flood control and water purification were paid for by the beneficiaries—then habitat conservation would be truly valued in the marketplace.

If you think this probably sounds too good to be true then you're right. In practice, a central problem is "getting the prices right." Even if the government had the authority to charge a factory for the damage its pollution caused, how much would that be? As with clean air, there are no markets for environmental harms, either; thus their costs must be estimated. And if a business seeks to incorporate its own negative externalities in its cost of operations, will it remain competitive with other firms that don't?

One of the key goals of environmental governance is thus to bring environmental externalities into the marketplace. We discuss PEG strategies to do this with payments for ecosystem services and certification standards in Chapter 11, and supply chain contracting in Chapters 8 and 10.

C. Tragedy of the Commons

Assume you have given up the difficult environmental management challenges of running a chemical factory and have turned to the simpler and bucolic life of a shepherd. Surely no environmental challenges will haunt you there, right?

Every morning you lead your flock of sheep to graze on the village common while you sit back and think big thoughts, blow on your pan pipes, and enjoy your bag lunch. So long as the number of sheep on the common remains small, the grass remains plentiful and the sheep contentedly munch away. Assume, though, that shepherds from over the mountain have heard of the wonderful grass in the common and bring their flocks. With each hour these sheep graze, there is less grass available for future grazing. In fact, you realize that this increased level of grazing will soon nibble the grass down to the roots, with the result of not enough forage in the future for anyone's flock, including your own. Yet you and the other shepherds will likely continue to allow your sheep to overgraze. Why?

The answer lies in the economic incentives. The more the sheep graze the fatter and more valuable they will be when they come to market. You could stop your flock's grazing, of course, to try and preserve the pasture for future days; but there is no guarantee your fellow shepherds will be similarly conscientious. In that case, you're a chump, sacrificing your own interests for no benefit. As a result, you may well encourage your sheep to graze *as much as possible*, and your neighbors will do the same. "Might as well get the grass in my sheep's tummies before it disappears in others'," you think. The result is individually rational in the short term—if the resource will be depleted, you might as well ensure you get your fair share—but collectively disastrous in the long term. It would be far better for each shepherd to restrain her flock's grazing, but seeking to maximize immediate economic gain ensures long term economic—and environmental—collapse.

This same phenomenon, known as *the tragedy of the commons*, can be identified in many open access resources, as farmers race to pump water from a shared underground aquifer, fishing boats with ever larger nets chase fewer and fewer fish, and wildcat drillers race to pump out oil as fast as they can. In each case, individually rational behavior is collectively deficient. Individuals' personal incentives work *against* the best long-term solution.

D. Collective Action and Free Riders

So what is to be done? Perhaps you could negotiate with all the shepherds and collectively agree to graze less. This may work when there are a handful of shepherds who all come from the same village. In fact, the Nobel prize winner Elinor Ostrom showed that in many communal property regimes around the globe local resource users have come together to manage water, grass, and lobsters sustainably over long periods of time.

But it becomes increasingly difficult to reach agreement as the number of shepherds increases (and more difficult still if they come from different places without shared cultural norms and informal means of enforcement). This obstacle is known as a *collective action problem* and is due to the increased transaction costs in negotiating solutions as the number of parties increases. At a certain point, it's simply too expensive and difficult to reach consensus agreement. To see this in action, try to decide on which movie to see or settle a restaurant check with more than four friends.

Perhaps, as a last resort, in frustration at the inability to agree on a common solution, some of you decide to stop grazing your flock so that the grass on the common can grow back. Noble intent, no doubt, but there is a risk that other shepherds will take advantage of your generosity and keep their sheep on the common. More food for their flocks, they may smirk. These shepherds benefiting from your sacrifice are known as *free riders*. A similar phenomenon might occur even if all the shepherds agreed to graze less. New shepherds might come in and start grazing all the time, free riding off of your sacrifice.

Do you see how companies that pollute may face a free-rider problem? It may be in the interest of all of the companies in an area to reduce pollution to protect the health of local populations, but any one company can outcompete the others by not reducing emissions when the others do. In the absence of an external authority or collective action by all of the companies, each company has an incentive to avoid reducing emissions, even if it is in the interest of all companies to do so.

Thus any solution to commons problems must overcome both the high transaction costs in reaching agreement among many parties (collective action) and counterproductive behavior by parties outside the agreement (free riders). Environmental law and policy has developed under the assumption that collective action is difficult and that government is the sole source of external authority, and that is often the case. But PEG initiatives have demonstrated that sometimes private organizations can address this by serving as the external authority or helping the companies act collectively. We discuss the role of employee initiatives in Chapter 7, shareholder pressure in Chapters 7 and 8, and certification schemes in Chapter 11.

II. Why Are Environmental Problems Difficult to Manage?

Understanding why we have environmental problems is a key first step in environmental management. After all, you can't figure out how to solve a problem if you don't know what the cause of the problem is. But even if you understand the nature of the problems, effective management faces a separate set of challenges. This section explores the main barriers to be overcome.

A. Uncertainty

In many respects uncertainty is *the* defining feature of environmental policy. Most environmental problems involve complex technical and economic issues. But decision makers rarely have anything approaching perfect knowledge when asked to make specific decisions. Certainty may come too late, if ever, to design optimal legal and policy responses. And most of us have an intuition not to act in the face of uncertainty, maintaining the status quo ("the devil we know") even if action is the rational choice.

In the context of climate change, for example, the detailed mechanisms of global warming are still only partly understood. Will increases in the earth's temperature lead to greater cloud formation, acting as a negative feedback to warming? Are measured temperature increases over the last century due to increased carbon in the atmosphere, the onset of an unrelated global warming trend, or a combination of the two? If atmospheric carbon dioxide concentrations continue to increase, what will the mean global temperature be in 20, 30, and 40 years, and what will this mean for sea level rise and local climates?

All of these questions bear directly on our decisions *today* to reduce emissions of greenhouse gases or introduce carbon taxes. The United Nation's Intergovernmental Panel on Climate Change has provided estimates based on the best judgment of over 2,000 scientists researching these issues from around the globe, but no one can claim one hundred percent certainty. They are simply the best projections we have.

Similarly in the case of using pesticides near drinking water sources, experiments may show that exposing mice to very high levels of a pesticide causes cancer. But we typically have little baseline data to understand what happens to humans exposed to the pesticide at everyday levels, orders of magnitude lower than those that harmed the mice. And mice, of course, aren't people, so perhaps the effects observed in mice would not occur in larger mammals.

Troubling levels of uncertainty are present when conserving natural resources, as well. Perhaps developers have proposed setting aside an acre beside a new shopping center to provide habitat for an endangered salamander population otherwise threatened by the shopping center's construction. Will an acre provide sufficient habitat for its survival? Is the main reason for the salamander population's collapse not loss of habitat but, rather, predation by cats? We do not always know enough about the salamander's life history or recent population declines to be certain, yet such information is critical to designing effective responses to proposed developments such as a new shopping center.

Another source of uncertainty lies in the complex interrelations among causes of environmental harms. Rather than resulting from a single, identifiable action, many environmental harms are caused by the cumulative effects of multiple actions. Addressing one cause may have little effect or, even worse, exacerbate another problem. Take the example of endangered salmon in the Pacific Northwest. Why are so many stocks collapsing? One can point to overfishing, damming of rivers, logging practices that lead to erosion and silt in the rivers, coastal pollution, and over-reliance on hatchery fish. To conserve and restore salmon populations, we must address most, if not all, of these causes. Yet there is enormous debate over which particular action will be most effective, not to mention the risk that solving one problem may cause another to appear somewhere else. Or consider acid rain. Did the emissions of a particular coal-fired plant in the Ohio Valley contribute to the acidification of a mountain lake in the Catskills? Most likely yes, but good luck figuring out *how much* harm it contributed and, therefore, how much its emissions should be reduced.

In fact, uncertainties over the magnitude of environmental problems, their causes, and future impacts bedevil management. What we would like to know as decision makers rarely approaches our actual knowledge. But if we do not understand well the current situation, then how can we predict the future impacts of our actions today? Does prudence dictate waiting until we have better information or taking early action in the face of potentially serious threats? Comfort with the status quo, no matter how flawed, runs strong in groups that benefit from business as usual.

In the climate change debate, for example, some industry-sponsored trade groups have argued that scientific uncertainty counsels prudence. The "problem" of global warming has not been rigorously established, they argue, and our limited knowledge of atmospheric physics severely restricts our ability to predict future temperatures or climates. And even if global warming is happening, there are enormous unknowns over how much warming will occur and at what rate. If the threat of global warming turns out to have been an exaggerated threat, then actions taken today to reduce fossil fuel consumption will have been an overreaction. Spending money to reduce fossil fuel use, it follows, may cause more harm than good because of increased unemployment and diversion of resources away from other worthy causes. The best response is more research and development. After all, how can one craft an effective policy without clearly understanding the problem we're trying to solve?

The obvious response to such arguments is that waiting for more certainty, if it ever comes, imposes costs of its own. In the face of a credible and significant threat, the opposing argument goes, we must act today so as to avoid the present and future harms (which may well be greater) imposed by delay. To employ a nautical metaphor, we should be bailing water out of our sinking ship as fast as possible, not standing on the deck studying the angle and rate of descent.

The same dynamic is at work in the examples of pesticides and endangered species. Delay while we study the toxicology of a pesticide may result in an increase in cancers that could have been prevented. Delay in the case of an endangered species may lead to greater understanding, but of a now-extinct species. Yet, as the voices of caution warn, overreaction imposes its own real costs in the form of higher prices and scarce public monies that could have been better spent elsewhere. In these and countless other examples, there are good reasons to wait and reduce the uncertainty, and good reasons to avoid potential future costs by acting now. Thus perhaps the first question of environmental management is how to act in the face of uncertainty.

There are two basic strategies to address this intractable problem. The first is to develop better information. A second is known as the *precautionary principle*. In its simplest form, the principle counsels caution in the face of significant but uncertain threats. As the Rio Declaration states, "Where there are threats of serious or irreversible damage, lack of full scientific certainty shall not be used as a reason for postponing cost-effective measures to prevent environmental degradation."

It's hard to argue against such an obvious rule of conduct, but people differ significantly over how the principle should be applied in practice. In its most extreme form, the principle would forbid any activity that potentially could produce significant harms, regardless of the likelihood that these harms may occur. The strategy, moreover, offers no help in the context of risk-risk choices, where every alternative poses significant risks, and the costs and delays involved in assessing those risks may be impractical. Yet one must still choose among them. Such risk-risk choices arise commonly in the environmental field, such as deciding whether to build a nuclear power plant or a natural gas-fired plant. There is no obvious "perfect" choice because each option poses environmental concerns and potential harms.

In the international context, the precautionary principle generally has been viewed as shifting the burden of proof from those who would challenge an offending activity to those who wish to commence or continue the activity. This shift in burden could shorten the time period between when a threat to the environment is recognized and a legal response is developed. In the climate change context, for example, the burden would fall on oil companies to establish that global warming is not a serious and credible threat before drilling new wells. In the salamander example, the developer would shoulder the burden of proving that the loss of habitat will not threaten the salamander's survival before clearing land for a mall. Chemical manufacturers would bear the responsibility of justifying that the use of particular pesticides would pose no significant health risks before allowing the pesticides to be sold and used.

A key difference between public and private environmental governance is speed. PEG initiatives often can respond much more quickly than governments to environmental problems with significant uncertainties. Government agencies are often constrained by statutory or regulatory standards for the level of scientific support and certainty necessary to promulgate a regulation or ban a chemical or action, as well as the time necessary to develop and adopt regulations and laws. In contrast, companies can put initiatives into effect very quickly in response to pressure from consumers, employees, managers, and investors. These groups may demand action and have little or no concern for uncertainties.

Companies are thus more nimble than agencies, but they are also more vulnerable to over-reaction or under-reaction in responding to calls for action that do not reflect considered judgments about risks, risk-risk tradeoffs, or costs and benefits. Consider, for example, how food companies should respond to consumer or NGO concerns about particular additives that are unregulated or lightly regulated, or about genetically modified plant ingredients.

Saying that a business fully complies with government regulations is often an inadequate strategy to manage uncertainties when pressure groups (or market opportunities) demand action now. We mentioned the social license to operate in Chapter 1. Naming-and-shaming campaigns may require companies to act in the face of incomplete knowledge ahead of government action (or considered inaction), and many companies appear to participate in PEG activities as a way to secure what we might call "brand insurance" against these kinds of possible but unpredictable events. This is particularly relevant for procurement policies and supply chain contract provisions, discussed in Chapters 8 and 10, and for the standards and certification systems discussed in Chapter 11.

B. Mismatched Scales

The boundaries of nature rarely track political or market boundaries. A map of the western United States shows states and counties with straight lines and right angles. Map the region's watersheds, ecosystems, or forests, however, and nary a straight line will appear. Ecological concerns were, not surprisingly, far from the politicians' and surveyors' minds when these legal jurisdictions were created, but the mismatch between natural and political scales poses difficult challenges for environmental management. Air pollution, water pollution, and wildlife certainly pay no heed to state (or national) borders, with the result that often the generator of the pollution is politically distinct from those harmed.

Acid rain was hard to control in the 1970s and 1980s because of a mismatch between environmental impacts and political jurisdictions. The costs of reducing emissions downwind were borne by those who received no benefit and, similarly, those benefiting from reduced pollution upwind did not have to pay for it. Midwestern power plants were far removed from the polluted lakes and forests of the Northeast and Canada. New York, Vermont, and certainly Canadian voters couldn't vote in Ohio or Pennsylvania. Thus those with the greatest cause for concern did not live in the areas where their concerns could be most effectively expressed through the local ballot box. Similar problems of scale are evident in wildlife protection, where draining or filling prairie potholes in the Great Plains, for example, may benefit the local farmers but imperil migratory birds from Mexico to Canada. Pumping carbon dioxide into the air may not seem significant to a company operating a coal-fired power plant in Montana, but to an islander on a low-lying Pacific atoll the prospects of sea-level rise are a good deal more unsettling.

As a result of these *geographical spillovers* across jurisdictions, transboundary environmental problems often pose the challenges of collective action (the high transaction costs to bring differing parties together), equity (ensuring that the parties enjoying the benefits of environmental protection also bear a share of the costs), and enforcement (monitoring compliance at a distance from the source of authority). This is as true with national as international environmental harms.

Mismatched political and natural boundaries also pose challenges of management authority. This is often expressed as a problem of federalism. Who should control pollution and natural resource management: local or national authorities? Locals are closer to the problems, often understand them better, and have to live with the consequences of the environmental policy. At the same time, if the problem is one of transboundary pollution, the locals don't live with the consequences of their pollution. Those downstream do. We discuss the strategy of payments for ecosystem services to overcome mismatched scales in Chapters 11 and 12.

A different type of mismatched scale problem can emerge when markets encompass multiple political jurisdictions. Imagine, for example, that in order to attract business Arkansas decides to lower its standards for air pollution. All else being equal, lower compliance costs for environmental regulations should translate into higher corporate profits. This not only poses a transboundary concern for the border states of Louisiana and Alabama; it also pressures states with similar industries, such as North Carolina, to lower their standards, in order to prevent industry relocation. The dynamic of local jurisdictions competing with one another by lowering environmental standards to attract industry is known as the *race-to-the-bottom*.

Realize, as well, that concerns over the race-to-the-bottom can not only pressure jurisdictions to lower their standards but can also chill efforts in states seeking to strengthen standards (because industry will threaten to relocate if their costs of regulatory compliance are increased). The same phenomenon can occur in the international context as well, as nations compete with one another for business investment.

The fact that companies choose their locations based in part on costs of doing business is indisputable. There is a strong debate, however, over the extent to which a race-to-the-bottom really occurs in the environmental field. For one thing, states can compete on many grounds, perhaps lowering tax rates or workplace safety requirements to attract business. Hence it's not a given that they would reduce environmental standards to attract industry.

Indeed, the race-to-the-bottom argument may be upside down. Because environmental quality is an important amenity, there's a strong argument that local jurisdictions are more likely to engage in a "race-to-the-top," competing for industry by offering *higher* environmental quality. The data on international industry relocation suggest that stringency of environmental regulation is less important to companies than proximity to markets, labor costs, raw material costs, political stability, etc. And this makes sense, since environmental costs are usually a small percentage of total business costs.

The race-to-the-bottom is not universal, but it is real. In those industries where environmental costs are relatively high, such as in the chemicals sector, there is evidence that companies have relocated with environmental compliance costs in mind. Perhaps more important, though, is whether regulators believe the race-to-the-bottom occurs, supported by fact or not, and act accordingly.

An important potential benefit of PEG compared to public governance is that many business firms, like ecosystems, operate independent of political jurisdictions/state lines. Walmart's decision to promote LED light bulbs does not stop at the county or state border. Its global supply chain policies extend beyond national jurisdictions.

Problems of scale occur in time as well as in space. Decisions must be made today that may prevent harm ten or twenty years from now or, indeed, in generations not yet born. Ozone depletion and climate change are two examples. CFCs (which are the major cause of stratospheric ozone depletion) and greenhouse gases we emit today will cause impacts over the next 50 years or longer. The same distributional asymmetry is at play here as with physical scale. The costs of refraining from an action fall on us today, while the benefits are enjoyed (most likely by others) far in the future. Yet these future beneficiaries can't express their preferences in today's voting booth or marketplace.

In the context of PEG, the temporal mismatch of long-term harms with the demand for short-term quarterly results can lead companies to act in environmentally harmful ways or to greenwashing. In other cases, PEG can allow retail customers, managers, employees and other to express preferences for intergenerational justice in ways that politicians in a polarized system seem unable to reflect. Some institutional actors, such as pension funds, may have a longer time horizon than most politicians or companies and can take a more patient (and potentially more environmentally responsible) investing approach.

C. Polarization

Political polarization—strongly opposing stances on political issues by individuals and political parties—can feel like the cranky uncle who comes to your family holiday dinner and causes trouble, but afterwards everyone is too embarrassed to talk about what happened. Family cohesion and planning have been disrupted, but no one wants to admit why. To understand why governments struggle to address many environmental problems, though, we need to understand the role of polarization since it plays a key role in calls for both more and less reliance on PEG.

Political parties have been taking opposing stances on policy issues for generations, so why is polarization a particularly important barrier now? In Congress, polarization has made it increasingly difficult to assemble the coalitions necessary to adopt major new environmental laws. The League of Conservation Voters (LCV) is an NGO that scores members of the House and Senate based on how they vote on environmental legislation. From 1970 through 1990, Democrats were more supportive of environmental laws (60%) than Republicans (40%), but not by much and the difference was stable. But LCV scores show that a major gap opened between Democrats and Republicans on major environmental legislation after 1990, and that gap has continued to widen over the following three decades. In recent years, only 10% or fewer of Republican members of Congress have supported new LCV-scored environmental laws versus 90% or more of Democrats. This doesn't leave any room in the middle for the compromises necessary for legislation.

Consider that Congress enacted more than a dozen major federal pollution control statutes between 1970 and 1990, but only one between 1991–2022. During this period overall public support for environmental protection remained roughly the same, so the post-1990 gridlock cannot be attributed to waning public support.

Instead, the constitutional design, sorting, and psychological factors have combined to make polarization a barrier to major new environmental laws. Let's begin with the constitutional design. Climate change is one of the most polarized issues in the U.S. Over 50% of voters support climate action, though, so why has major climate legislation failed? Shouldn't we expect majority support of voters to lead to new laws, as it did in the pre-1990 period?

Increasingly, the answer is no. The U.S. constitutional design over-weights the influence of conservative voters in rural states, who tend to oppose government climate action. Two Senators are elected from each state, which means that a low-population, rural—often more conservative—state has the same number of Senators as a populous, urban—often more liberal—state. The result is that roughly 18% of the U.S. population controls 50 votes in the Senate. Since the Senate has the power to confirm Supreme Court justices, voters in these low-population, rural states also have over-weighted influence on the Supreme Court. Because the Senate is skewed toward low-population, rural states, the Electoral College, which consists of one elector for each member of Congress, results in a skewing of the Executive Branch toward these voters as well. Politicians also have incentives to take extreme positions because of the effect of partisan primaries, where the voters are more polarized than the general public.

These constitutional barriers have existed for two centuries, but two additional factors have contributed to the legislative gridlock. The first is sorting. When substantial numbers of Republicans and Democrats lived in the same geographic regions and when both parties included liberals and conservatives, the over-weighting of small, rural states did not necessarily result in gridlock on environmental issues. Bipartisan compromises could occur between liberals and conservatives, and compromises did not signal defection from a political party. It was possible to be a Republican who supported new federal environmental laws, and it was possible to be a Democrat who opposed them. Compromises were policy trade-offs, not defections from the party or identity group. The result was bipartisan coalitions on more than a dozen environmental statutes.

In the last several decades, partisan sorting has resulted in fewer Democrats identifying as conservative and fewer Republicans as liberal. Geographic and social sorting also have occurred—liberals more often live in urban areas in coastal states and conservatives in rural or ex-urban areas away from the coasts. Social, cultural, and religious groups are much less likely to include both liberals and conservatives than in earlier decades. The result is that liberals and conservatives typically only interact with people who share their worldview.

Sorting also has occurred in the way people receive information and communicate within social groups. Far more than in the pre-1990 period, people get their news from sources that are only trying to reach a liberal or conservative audience, rather than a broad audience. Three networks dominated television in the 1960s and 1970s when the explosion in new environmental statutes began, and these networks only survived by reaching a broad audience. Today, liberals watch MSNBC and CNN, and conservatives watch Fox News, Newsmax, and OANN. Social media emerged in the 2000s and has had similar effects, creating closed information networks that only expose people to messages and messengers targeting their group, not those that might appeal across multiple groups.

The constitutional design and sorting would be a challenge on their own, but they interact with several features of human psychology to make it hard to build the support necessary for new laws. For instance, receiving information only from favored sources might not be such a big problem if more accurate and thorough communications about climate change could counter damage done by biased media. One might assume that receiving accurate information about climate change can improve support for climate action, but almost no research supports this. A thorough and accurate understanding of climate change does not reliably lead to climate policy support. Instead, people begin with a political ideology—our values and worldview about what the role of government should be in climate action—and a partisan identity—our affiliation with a political party—and then engage in motivated reasoning and confirmation bias. We seek out information that fits with our worldview and toss out conflicting information. For instance, climate skeptics report that they are twice as likely to closely follow science and technology news.[1] But they don't have an accurate view of climate science; they've simply focused on those isolated nuggets of information that support their view and dismissed all the rest.

Motivated reasoning and confirmation bias make it easier to persuade people to believe things that are not true and to resist new information. This is a problem for adopting new environmental laws because political and media elites who oppose these laws can send signals about what the members of their political groups should support and what they should reject.

One consequence is that people will deny that a problem exists or is serious when they do not like the anticipated solution. If liberals hear that the solution to climate change is more nuclear power, they express less concern about climate change. If conservatives hear that the solution to climate change is more government regulation, they express less concern about climate change. Because polling shows that over 70% of Republicans and more than half of Democrats believe that big government is a greater concern than big business or big labor, the aversion to government regulatory solutions is a particularly important barrier for environmental law. Leaders and lobbyists who oppose new environmental laws can simply characterize a new climate law as an example of big government.

People look to group leaders—politicians, media commentators, and celebrities—to learn what the beliefs and social norms of their groups are and determine how to align their policy stances with the stances of their groups. This effect is so strong that people form their policy support more based on cues from their group leaders than on what a policy actually says. For instance, when Republicans learn that other Republicans support X policy, they support X, but when

---

[1] ANTHONY LEISEROWITZ, ET AL., YALE PROJECT ON CLIMATE CHANGE COMMC'N & GEORGE MASON UNIV. CTR. FOR CLIMATE CHANGE COMMC'N, GLOBAL WARMING'S SIX AMERICAS IN MARCH 2012 AND NOVEMBER 2011, at 34 (2012).

they learn that other Republicans do not support X, they reject X, with little regard for the content of the policy. The same occurs with Democrats. In other words, their policy support is driven more by what they think their group supports than by reasoning to a conclusion about it. This is a barrier to environmental action when people in a group believe (often incorrectly) that most group members don't believe the climate change problem is serious or don't support government action to address it.

When we put these psychological factors together with the constitutional design and sorting of groups and information, we can see why polarization is such a strong barrier to government environmental action. In the 1970–1990 period, agreement could be reached on environmental policy because coalitions could form across party lines and members of both parties benefitted by being seen as solving problems. Media outlets catering to a broad audience reported favorably on major new environmental statutes. And politicians did not have to reject their partisan identity to support the legislation—compromise did not require stepping outside of their group.

But solutions are more difficult now when the signals from political and media elites suggest that their group does not believe in a problem or support a particular type of government solution. Now reaching a compromise involves risking exclusion from a valued social or political group. Politicians and media leaders have incentives to take polarizing positions. And core psychological processes enable polarizing leaders to have widespread effects on the public. When differences occur, they occur between groups, not within groups, and we all are susceptible to attributing good characteristics to those we consider to be in our group and bad characteristics to those in other groups. The product of this polarization is government gridlock on major environmental laws and a growing gap between the preferences of most people for environmental protection and the actions that governments can take.

Importantly, this polarization and government gridlock has led to greater calls for business and non-governmental organizations to step in and take a lead role in solving environmental problems. PEG has thus emerged to fill some of the gaps in public governance.

D. Who Has a Seat at the Table?

Companies' actions that affect the environment are, of course, subject to laws passed and enforced by the government. Rules determine how much Dimethyl Terrible a factory may emit into the air or whether development can be halted because of threats to the Furbish Frog. Even if we assume high compliance with environmental laws, that may not ensure high environmental protection. Why not?

Consider the six inch high jump.

The rules may be set at very low levels. Or most activities may be excluded from coverage. In both instances, and many others, interests that are affected by the rules may lobby Congress or agencies in favor of weak rules. So long as bribes are not involved and lobbying disclosure rules are followed, this is entirely legal. Regulated interests have just as much right to argue for weak regulations as environmental groups to argue for strong regulations.

One might argue that environmental interests are at a disadvantage because protected interests frequently do not have a voice of their own. We already have discussed the importance of future generations' interests in the preceding section on mismatched scales. If we could make use of a time-travel machine and bring them back from the future, they surely would have strong views on how decisions taken by us today will impact their health and welfare. Absent such science fiction technology, though, their theoretical interests can only be voiced by those in the present. This is sometimes described as a matter of "intergenerational equity."

Endangered species litigation is brought technically on behalf of an affected person (perhaps a researcher of the species) but in reality is brought on behalf of the species as well. It goes without saying, of course, that these entities cannot bring a lawsuit on their own behalf, much less appear in court. Proxies therefore must bring the litigation on their behalf.

This innovative inclusion of interests, however, poses its own challenges. Who should speak for the trees in the halls of Congress?

The challenge of whose interests are protected goes beyond humans versus nature. Some human interests seem to be much more protected than others. We discuss the challenge of environmental justice, protecting the environmental interests of poor communities, in the next section. Here, though, we consider a different question: Why are seemingly small private interests disproportionately powerful in the political arena?

"Public choice theory" provides one explanation. In brief, concentrated economic groups can focus their resources on lobbying Congress or an administrative agency to protect their own interests. This may take the form of erecting barriers to entry from competitors (such as limiting the number of liquor licenses in a community), distributing narrow subsidies (such as crop supports to sugar growers near the Everglades), or creating special protections (such as imposing tariffs or import restrictions on foreign steel).

Each one of these policies may well make the country worse off overall. So how do they happen in a democracy?

Parties that benefit from targeted policies or regulations will often form more concentrated and effective advocacy than the diffuse public interest that suffers. Sugar subsidies might make my taxes a penny more expensive and harm the Everglades restoration because of polluted runoff from sugar cane plantations, for example, but the injury to me is too small to warrant the cost and hassle of organizing with many others to oppose these policies. Public choice theory flows from these problems of collective action. Because it's much more difficult to organize diffuse public interests that are only marginally affected than concentrated interests that are directly affected, we can expect concentrated interests to dominate the regulatory and legislative process.

Perhaps surprisingly, the strong influence of business interests in government make PEG all the more important. PEG can be undemocratic, in the sense that actions by just a few major companies can significantly influence behavior but are untethered to government democratic processes. The Swedish retailer, IKEA, purchases about 1% of global timber. Its supply chain requirements arguably have as much or even greater influence on forest management as some forestry laws, but the requirements are not adopted by elected officials or agencies that report to elected officials. At the same time, IKEA faces pressure on climate and other environmental issues from its employees, customers, investors, lenders and insurers, and the communities in which it operates, just as politicians face pressure at the ballot box. In areas of the world where governments are not responsive to the preferences of their populations on environmental issues, PEG actions have the potential to be more responsive to those preferences than governmental actions because these pressures impose new, direct costs on the targeted entities. We discuss the drivers of corporate PEG climate change initiatives in Chapters 7 and 8.

III. Measuring Success

Once we have identified the misaligned incentives of free riders, externalities, polarization and other barriers to environmental protection, we still need to decide what we are managing for. We are managing for a cleaner environment, of course, but environmental protection inevitably requires trade-offs. How can we know which trade-offs to accept?

Imagine, for example, that a company is trying to decide whether to manufacture and sell a new pesticide. Should the only question be whether it is legal to do so? What if the pesticide increases food production but injures human health? What if the pesticide would not injure humans but might harm wild animals that come into contact with the substance? Should this depend on the scale of the benefits of the pesticide? Should it matter, for example, how much the pesticide would increase crop yields?

Assuming that the pesticide could harm human health, does the distribution of the harm among individuals matter? Should harm to farmworkers, many of whom might be poor migrant workers, be viewed differently than harm to consumers? If the company decided not to sell the pesticide within the United States, should it manufacture here and sell to developing countries where use is still legal?

Or should all these concerns be irrelevant to the company so long as it complies with government laws and regulations?

In evaluating environmental choices such as these, three broad frameworks provide different, yet sometimes overlapping, answers to these questions. Business leaders may focus on the short term costs and benefits of managing environmental problems while selling goods and services for the benefit of the shareholders of the firm (*shareholder value*), on longer term measures of value and the interests of parties beyond shareholders who are affected by the actions of the firm, including employees, customers, or the environment itself (*stakeholder value*), or on whether the costs and other burdens of environmental harms and solutions are equitably distributed among individuals and groups throughout our society and future interests (*environmental justice*).

In the pesticide hypothetical, the short-term "shareholder value" decisionmaker would want to know specifically whether and how manufacturing and selling the pesticide would affect the firm's bottom line and stock price in the near term. A more robust understanding of shareholder value might take a longer-term perspective on the need for the decisions to benefit shareholders and be willing to accept some losses in the short term, so long as the long-term gains are real. Those concerned with "stakeholder value" would be interested in not just the impact on shareholders, but how the decision will impact relations with employees, customers, the local community, and perhaps the environment itself. Those focusing on environmental justice would consider whether the harms from the pesticide use would fall primarily on minorities or less powerful members of society, such as farmworkers and future generations.

These frameworks do not exhaust all of the potential modes for analyzing environmental management decisions, nor are they necessarily mutually exclusive. Virtually every argument around conference room tables in companies, though, builds off of one or more of the basic frameworks outlined above.

Whenever you hear or read about an environmental management decision, you should ask yourself which framework is being used. Disagreements over management often stem more from disagreements over the correct framework (what are we managing for?) than from disagreements over the facts. Indeed, at their base, many environmental conflicts are driven by conflicting values. In reading the sections that follow, you will gain a clearer understanding of why certain issues are so difficult to manage.

A. Shareholder Value and Stakeholder Value

Many of the key players in environmental management are business firms, not individuals, and their actions are legally restricted. A set of rules defines what corporate managers must, must not, or may take into account in their day-to-day decisionmaking. In our discussion of the tragedy of the commons, we offered the example of a company that could choose voluntarily to reformulate its products in favor of more costly organic or more sustainably sourced materials, but recognized that if it had to raise its product prices and lose market share, the firm's managers might think twice before taking the more environmentally friendly action. If the firm's competitors do not reformulate their products as well, the environmentally friendlier firm could be at a competitive disadvantage.

But even setting aside what its competitors might do, a firm's managers may still not believe they can make the environmentally beneficial choice. The firm's managers are constrained by state corporate law that provides the "rules of the road" for how corporations must operate. While we will discuss state corporate law in some detail in Chapter 5, we want to set the stage here by explaining the central debate over the purpose of a corporation.

Put simply, the debate concerns whether corporate managers owe duties only to maximize profits for the benefit of the *shareholders* of a firm—a view espoused most prominently by the economist Milton Friedman, or whether corporate managers owe broader duties to other *stakeholders* of the firm as well. Other stakeholders can include the firm's employees and customers, the local community, and even the environment itself.

Proponents of the shareholder value maximization view contend that a firm's manager evaluating whether to reformulate its products in favor of more sustainably sourced materials should consider only the costs and benefits of the choice for the shareholders of the firm by increasing the price of its stock or the value of the firm overall. There are multiple versions of this view. One focuses more on short-term profit and stock price. One can easily see how this view is less likely to lead the managers to choose the more sustainably sourced materials, especially if they are more expensive in the short term.

A more nuanced view of shareholder value tends to look at the long-term value of the firm rather than only the next quarter. Importantly, there is not always a clear tradeoff between choosing greater levels of environmental protection versus firm profits. In some cases, though not always, the two can go hand-in-hand. Michael Porter and Mark Kramer have famously described this as the concept of "shared value" in which creating value for a firm and its shareholders also creates value for the environment and society.[2] For example, a business firm might innovate in recycling and create a profitable market for goods that would otherwise become waste. Others, including Oliver Hart and Luigi Zingales have argued at a more conceptual level that many shareholders have pro-social or pro-environmental concerns, especially when these shareholders feel some sense of responsibility for the action that might be causing social or environmental harms.[3] They argue that management should take shareholders' pro-social and environmental concerns into account in their decisionmaking (including by seeking to reduce the firm's externalities), and encourage more shareholder voting to imbue this sense of responsibility. In their view, firm directors have a duty to maximize shareholder welfare, not the firm's market value. Other scholars have likewise offered versions of an argument that squares the circle between a shareholder-focused approach and one that takes broader social goals and stakeholders into account. Under this, more nuanced approach—which is still focused on shareholders—the managers may choose the more sustainably sourced materials, even if they are more expensive in the short term, if there is an expectation that there will be longer-term benefits that accrue to the shareholders in the form of acceptably higher prices for the product, the ability to attract new environmentally conscious customers, or preservation of supply chains for raw materials that are essential for the firm's long-term health.

In contrast, a stakeholder-based view of corporate purpose leaves a great deal more discretion to managers to take into account not only the short-term cost of the sustainable materials, but also the longer-term benefits to all of the firm's stakeholders, not just those who own shares. For example, the environment and local community may benefit greatly if the firm chooses to use fewer toxic chemicals. Empirical studies have demonstrated that employees of corporations

---

[2] Michael E. Porter & Mark R. Kramer, *Creating Shared Value*: How to Reinvent Capitalism—and Unleash a Wave of Innovation and Growth, HARVARD BUS. REV. (Jan.–Feb. 2011).

[3] Oliver Hart & Luigi Zingales, *Companies Should Maximize Shareholder Welfare Not Market Value*, 2 J. OF LAW, FINANCE, AND ACCOUNTING 247 (2017).

with a purpose—including those that prioritize the environment—report greater job satisfaction. And numerous studies have demonstrated that customers report a willingness to pay higher prices for more sustainable goods. If managers may take these stakeholder interests into account in their decisionmaking, that is likely to create more favorable conditions to choose the more sustainable path. The key distinction between the more nuanced shareholder value approach and a stakeholder approach is that even if the action is not going to be profitable in the long term, but it benefits other stakeholders like employees, customers, or the local community, a firm with a stakeholder orientation may choose to pursue this path.

B. Environmental Justice

Layered across all of these measures of success is the question of how the benefits and costs of environmental protection are distributed throughout society and who has the opportunity to participate in environmental decisions. For climate change and some other environmental issues, environmental justice is not only a core *intragenerational* concern—accounting for implications in the current generation, but also an *intergenerational* justice problem because a failure to take rapid, major actions will harm the descendants of disadvantaged communities for dozens or hundreds of generations, and they are not at the table in discussions about environmental governance.

Ordinarily, we might think of environmental justice as only a concern for public regulators, but it is an important value against which to measure PEG as well. Are the benefits—in the form of access to nature, better air, cleaner water, etc., concentrated in geographic regions or along class or racial lines? Are the costs being imposed on marginalized groups? Does the process of making decisions include meaningful participation by all stakeholders?

For the last several decades, the focus of environmental justice efforts has been on how the burdens of environmental harms and government regulations are allocated among individuals and groups within our society, as well as the extent to which the ability to participate in government decisionmaking about environmental regulations and permits is inequitable. Environmental governance at the federal, state and local levels historically ignored distributive issues. Supporters of strong environmental protection emphasized overall reductions in pollution; virtually no one asked how environmental harms, benefits or regulatory costs were distributed in the population.

That changed in the 1980s with a series of high profile media accounts demonstrating how some communities were bearing inequitable burdens of toxic air and water pollution and the siting of toxic waste disposal sites. Many studies conducted over the last several decades indicate that economically disadvantaged and minority communities bear a disproportionate share of environmental burdens. For example, minority groups disproportionately populate communities that are host to treatment, storage, and disposal facilities for hazardous waste. Minority communities disproportionately suffer from substandard air quality and are home to a higher number of Superfund sites that are contaminated by hazardous substances. As the case of lead contamination in Flint, Michigan, drinking water demonstrated, poor communities of color also suffer greater levels of environmental injuries, such as lead poisoning and pesticide exposure. The sheer number of studies, and the consistency of their results, suggests a disturbing maldistribution of environmental burdens in the United States.

Environmental justice focuses both on the distribution of environmental burdens and benefits (substantive environmental justice) and also on the process by which environmental decisions are made in the United States (procedural environmental justice). In the view of most advocates of environmental justice, local communities should have a significant, if not controlling, voice in decisions and activities that impact their residents' lives. Decision making processes in turn should be open to all residents, and everyone should have access to the scientific and other resources needed to understand and assess policy proposals. Environmental justice advocates thus push for decisions to be made through democratic processes involving local governments. This runs counter to the modern emphasis in American environmental policy on *federal* decision making by *expert* agencies. Environmental justice advocates also typically have little faith in traditional environmental groups, which have tended to have few minority employees and accomplish much of their work in the courts and the halls of Congress rather than in local communities.

The federal government has taken a number of important steps on environmental justice since the issue received major media attention in the 1980s. By 1994 President Clinton had signed an executive order requiring federal agencies to study and account for environmental justice in decisionmaking. More recent executive orders and policies have broadened and deepened efforts by the federal government to address environmental justice. States and localities vary widely on the extent to which they account for environmental justice, but some have adopted more extensive requirements than those adopted by the federal government.

As this discussion suggests, it is easy to assume that environmental justice is only a concern for governments and public policymakers. Many view justice concerns as a matter for public governance and public sector organizations, and, if so, the questions are which level of government should address these issues and how should they do so. In this view, the private sector responds to government requirements that reflect justice concerns, but achieving justice is not on—or should not be on—the radar screen of companies and other private sector organizations.

This is changing, though, as private sector organizations increasingly play a governance role in environmental protection, not just a role as regulatory targets. Governments respond to the environmental justice concerns of voters. Companies and other private sector actors do not face voters directly, but they respond to the values and norms of their employees, customers, investors, and local communities and these concerns often focus on the equitable distribution of environmental harms and regulatory costs, and equitable participation in environmental decisionmaking.

In recent years, concerns about environmental justice have become a more prominent and explicit aspect of private sector decision-making, actions and disclosure. Investors, NGOs, and local communities often hold companies accountable for equitable implications of their environmental performance. In particular, the growth of the environmental, social, and governance (ESG) movement among investors and companies has placed social concerns such as equity on the table with the same or greater emphasis as environmental concerns.

Case Study: Oil Companies' Climate Strategies

In recent years, the challenges of climate change have moved to the boardroom as more and more companies feel pressure to develop climate strategies. Perhaps nowhere is this more challenging than for traditional oil companies. These businesses were created expressly for the purpose of extracting, refining, and selling fossil fuels—the very activities that must be drastically reduced in the coming decades if global warming targets are to be met.

ExxonMobil is the largest oil company in the world. It has not been an industry leader in addressing climate and, indeed, has been accused of funding climate denial groups. In 2021, the company announced four corporate climate policies. It pledged to reduce emissions in its operations, provide products to help customers reduce their emissions, develop technologies to reduce carbon

among field workers and even people living in the vicinity of the farms. Should a chemical company produce this pesticide in America and sell it overseas to poorer countries where the pesticide's use is legal? Should it depend on whether the pesticide leaves residues on fruits and vegetables that are then exported back to the United States (sometimes known as the "circle of poison")?

Chapter 3

THE ACTORS, TOOLS, AND PROCESSES OF PRIVATE ENVIRONMENTAL GOVERNANCE

I. Challenging Traditional Assumptions

Ordinarily, when we think about the traditional model of environmental law and governance the roles and responsibilities seem obvious. We know who the regulator is, what tools that regulator has at its disposal to address environmental challenges, and the background legal rules that govern how the regulator can adopt substantive environmental standards. Congress adopts environmental statutes (subject to the veto authority of the President), and the EPA sets the specific pollution limits that factories need to meet. As we will see in this Chapter, though, PEG upends many of these traditional assumptions. Neither the key actors, the tools, nor the processes of environmental governance are obvious. This new model opens the door to new ways for lawyers, managers, and advocates to solve some of the most persistent environmental problems.

A. The Traditional Model of Environmental Law and Governance

In the traditional model, it is clear *who* is the source and enforcer of environmental standards: the government. That government actor could be Congress or a state legislature that passes a statute like the Clean Air Act, the Clean Water Act, or the National Environmental Policy Act. In many cases, these statutes require further detail to become capable of enforcement. So Congress delegates authority to interpret the statutes to a regulatory agency like the Environmental Protection Agency (EPA), the Department of Transportation, or the Department of the Interior. State legislatures do the same, delegating authority to the equivalent state or local regulatory agency. These agencies then promulgate more specific environmental regulations like the New Source Performance Standards under the Clean Air Act or Corporate Average Fuel Economy (CAFE) standards for new motor vehicles under the Energy Policy and Conservation Act. These detailed regulations make clear both to the regulated parties and the enforcement officials what is required to comply.

The "enforcers" of environmental standards set forth by legislatures and regulatory agencies are also clear: they are part of the executive branch. The EPA and its state equivalents typically monitor compliance, conduct civil or criminal investigations, and have the power to impose fines or enter into consent agreements for some violations. For the most serious violations, the Department of Justice and its state equivalent work with the environmental regulatory agencies to prosecute environmental crimes or engage in civil environmental enforcement.

Courts also play a part. Both state and federal courts decided early environmental cases under the common law doctrine of nuisance. When local landowners contended that nascent industries like copper smelting plants were belching smoke that harmed their crops, livestock, and their own health, they filed lawsuits against those companies, as in the famous 1904 case of *Madison v. Ducktown Sulphur, Copper & Iron Co.*[1] Courts could determine damages or issue injunctions to address these legal claims of environmental harm. Even the Supreme Court has played the role of environmental regulator. For example, in 1906 it was called upon to decide an environmental dispute between states in the case of *Missouri v. Illinois*.[2] In that case, the Court had to determine whether to issue an injunction when the State of Missouri claimed that the City of Chicago's dumping of sewage in a river was responsible for an increase in cases of typhoid fever downstream in St. Louis (it did not issue the injunction).

The notion of courts as sources of environmental standards is not merely a historical curiosity. Recently, the common law of nuisance has seen a resurgence of activity in which cities across the country have sued fossil fuel firms, seeking damages to fund resilience and adaptation measures to address the harms of climate change. Beyond the law of nuisance, in *Juliana v. United States*, the plaintiffs have asserted that the U.S. Constitution's guarantee of life, liberty, and property requires the government to limit greenhouse gas emissions more stringently for the benefit of our nation's youth. Whether or not individual cases succeed, the fact is that courts continue to play a role in deciding environmental disputes even today.

Moving past the question of "*who?*" in the traditional model of environmental law and governance, there are background rules that govern "*how?*" environmental standards can legitimately be adopted. For example, if the regulator is Congress, we know that the Constitution requires legislation—such as the Clean Air Act or the Clean Water Act—to be adopted in the same form by both chambers of Congress (bicameralism) and that it must be either signed by the President (presentment) or both chambers of Congress must vote to

---

1 83 S.W. 658 (Tenn. 1904).

2 200 U.S. 496 (1906).

override a presidential veto by a two-thirds majority. In addition, each chamber has its own procedural rules (such as the filibuster in the Senate) that govern the process of how legislation must be adopted. States have their own equivalent rules for legislation.

Regulatory agencies like the EPA or the Department of Transportation also have rules for adopting environmental regulations, set forth primarily in the Administration Procedure Act of 1946 (APA). The APA's process for "notice-and-comment" rulemaking, for example, requires an agency to issue public notice of a proposed rule, seek public comment on the rule, and explain its reasoning for the rule. In addition, the APA governs the adjudicatory proceedings that regulators can hold to determine whether penalties or other sanctions are appropriate in enforcement proceedings. So, too, are prosecutors enforcing environmental rules and regulations bound by certain legal standards, such as those governing when evidence is sufficient to bring a criminal or civil case. And background legal rules such as the Federal Rules of Evidence and the Federal Rules of Civil Procedure govern civil court proceedings in which enforcement of these environmental standards take place.

Finally, when we assume a government regulator, we understand *"what?"* environmental regulations and standards look like. As set out in Chapter 2, the public law "toolkit" of regulatory options can be understood through the "Five P's" framework: **P**rescriptive Regulation, **P**roperty Rights, **P**enalties, **P**ayments, and **P**ersuasion.

Prescriptive Regulation refers to commands about what a party must or must not do, technology that must or must not be used, or performance standards that must be met. The **P**roperty Rights tool is especially useful in cases in which an environmental resource is a "commons" open access resource that is subject to overuse—such as a fishery or public grazing lands. The government can allocate property rights in the resource—such as a grazing permit or a catch allowance—to provide incentives to those with such rights to steward the resource and limit overuse.

Payments and **P**enalties are two sides of the same coin, like subsidies and taxes. The government can pay people or institutions like corporations to encourage certain behavior, like the purchase of electric vehicles, and impose penalties or charges on behaviors it wants to discourage, like a carbon tax on greenhouse gas emissions. **P**ersuasion is the least intrusive tool. It relies on information disclosure or "nudges" to encourage environmentally preferable behavior, such as in the case of the EPA's Toxics Release Inventory (TRI) program. TRI requires entities releasing more than a threshold amount of certain toxic chemicals to publicly disclose such releases in an annual report. Purely informational governance, lacking any substantive requirement to reduce releases of toxic chemicals, TRI's information disclosure requirement has nonetheless coincided with dramatic decreases in the releases of such chemicals since EPA began public disclosure of TRI data in 1987.

B. The Actors, Tools, and Processes of PEG

By contrast, PEG upends many of these assumptions. The "Who" of environmental governance becomes much broader and unexpected when we include private actors in the mix. In addition, actors have additional tools in their governance toolkit that force us to broaden the set of tools available as part of the "What" of environmental governance. Finally, private actors are not bound by the background legal rules like the APA that govern the process of public environmental regulation. Many private organizations have developed procedural standards that parallel the APA, and some private "meta-standards" exist to create greater consistency in procedures across organizations and broader stakeholder participation in "How" private actors set PEG standards. Many of the examples mentioned in the sections below are described in detail in Part II of the book.

To paraphrase Alice in Wonderland, we need to pass through the looking glass. PEG can be as effective as public governance, sometimes more so, sometimes less, but we must recognize that we are in a different landscape. Or, as Dorothy memorably remarked to Toto, we are not in Kansas anymore.

1. The PEG Actors

By definition, the "Who" in PEG must look beyond government. The key players include a surprising range of organizations, such as business firms, environmental advocacy groups and other non-governmental organizations (NGOs), multi-stakeholder organizations, industry associations, investors and asset managers, banks, and insurance firms, among many others at local, national, and international levels.

Table 1: Key Actors in Public and Private Governance

Public Environmental Governance	Private Environmental Governance
International Agencies	Global and domestic business firms

Federal Government	Environmental advocacy groups and other non-governmental organizations (NGOs)
State Governments	Multi-stakeholder organizations
Local Governments	Industry associations
	Investors and asset managers
	Banks
	Insurance firms
	Others (religious, civic and cultural groups, universities, nonprofit medical centers)

The following paragraphs describe some of the key types of PEG players with short examples of how they shape behavior to protect the environment.

Business firms of many stripes are, of course, key actors in private governance. While business firms can take the form of a corporation, a partnership, or a sole proprietorship, the most active players in PEG have often been publicly traded corporations. The managers of publicly traded corporations have become increasingly sensitive to environmental considerations (both independently and as part of a broader movement to consider environmental, social, and governance or "ESG" issues). While the managers of a corporation—the so-called "C-Suite" like the CEO (Chief Executive Officer), CFO (Chief Financial Officer), and CSO (Chief Sustainability Officer)—manage the day-to-day affairs of a corporation, ultimately it is the firm's board of directors that is responsible for its major decisions and overall direction. The board of directors owes a fiduciary duty to the shareholders of the firm to ensure that the firm is managed in a way that maximizes shareholder welfare. While the question of what precisely must be maximized (a narrower view of shareholder value vs. a broader view of shareholder welfare) and over what time frame (short-term or long-term) has long been a subject of debate (topics we explore in detail in Chapter 5), shareholders—both retail and institutional investors—are increasingly demanding that firms take both their long and short-term environmental and climate impacts into account. Investors and other members of the public have likewise increasingly demanded improved environmental and climate-related disclosures, both through public regulatory filings and in PEG disclosure platforms like the CDP (formerly the Carbon Disclosure Project).

As a result, these corporations, which include major *consumer-facing retailers* like Walmart, Target, Best Buy, and Home Depot, among others, can use their significant market power to adopt and enforce environmental standards when they sell goods in the marketplace, or purchase goods and raw materials from their suppliers. They can unilaterally adopt environmental standards that apply to their own conduct, such as committing to reduce onsite greenhouse gas emissions or declaring their commitments to purchase only renewable energy to power their facilities. But they can also use their market power to impose environmental conditions on suppliers or others within their value chain through contracts. For example, retailers such as Target and Walmart have unilaterally declared their intention to reduce greenhouse gas emissions within their supply chains. These commitments require suppliers both to set emissions reduction targets and publicly disclose their emissions. Other firms, such as Hewlett Packard, have employed similar techniques to force their suppliers to stop using certain toxic chemicals or metals in their products even when those materials remain legal to use in the United States. These examples are described in detail in Chapter 8 and Chapter 10. Firms sometimes act alone to set such standards, but often they act in partnership with an environmentally minded NGO or multi-stakeholder group focused on a particular aspect of PEG. And sometimes they act in concert with an entire industry.

Thus, a second important category of actor in the PEG landscape includes *NGOs, multi-stakeholder organizations,* and *industry associations*. These types of private organizations play a role in setting and enforcing private environmental and climate governance through information disclosure, industry standards, or certification programs. They lie along a continuum from NGOs (which tend to be "public interest" organizations that do not have any industry representation), to multi-stakeholder organizations (which may include representation from NGOs and industry as well as international organizations or government), to industry associations (which are organizations designed to represent industry interests as a collective).

These organizations are not beholden to private shareholders like corporations; rather, they tend to be not-for-profit private organizations that represent stakeholders ranging from members of the public who seek to conserve a specific resource (as in the case of the Marine Stewardship Council or the Forest Stewardship Council), to specific industries like logging or the automotive industry. Importantly, industry associations are likely to represent industry interests on many issues—not just environmental ones. NGOs and multi-stakeholder organizations tend to be more focused around a particular issue, such as environmental protection broadly conceived, climate change (such as the Science-Based Targets initiative) or the fashion industry more specifically (such as the Sustainable Apparel Coalition), or even narrower issues like forest or fishery conservation or sustainable coffee or palm oil harvesting. Other examples of certification programs created by NGOs include the MSC's certification program for sustainable fisheries discussed in Chapter 1, the U.S. Green Building Council's Leadership in Energy & Environmental Design (LEED) certification discussed in Chapter 11, and the FSC's certification program for sustainable forest management, also discussed in Chapter 11.

It is worth noting that unlike in the public law context where there is often a single set of environmental standards to follow, in the PEG context with multiple actors, there may be multiple conflicting certification programs and standards. For example, in the forestry context, the FSC's more stringent certification standards compete with the less stringent industry association standards adopted by the Sustainable Forestry Initiative.

Industry associations have long played a role in PEG not only through the setting of environmental performance standards, but also for intermediate steps, such as the publication of best practices or methodologies for calculating an environmental footprint. Industry associations have played complex roles in environmental protection. In many cases they have responded to their least-motivated members and have lobbied against government requirements, but in others they have supported progressive industry-wide standards. One industry association that has received considerable attention in scholarship on PEG is the American Chemistry Council (formerly the Chemical Manufacturers Association), which created the Responsible Care Program in the wake of the Bhopal chemical plant disaster in India. The Responsible Care Program sets forth a standard that member chemical manufacturers must meet with respect to the safety of toxic chemicals. While many scholars have criticized the program for its lack of enforcement sanctions, and some recent scholarship has found that participating firms increased, rather than decreased, pollution as compared to firms that did not participate in Responsible Care, another recent study found that firms participating in Responsible Care had a significant reduction in industrial accidents.

A *multi-stakeholder organization*, process, or alliance is slightly different from an industry association, because its membership is not limited to industry, though such organizations often include significant industry representation. For example, the Sustainable Apparel Coalition (SAC) describes itself as a "global, multi-stakeholder non-profit alliance for the fashion industry." Originally founded by Walmart and Patagonia, the SAC now comprises more than 250 members, including major private firms in apparel, footwear, textiles, and the retail sector, as well as industry associations, NGOs, and academic institutions. The SAC has developed a metric for measuring sustainability in the apparel and footwear value chain both for environmental impact and social impact (labor standards). Other standards adopted either by industry associations or multi-stakeholder processes include the International Rubber Study Group (focusing on sustainable rubber harvesting), the Roundtable on Sustainable Palm Oil (focusing on sustainable harvesting of palm oil), and many others.

Sometimes NGOs or industry groups merge into larger multi-stakeholder "initiatives" like the Science Based Targets initiative (SBTi), which was formed as a partnership by CDP, the United Nations Global Compact, World Resources Institute (WRI) and the World Wide Fund for Nature (WWF). SBTi works with business firms to set targets based on the latest climate science to reduce greenhouse gas emissions in line with the goals of the Paris Agreement. To date, more than 800 business firms have set science-based targets based on this private initiative. As a second example, the Partnership for Carbon Accounting Financials (PCAF) is an "industry-led partnership" that aims to facilitate transparency about the emissions within financial institutions' lending portfolios. PCAF has developed a methodology for financial institutions to account for emissions within their lending portfolios so that they can ultimately align their portfolios with the goals of the Paris Climate Agreement. PCAF began as a collection of global banks and financial institutions, but it has become a multi-stakeholder organization that includes the participation of NGOs like CDP, the UN-convened Net-Zero Asset Owner Alliance, and the SBTi. This broad-based participation ensures that the metrics adopted by PCAF both facilitate and are harmonized with these other reporting and certification platforms.

A third major category of actors in PEG includes *investors* and *asset managers*. Investors and asset managers have been especially active in pursuing PEG. Their actions have included public statements by the leaders of major asset management firms like BlackRock CEO Larry Fink's statement in his annual letter to CEOs in 2021 that "climate risk is investment risk," as well as initiatives by major asset managers and investor groups to promote better disclosure and management of climate risk by corporations whose shares they own. Investors and asset managers play a unique role in PEG as holders of equity (shares or stock in a firm within their portfolio), as holders of equity have unique rights vis-à-vis a business firm. Ownership of equity gives those owners—investors (both institutional and retail) and asset managers—the right to take certain steps that can influence how the firm is managed. These steps include the right of investors to elect directors to a corporation's board, the right to offer shareholder resolutions or proposals that would require a firm to address environmental issues more aggressively, and the right to vote on such proposals. If the firm fails to comply with such resolutions that the investor or asset manager favors, the investor or asset manager can sell (divest) its shares. Although a single individual investor selling shares may have little impact, some of the larger institutional investors and asset management firms can attract negative public attention through divestment or even affect the share price if the investor owns a large enough percentage of the firm's equity.

One important recent example of the role that asset managers and investors can play includes the highly publicized 2021 campaign by activist investment firm Engine No. 1 to seat several new members on ExxonMobil's twelve-seat board of directors who would be more proactive about focusing on climate change and long-term sustainable value creation. While Engine No. 1 owned a mere 0.02% of ExxonMobil's shares, the firm was able to convince a substantial number of other institutional investors, including BlackRock, Vanguard, and State Street (who collectively owned 20% of ExxonMobil's shares), as well as the California State Teachers Retirement System, the California Public Employees' Retirement System, the New York State Common Retirement Fund, the Church of England Investment Fund, Institutional Shareholder Services, and Glass Lewis, to support between two and four of the proposed directors. Ultimately, the campaign was successful in seating three new members on Exxon's board. Likewise, at around the same time, investors in Chevron, ConocoPhilips, and Philips66 successfully adopted shareholder resolutions advising these firms to reduce not only their operational emissions, but also emissions in the firms' value chains that arise when its oil and gas products are purchased and used by customers.

Although investors and asset managers have certain powers to engage in PEG as owners of shares in various firms, *banks* are also beginning to play an important role in PEG through their lending function and the issuance of debt. Banks have long played a significant role as monitors of their lenders' behavior. They have three primary debt-related tools at their disposal, each of which is different from those in the arsenal of shareholders or asset managers owning equity (shares of stock in a company).

First, banks can use the loan underwriting process to manage risk, and simply decline to lend to high-risk projects or choose to lend to low-risk projects. For example, in 2020, all major U.S. banks announced that they would restrict future financing of new coal-fired power plants and coal mining, as well as decline to finance new oil and gas development in the Arctic. On the opposite end of the spectrum, banks can direct capital flows in a positive direction toward clean energy and low-emissions projects or new technologies. Major banks have mobilized substantial capital funds—in the hundreds of billions of dollars—to clean-tech and renewable energy investments, green buildings, green bonds, and electric vehicles. Second, banks can decide to provide debt but include debt covenants with environmental conditions that must be met by borrowers. For example, major banks have begun to include loan terms that are designed to decrease the cost of borrowing when the borrower reduces greenhouse gas emissions at certain levels, and to increase the cost when the borrower fails to meet these targets. Finally, they can engage in active monitoring of borrowers during the lifecycle of a loan to implement PEG, including through their softer powers of advising.

One way in which major banks operationalize some of these environmental risk-management strategies and commitments is through the Equator Principles. We discuss the Equator Principles in more detail in Chapter 9, but for now it is important to know that it is a multi-stakeholder initiative that most of the major global financial institutions have adopted. It requires participating financial institutions to engage in environmental and social impact assessment before providing financing to major projects like pipelines and dams that are likely to have significant environmental and social impacts. In some ways, the Equator Principles mirror the National Environmental Policy Act's requirements that federal agencies engage in environmental impact assessment before undertaking, permitting, or financing major projects like roads, bridges, pipelines, or levees in the United States. However, the Equator Principles go one step further to require participating financial institutions to mitigate negative environmental and social impacts.

One final major set of players in PEG worth pausing to understand is *insurance companies* and *reinsurance companies*. Insurance companies operate by pooling risk. They charge insured clients a set amount of money on a regular basis—called a premium—and pay the insured funds if they suffer specified damages. An individual or firm is willing to purchase insurance to smooth their income because they may not otherwise have access to sufficient capital in a disaster situation to address the damages. In other words, insurance works by transferring risk. Insurance can promote activities that are socially beneficial but risky and that might not otherwise be undertaken in the absence of insurance. *Reinsurance* operates as a form of insurance for insurance companies—insurance companies purchase reinsurance to pool their risk in the event of a disaster that is so costly that the payouts would exceed their ability to pay.

Insurance companies will only issue policies if they can guarantee themselves a reasonable rate of return. Accordingly, they will only insure risks that are: (1) sufficiently well understood to make it possible to price the premium; (2) due to random chance (meaning that there is a risk, not a certain outcome); (3) independent and not correlated (meaning that large populations do not suffer the same loss at the same time, which could strain a firm's resources to pay out simultaneously); (4) subject to minimal levels of moral hazard (meaning that the ability to obtain insurance does not increase risky behavior); and (5) subject to minimal levels of adverse selection (meaning that the entities that purchase insurance cannot only be those most likely to suffer the damage), which would lead to unraveling of the market.

Insurance companies, like banks and investors, can exert substantial pressure on their insureds (or potential insureds) when it comes to their ability to undertake projects with a significant environmental footprint. Such projects might include carbon-intensive projects like oil and gas drilling, pipeline construction, or mines. Thus, whether and how insurance firms are willing to insure such projects can have significant implications for decarbonization and other environmental impacts. For example, some major global and U.S. insurance firms now decline to insure coal-based business models, the construction of new coal-fired power plants, and coal mines. In addition, many of these firms have stated publicly that they will not underwrite loans for firms that generate more than thirty percent of revenue from coal mining or energy production from coal.

The three largest *reinsurers* (firms that provide insurance to insurance firms)—Swiss Re, Munich Re and Lloyds of London—likewise have limited their coverage of coal mining. These actions have increased the cost of insurance for coal mining as the number of potential insurers has declined. In addition to these negative screens for greenhouse gas emissions, insurance firms can exert substantial power over individual land-use and siting decisions by declining to insure properties in high-risk fire or flood zones or by substantially increasing premiums.

Insurance can also promote environmental and climate resilience. For example, insurance firms can reduce premiums (the amount that an insured pays under a policy) for behavior and actions that promote protection of properties against certain environmental risks, such as proactive landscaping to reduce fire risk, moving electrical panels or equipment to higher levels of buildings in flood-prone areas, or constructing or retrofitting properties to be more resilient to hurricane-force winds.

More recently, some insurers have begun to take creative steps to protect ecosystems that themselves promote climate and environmental resilience. It is well established, for example, that coral reefs act like natural sea walls—protecting a beach and its upland properties from coastal storm surges. If the coral reef is healthy, it can significantly reduce the impact of storm surges on the beach and coastal properties. A damaged reef provides far less protection. However, coral reefs can be quickly repaired after they are damaged if corals are reattached promptly. An insurance firm could write an ordinary indemnity insurance policy for damage to the properties caused by a storm, but there is another creative option. Insurance firms can insure the coral reef itself against damage. The first such policy of its kind was put in place in 2019 in Mexico to insure a coral reef adjacent to the Yucatan Peninsula. The insurance policy guarantees immediate funds to repair any damage to the coral reef caused by high winds above specific speed thresholds and is described in Chapter 11.

2. *The PEG Tools*

PEG encompasses the actions that these private actors and institutions take to manage common pool resources like forests and fisheries that are subject to overuse, to reduce negative externalities such as those from toxic chemicals and greenhouse gas emissions, and to improve environmental resilience, among other goals. Private actors employ a number of different tools or "instruments" to achieve these environmental goals. In fact, many of the tools that private actors employ parallel the policy instruments used by public regulators. And some of the tools that private actors employ suggest that an environmental governance toolkit including both public and private options has more than Five P's. We described the Five P's of public governance in Chapter 2, and Table 2 below sets out their private sector version.

Table 2: Parallel Tools in Public and Private Environmental Governance

Public Environmental Law	Private Environmental Governance
Prescriptive Regulation	Private, legally enforceable prescriptive standards including certification systems, and other contractual provisions such as supply chain agreements, M&A contracts
Property Rights	Property rights
Financial Penalties	Private charges & fees, Negative Screens
Financial Payments	Investment, green bonds, climate philanthropy
Persuasion	Information disclosure, environmental labeling
Insurance (pooling risk through public or mandatory private insurance)	Insurance (private, non-mandatory insurance)

Just as government regulators can employ Prescriptive Rules, so, too, can private actors. For a private standard to qualify as prescriptive, it must have two characteristics. The first is that it mandates a standard for behavior—either a technology-based standard or a performance standard, similar to a public prescriptive rule. Second, it must be enforceable either as a contract (legally enforceable) or by the third-party entity adopting the certification standard through other enforcement mechanisms. Among the examples noted above, both the Marine Stewardship Council's standards for sustainable fisheries and the Forest Stewardship Council's standards for sustainable forest management operate as a parallel form of prescriptive rules. The MSC and the FSC set forth what forest and fishery managers "shall" and "shall not" do to ensure sustainable management. These are performance-based standards set forth by private rather than public organizations. Adherence to these standards yields the benefit of a certification, while failure to meet the standards can lead to the enforcement mechanism of a loss of certification. Another example of prescriptive private certification standards is the LEED certification for buildings, which sets forth both performance- and technology-based standards.

In addition to these private certification programs, private environmental standards are embodied in contracts, such as provisions in merger and acquisition agreements, commercial real estate leases, or supply chain contracts. Each of these mechanisms provides a way for one private entity—such as the firm engaging with its suppliers—to dictate to suppliers what environmental standards they must meet. Major firms with significant supply chains like Walmart and Target, major auto manufacturers, computer and technology firms like HP, and others in different specific industries routinely employ supply chain contract strategies to reduce environmental externalities. They do this through prohibiting suppliers from using certain chemicals in the supply chain, requiring suppliers to disclose and set reduction targets for greenhouse gas emissions, and declining to enter into contracts with potential suppliers who fail to meet these standards. Of course, unlike in the case of a public prescriptive rule, a supplier that does not wish to meet the standard can simply decline to sell its goods or services to the firm setting the environmental standards. Or in the case of a lease or merger, the private actor facing the prospect of environmental enforcement can simply decline to agree to the contract and seek a lease or merger partner elsewhere.

Private governance approaches can also employ **P**roperty Rights. While public authorities can split a commons—like grazing land—into parcels of private property, or can issue licenses to graze for a fee, private governance use of property rights may look a bit different. Private firms can employ property rights or entitlements within the firm itself to avoid problems of split incentives. For example, when a firm owns a resource like office space, it can pay centrally for a resource used by the firm such as its electricity. Divorcing the cost from usage can lead to misaligned incentives to conserve the resource. A property-rights approach could involve the firm allocating to each business unit a certain amount of power per quarter or year (or the resulting emissions from the generation of electric power) and charge a fee for usage over the limit. The same approach could be used for water use, the creation of a carbon budget for employee business travel, or other environmental externalities, in each case providing better incentives for the actual end user of the resource to manage it more effectively.

Some firms have even combined the use of property rights with internal trading mechanisms, such as through the adoption of internal carbon trading, in which different business units are allocated emissions "allowances" just as they would be in a public emissions trading market like the European Union's Emissions Trading System. In the private context, however, it is the firm that sets an emissions cap, and business units can trade only with other business units within the firm. They purchase allowances when the marginal cost of abatement for the business unit is higher than the cost of an allowance in an internal market. Notably, British Petroleum briefly employed such an internal private trading market in the late 1990s.

While in the public law context **P**enalties generally consist of taxes, fees, and charges, in the private governance context the notion of Penalties is broader, also encompassing market-leveraging approaches that increase the costs of undesirable behavior. At the closest parallel, a private organization can employ a private fee for environmentally undesirable behavior, such as Yale University's use of a private carbon charge to reduce the University's overall greenhouse gas emissions. Beginning with a pilot study, Yale University has adopted a private fee of $40 per ton of CO_2 emitted by its buildings (based on electricity, chilled water, natural gas and steam consumption), and it then sends each participating building a monthly report containing information about its energy consumption. Buildings that outperform or perform equally to Yale's overall average receive a net return of their fee; buildings that perform worse than Yale's overall performance receive a net charge. Other private actors, including Microsoft and Disney, have likewise instituted private carbon fees. In Microsoft's case, the fee was assessed globally across the firm in more than 100 countries and on more than a dozen different business units within the firm, and the funds were dedicated to the purchase of carbon offsets and other clean infrastructure investments for the firm.

Penalties can also encompass debt covenants by banks that increase the cost of capital for firms with a higher emissions profile. At the extreme end of the spectrum, actions by banks to decline to loan to coal-fired power plants, or by insurance firms to decline to insure coal-mining projects qualify as penalties. At the very least, these actions—especially when undertaken by most major players in an industry—increase the cost of such environmentally damaging projects. At most, they could render such fossil-fuel intensive projects impossible to undertake as simply cost-prohibitive.

Incorporating private governance into the notion of the toolkit likewise should expand our understanding of **P**ayments. In the public sector, payments are largely subsidies in which the government grants a benefit such as a tax credit or low-interest loan to a firm that is engaging in environmentally beneficial behavior such as government subsidies for solar energy production. Or, the government may grant the benefit to consumers who purchase environmentally preferable products such as electric vehicles. This is the strategy that Congress adopted in the 2022 Inflation Reduction Act. In the private governance context, Payments can exist at multiple levels. Payments most certainly encompass actions by major banks and asset managers to direct capital flows to clean tech, renewable energy, and other environmentally positive industries either directly through loans, through newly established Green Funds specifically earmarked to promote such ends, or through other financial instruments like Green Bonds. They can also include "climate philanthropy" by banks or other major financial institutions, in which the financial institutions provide financial support to NGOs that are then seeking to promote environmental ends. And Payments—whose aim is to make cheaper environmentally beneficial activities—can also include loan terms and debt covenants that make access to credit cheaper for firms with a better environmental footprint.

Many forms of **P**ersuasion have emerged both in public and private environmental governance. The clearest example that exists in parallel across the public and private sectors is the use of information disclosure to promote positive environmental behavior through transparency. As Supreme Court Justice Louis Brandeis once remarked, sunlight is the best disinfectant. And as any management consultant will tell you, "You can only manage what you measure." Thus, just as the Securities and Exchange Commission requires publicly traded firms to disclose certain environmental risks, so too does the CDP provide a platform for firms to disclose to investors and the public much more detailed information about each firms' risks and opportunities related to climate, water use, and forest management.

In other cases, the information disclosure may be accompanied by some form of prescriptive standards, resulting in a hybrid of **P**ersuasion and **P**rescriptive Rules. Arguably the MSC and FSC certification standards, which combine prescriptive standards for fishery and forest management with information disclosure in the form of a certification and labelling system, are such hybrid instruments. The Equator Principles are another example of such a hybrid instrument. As we discussed above, most of the major global financial institutions have publicly committed to these principles, which were designed by commercial lenders in response to pressure by NGOs to develop standards for financing of major global infrastructure projects—like pipelines and hydroelectric dams. The Equator Principles are similar to the environmental impact assessment requirements of the National Environmental Policy Act but go one step further in requiring certain forms of mitigation.

Because it would be too convenient for all the instruments to begin with the letter P, we should include a final important instrument that has parallels in both public and private governance: **I**nsurance. Because insurance operates to pool risk, we could label this instrument **P**ooling Risk to get our treasured "P", but we think Insurance is a more recognizable label. As noted above, insurance firms have the power to affect behavior by insured parties in ways that are either more or less environmentally friendly. Just as insurance firms can increase your homeowner's insurance premium if you own a trampoline or fail to install a home alarm system—both of which make it more likely that you will have to file a claim—insurance firms can increase premiums for or decline to insure environmental risky behavior. Such behaviors might include building new homes in a fire- or flood-prone area. They can entirely decline to insure projects that are the most environmentally harmful, such as the construction of a new pipeline or coal mining project. They can reduce premiums for environmentally beneficial behavior that either mitigates environmental externalities or increases environmental resilience, such as when insureds undertake landscaping to reduce fire risk or otherwise harden their properties against storm and wind damage. Some insurance companies issue policies that insure against the costs of unknown environmental problems that may arise after a company acquires a facility or that exceed the expected costs of cleaning up a known environmental problem. These policies create incentives for an insurance company to investigate their potential insured's environmental risks before entering into the policy, and to monitor the activities of their insured and reduce the environmental harms they cause during the term of the policy. And insurance firms are increasingly undertaking creative approaches not only to insure properties, but to insure nature itself.

Why are these insurance activities, which arguably increase or decrease the cost of environmentally risky or beneficial action, not simply categorized as **P**ayments and **P**enalties? Insurance is qualitatively different. It is a tool that can smooth income over time—the insured pays a set amount in the form of a premium over time to guarantee access to funds in the event they suffer damages that are covered by their insurance policy. It is a form of risk management through pooling of risk, rather than an independent source of funds from a third party in the form of a government or private subsidy, bank loan, or cash, although in some cases it puts the insurer in an environmental investigating, monitoring, and oversight role more typically played by governments.

In addition to parallel actors and tools, over the last several decades PEG initiatives have targeted many of the same subject matter areas as public environmental laws and policies. We will be discussing these PEG subject matter parallels throughout the book, but Table 3 provides some initial examples.

Table 3: Parallel Subject Matter in Public and Private Environmental Governance

Subject Matter	Public Governance	Private Governance
Forests	• National Forest Management Act • Clean Water Act Non-point Source Provisions Applicable to Silvaculture	• Forest Stewardship Council • Sustainable Forestry Initiative
Fisheries	• Magnuson-Stevens Fishery Conservation Act	• Marine Stewardship Council
Toxic Chemicals and Pesticides	• Toxic Substances Control Act • Federal Insecticide, Fungicide and Rodenticide Act Pesticide Registration and Application Requirements • Federal Food Drug and Cosmetic Act Product Approval Requirements	• Supply Chain Contract Terms • Good Neighbor Agreements Prohibiting Use of Listed Toxic Chemicals • GRI Corporate Toxics Disclosure • Eco-Labeling Programs
Climate Change	• EPA Mandatory Greenhouse Gas Reporting Rule • Clean Air Act Stationary Source Regulations • Clean Air Act Mobile Source Regulations	• Carbon Disclosure Initiatives by CDP, CERES, and Others • Science Based Targets Initiative • Carbon Investor, Lender and Insurer Initiatives • Clean Energy Buyers Alliance
Environmental Impact Assessment	• National Environmental Policy Act	• Equator Principles

Building Standards	• State and Local Land Use/Zoning Laws • Building Codes	• U.S. Green Building Council LEED Standards • Provisions in Real Estate Leases and Finance Agreements
Hazardous Waste Remediation	• Resource Conservation and Recovery Act • Comprehensive Environmental Response, Compensation & Liability Act (CERCLA or Superfund)	• Provisions in M&A Agreements, Commercial Leases, Credit Agreements, Supply Chain Agreements • Environmental Insurance Agreements
Land Conservation	• Federal & State Parks and Forest Laws & Programs	• Easements and Purchases by Nature Conservancies and Land Trusts

3. *PEG Procedures and Processes*

The processes and procedures of public environmental law are well established and mandated by statutes. Agencies must follow notice-and-comment rulemaking in order to promulgate a regulation. For PEG, there are no government requirements on how an organization or a firm sets private environmental standards or goes about enforcing them, but that does not mean that PEG constitutes a free-for-all.

Many major PEG organizations have developed procedures to ensure that the ultimate standard adopted includes meaningful representation by industry, consumers, employees, the public, and others. (We address other legal limits and rules that govern what private firms can or cannot do in PEG in Chapter 5.) These procedural standards parallel the requirements in the Administrative Procedure Act but often include additional requirements about outcomes rather than just processes. For example, the ISEAL Alliance is an organization that governs the adoption of specific private environmental standards. It offers resources and standards, including a Code of Good Practice and Credibility Principles, and includes among its member organizations the Marine Stewardship Council, Fair Trade certification, the Forest Stewardship Council, Gold Standard (for carbon credits), Rainforest Alliance, BetterCotton.org, and the Responsible Jewelry Council, among others.

The ISEAL Credibility Principles aim to serve as a foundation of substantive environmental standards to ensure that they are both credible and effective. The Credibility Principles provide that a credible standard must make an impact, must be developed through a collaborative process that includes and engages with the relevant stakeholders, must create value for its users (provide a business case for users to participate in the standard), must include tools to measure progress, and must embody an approach of continuous improvement. In addition, the Principles require that a PEG standard be transparent, reliable, and impartial (avoid conflicts of interest), and require the disclosure of truthful information. Although the Principles operate at a high-level of abstraction, the ISEAL Codes of Good Practice (Standard-Setting Code, Assurance Code, and Impacts Code) drill down to offer more detailed instructions for organizations on how to develop, structure, assess compliance with, and monitor the impact of PEG standards.

QUESTIONS AND DISCUSSION

1. As noted above in Chapter 1, a constant concern with PEG is the lack of accountability or sanction. Do you think that relying on the procedures adopted by a certification system such as MSC or FSC adequately addresses this concern? How do these procedures compare to the procedures government agencies are required to follow? Would your view change if the procedures meet the requirements of "meta"-standards like the ISEAL Codes of Conduct? Why or why not?

2. Do you think that PEG suffers from a "democratic deficit"? In other words, do you think it is problematic that these environmental standards are written largely by private actors—even if there is widespread consultation with different stakeholder groups? How does the responsiveness of PEG to public preferences compare with the responsiveness of governments at the national, state, and local levels?

3. In what ways and along what dimensions are private actors likely to be better than public actors at setting and enforcing environmental standards? In what ways and along what dimensions are they likely to be worse?

4. Drawing on the PEG Five P's, can you develop initiatives for each P (including insurance) that promotes biodiversity conservation?

5. What incentives do investors, banks, and insurers have to pressure companies they interact with to reduce pollution even if the reductions are not required by a government agency? What incentives do they have to pressure companies to avoid government pollution controls?

Chapter 4

THE WHY AND WHETHER OF PRIVATE ENVIRONMENTAL GOVERNANCE

Imagine you are on the first day of a new job for an environmental advocacy group. The head of your team has asked you to find some way to reduce water pollution from agriculture, the leading cause of water quality problems in the US. Congress has been unwilling to impose standards on farmers, ranchers, and foresters, and federal, state, and local agencies have had limited success over the last 50 years. You can use any combination of tools and targets. What will you do?

What if you were just starting a new job at a law firm representing food retail companies that feel pressure to reduce their role in agricultural "non-point source" water pollution (such as pollution that does not come out of pipes)? Or representing companies or farmers who want to avoid the costs of reducing non-point pollution and have asked you to respond to pressure on this issue? What if you are a business manager trying to successfully position your business on this issue?

The last chapter outlined the new PEG actors, tools and processes that can help you develop new ways to implement—or defend against—a non-point source water pollution strategy. But to succeed as an environmental advocate, lawyer, or manager, knowing the actors, tools and processes is not enough, it is also important to have a mental model of how PEG works—to know why PEG occurs, what motivates the private sector to perform the roles that otherwise would be performed by governments, and how those drivers have led to the modern system of private and public governance that has emerged in the last several decades. In other words, why do private sector actors engage in environmental protection? How do they interact with other private sector actors? When do private sector actions enhance or undermine government actions, and vice versa? When we account for all of the effects of PEG, does it improve the environmental behavior of companies or improve environmental quality? Does it achieve or undermine environmental justice? With an understanding of how PEG works, you can develop effective strategies and avoid unintended consequences.

PEG is rapidly evolving, developing new tools, adding new actors, and addressing new areas every year. This Chapter explains what we know about the core features of the emergence of PEG—the motivations of the major actors, how we should evaluate PEG, its effects, and what we should worry about as PEG and public governance interact in the US and around the world. We will use non-point pollution as our test case, but the essential elements of the model we develop in this Chapter are important for understanding all the subject matter areas we will explore in later chapters.

Vocabulary—a Cautionary Note

We begin with a cautionary note on how our choice of words can be a trap in the environmental law and policy field and can limit our ability to understand the opportunities and limits of PEG. Word choice steers our ability to think about all types of problems. The terms that have developed over the last 50 years to describe environmental law and policy were developed at a time when environmental law almost always involved the exercise of public authority, with the private sector serving as the target of government environmental regulations, not as the creator and implementer of standards. As a result, the traditional terms of environmental law and policy assume that government is the regulator and private organizations are the regulated community. But these terms can get in the way of our ability to see new governance options as they emerge and to develop new solutions to problems in an era in which the exercise of private authority, not just public authority, is becoming increasingly common.

The first choice of words is demonstrated by the discussion in the last paragraph. Note how we begin by talking about "government" but end by talking about "governance." That small step can open the door to the idea that governance—the exercise of authority by one party over another—can involve the actions of many different actors, not just government. We use the term governance throughout this book to leave the door open to the wide range of actors who are performing the functions of governments, but it is important to be aware of other vocabulary traps as well.

For instance, a group of environmental advocates may meet to discuss ways to reduce non-point source water pollution. Using the language of public governance they may ask "What can government do?" They may discuss how they can encourage national, state, and local governments to adopt policies, laws, and regulations directed at farmers, ranchers, foresters, homebuilders, and other sources of non-point source water pollution. If they think of themselves as environmental policy experts, they may start by assembling a list of the available policy options, but for many people the term "policy" refers to *government* policies, and government policies may not be feasible or effective. Although policy does not necessarily mean government policy, because many of us equate policy with a government standard rather than a private sector standard, the term policy may limit thinking to the governance options that can be developed and implemented by government agencies. In this book, we often use more general terms like "initiatives" and "efforts" to avoid inadvertently shutting down our ability to think about the public and private governance options for environmental problems. These are somewhat clunky terms, but our modern vocabulary has limited our options if the goal is to keep an open mind about the governance options.

The term "regulation" poses even greater risks of limiting thinking about governance options. Most of the participants in our hypothetical non-point source water pollution discussion may assume that regulation means federal or state government regulation through an executive branch agency. The advocates may lobby for government regulation and assess whether their efforts are succeeding by reporting on the number of government statutes and regulations adopted, compliance levels with regulatory requirements, the number of enforcement actions taken, and the size of the fines imposed on violators.

But what if strong government regulation is not politically or legally viable (as is largely the case around the country), or is not the most effective way to reduce agricultural non-point source water pollution? In that case, using the term regulation may narrow the options that are discussed around the table. Whenever possible, we use the more general terms "standards" and "requirements" to signal that private as well as public actors may be the source of the coercion.

We also generally avoid the use of the term "voluntary," which is sometimes used as a broad term to refer to all private standards. Calling something voluntary can signal that the subject of the standard is not coerced. That surely is the case for some internal corporate policies that can easily be changed by the company, but private standards and other requirements are often accompanied by pressure that does not leave the target in a position to act voluntarily. If the pressure to act is the result of a supply chain contract, loan, or lease provision, it may be legally enforceable, whether entered into voluntarily or not. If the pressure to act does not produce a legally enforceable requirement but arises from a major corporate customer, investor, creditor, insurer, employee group, or NGO with the ability to affect the company's reputation, the response by the company is only voluntary in a limited sense.

Using the term voluntary in these situations is more of a signal that a government agency cannot issue an administrative order or file a legal suit to compel the company to act. Agencies may have more success with these actions and in some cases have criminal sanctions at their disposal that private litigants don't have. Although the term voluntary in this case may be an attempt to signal that something is "non-governmental" rather than "not compelled," it can leave the impression that private standards backed by strong pressure are not effective. That is certainly true in some cases but often is not, and it is an impression that should be subjected to rigorous testing, not simply created through use of a general term like "voluntary."

Similarly, framing transboundary pollution problems as "international" problems can limit our ability to develop new governance options. The term international means between nations, and using the term can induce us to think about a problem as a question that should be resolved through the United Nations or through bilateral or multilateral agreements between nation states. International law scholars have addressed this problem by using the term transnational to discuss forms of governance that bypass nation states. We often use the term global to avoid any implicit assumption about the role of nation states. Remember that the point is not that nation states or governments at any level cannot or should not work together to solve a problem, it is just that we do not want our choice of terms to shut down our ability to think about a broader set of actors and solutions. In all these cases, think "yes and. . ."

I. Why Does Private Environmental Governance Occur?

A. A Model of PEG

Understanding how PEG functions requires thinking of PEG as a system of governance that often complements and sometimes competes with public governance. As Louis Leonard, the World Wildlife Fund's former head of energy and climate programs, explains it, at the systems and initiative levels PEG includes several "operational functions" also found in public environmental law. Leonard's focus is on climate change, but a model of PEG has emerged that applies to many other environmental problems, including toxic chemical releases, non-point source water pollution, and natural resource management.

The operational functions of PEG include motivating organizations to participate by the threat of negative sanctions or the benefits of positive incentives; setting standards that align with science-based benchmarks (for instance, setting non-point source water quality discharge standards that will achieve water quality standards); assessing and disclosing data specific to individual companies to facilitate allocation of responsibility; driving implementation using tools such as subsidies, market-based instruments, and guidance; tracking progress to measure and publicly report progress against goals; and promoting the use of robust mechanisms to hold to account those that do not comply.

Leonard and other experts recognize that the system must be a legitimate form of governance that includes fair decision-making for participants and stakeholders, transparent decisions, and data to attract and retain participants and build public trust in the system, as well as equity and justice for participants and stakeholders.

1. The Standard Environmental Law and Policy Model

On the surface, this all seems like a matter of common sense—of course a successful private governance system should have comparable operational functions to a public governance system. But understanding how to navigate in a world that adds private governance to the more traditional public governance on environmental issues requires understanding several fundamental differences, not just similarities.

A first step is to understand how public support for environmental protection generates responses in the public and private governance models. For public governance, political scientists have noted how interest groups lobby government policymakers to shape how government agencies regulate companies. One example of such a theory is public choice theory, developed by political economists to explain how parties that will benefit or be harmed by regulation lobby for favorable government treatment. In this analysis, concentrated business interests often prevail over diffuse public interests, with exceptions that arise during times of high public concern about a particular subject matter. This analysis provides an explanation of the legislative gridlock that began in the early 1990s, in which concentrated interests such as the fossil fuel lobby have been able to block environmental legislation which would benefit a diffuse public. However, we find public choice theory to be less compelling as an explanation for the converse situation—the adoption of the major pollution control statutes from 1970 until 1990, in which a broad swath of the public was able to overcome concentrated interests opposed to such laws.

In the last several decades, scholars in fields like political economy, sociology, economics, and law have all begun to develop theories of why private actors adopt private environmental governance and how PEG interacts with public law. These include David Baron's theory of "private politics," Alan Wiseman's theories on business-government interactions, Sarah Soule and Brayden King's work on social movements, and Danial Diermeier's theories of strategic activism and nonmarket strategy, to name just a few. This body of research is large and growing. For those of you interested in a more theoretical deep dive, we offer a list of suggested readings at the end of our book.

2. *The New PEG Model*

In the last few decades, advocates of environmental protection have begun to bypass government altogether. Instead, numerous stakeholders create legal, social, and economic pressure directly on companies and other sources of environmental harms (for instance, universities, medical centers, and religious organizations) to improve their environmental performance.

PEG has emerged when government actions have not satisfied the preferences of the public, employees, shareholders, managers, community members, advocacy groups or others often labeled as "stakeholders" or "constituents." Instead of only expressing environmental preferences through voting, lobbying, and other efforts to influence politicians and agencies, some or all of these stakeholders can bypass lobbying governments to regulate businesses and instead create pressure directly on these businesses. What has emerged is a system of governance, so it might be better to describe these individuals or groups as constituents in a system of governance, rather than stakeholders in the marketplace, but stakeholders is the most widely used term and we use it in this book.

Corporate participation in private governance initiatives is motivated by a complex set of drivers, including avoidance of reputation or brand risks, response to employee and manager preferences and pressure, and response to retail customer demands. The prospects for financial gains from reducing costs through efficiency or increasing revenues through new business opportunities are also drivers of PEG actions. In turn, these drivers induce firms to govern other firms' environmental behavior and performance through investor, lender, and insurer pressure and, in some cases, legally-binding requirements such as supply chain contract provisions.

This is the core insight of the new PEG model: because widespread preferences for environmental protection are not being met by government, those preferences create pressure for action on numerous private sector actors, including companies, investors, lenders, and insurers and those private sector actors feel compelled to respond. These private sector actors often respond by becoming private "governors"—by requiring improved environmental performance from those they invest in, buy goods and services from, loan to, and insure.

The drivers for corporate PEG can be roughly divided into five broad categories.[1]

- Internal economic strategies based on recognition of how environmental risks and opportunities and efficiency improvements influence profits and losses;
- Public pressure felt from consumer boycotts, naming and shaming campaigns, and advocacy organization pressure;
- Evolving norms expressed externally by industry leaders and customers and internally by employees;
- Business-to-business pressures expressed through supply chain contracts and procurement policies; and
- Financial system pressure felt from decisions by investors, lenders, and insurers about specific business practices.

Together, these drivers help explain the extensive growth of PEG climate initiatives. But an important feature of the emerging system of PEG climate initiatives is that they build on themselves and cannot easily be attributed to a single cause. For instance, corporate climate commitments may occur initially because of the business case, public pressure, and evolving norms. Cascades may then occur as additional firms make climate commitments, and the growing number of firms announcing commitments strengthens the business case, retail consumer pressure, public pressure, and the perceived norms among managers and employees, and these motivations then induce firms to pressure others via business-to-business (B-to-B) and financial system pressure. In turn, the B-to-B and financial system pressure can further increase the business case for climate action, embolden advocates who conduct public pressure campaigns, and bolster evolving norms among employees and customers.

3. Overcoming Environmental Problems

To assess the extent to which the new PEG model explains the emergence and functioning of PEG, it is helpful to think about how in some cases PEG can address the core causes of environmental problems and reasons why these problems are difficult to address, which we discussed in Chapter 2. These causes and problems confront any system of governance, but knowing where PEG is likely to be effective and where it is not can provide a valuable foundation

---

[1] See Louis G. Leonard, *Under the Radar: A Coherent System of Climate Governance, Driven by Business*, 50 ENVTL L. REP. 10547 (2020).

for understanding the topic areas discussed in Chapters 7 through 12.

PEG can provide new ways to address the causes of environmental problems:

- *Externalities and Pricing.* As we noted in Chapter 2, while protecting the environment often provides a net benefit to society, the economic interests of individual parties involved often can encourage harmful activities. Whether society's interest is in the existence of clean air, the ability of the globe to produce a stable climate, or the environmental services that ecosystems provide, public goods are often over-exploited and are subject to negative externalities like pollution. When governments respond to environmental problems they often do so by trying to get the incentives right, such as by pricing greenhouse gas emissions and other negative externalities. PEG initiatives do the same, creating incentives for individuals and private sector organizations to act in ways that benefit society, rather than only themselves.
- *Collective Action, Transaction Costs, and Free Riders.* In the absence of government regulation or creation of property rights in public goods (resources that cannot be privately controlled, such as clean air), companies and individuals have incentives to extract resources and to pollute without paying a price. Collective action (the cost of organizing different actors to do something) is discouraged by transaction costs (the cost of getting them together and deciding to do something) and free riders (those who do not make commitments with the others and benefit as a result). To understand these economics terms in an everyday setting, getting everyone in an office to contribute to a coffee fund takes time and effort, and not all drinkers of their morning java may contribute. Yet many types of public goods are difficult if not impossible for governments to protect because of geographical and political boundaries, democracy deficits, and other problems. In some situations the transaction costs of acting in the private sphere can be lower and more effective than acting in the public sphere, such as when information flows via social and traditional media are easy, and when low cost options exist for consumer choices about consumer products, investments, loans and insurance. Free riders are a problem for any effort to drive public

or private governance, but the easy flow of information can reduce the number of free riders and enable those who are motivated to call out free riders for inaction. PEG initiatives have had some success filling gaps by using information and collective efforts to change the reward structures and incentives of polluters and users of common resources. Although a farmer may not have an incentive to reduce agricultural runoff to a local stream, pressure from the corporate purchaser of its products created through supply chain requirements by a food retailer responding to NGO brand pressure may better align the farmer's incentives with those of the general public's interest in a cleaner, more sustainable resource. These supply chain initiatives can bypass or reduce the need for collective action. Similarly, private markets have developed for ecosystem services, and these markets create economic incentives that might otherwise be created by government regulation or creation of private property rights.

PEG also can provide new ways to address the *reasons why* environmental problems are difficult to manage:

- *Uncertainty*. Many environmental problems pose not just problems of risk (a threat with some known probability of occurring) but uncertainty (a threat whose probability can't be quantified), and governments struggle to adopt, implement, and defend regulatory actions in the face of uncertainty. The precautionary principle suggests not allowing new products or activities that pose uncertain threats, the status quo may itself be worse, and uncertainty tends to delay the implementation of government regulation as it prompts litigation over whether the rules are really necessary. PEG actions can be taken more quickly—a retailer can ban a toxic chemical in the products it sells without going through the regulatory process. That enables quicker action but also can lead to harms that would have been identified with a slower, more deliberate process.

- *Mismatched Scales*. Environmental harms—including non-point source water pollution—often occur across wide areas and cross international, national, and local government boundaries. Governments typically lack the authority to coerce behavior change outside their boundaries. This creates the risk that a race-to-the-bottom will occur, where governments lower their environmental standards to attract business, and companies move or threaten to move to these areas. Collective action among governments is difficult because of the high transaction costs to bring differing parties together. Distributional justice with respect to environmental benefits and harms may falter in these cases of mismatched scales, with some geographies and communities faring much better than others. And the challenge of monitoring and enforcement at a distance from the source of authority remains present. While PEG actions lack the coercive power of national governments, they can transcend geographic and national boundaries in ways that can undermine race-to-the-bottom incentives and reduce these distributional inequities. Pressure from investor, lender, and corporate supply chain requirements can create pressure on farmers in Arkansas to reduce non-point runoff that flows into Oklahoma. Pressure on farmers in the U.S. can reduce non-point runoff into the Red River that flows from Minnesota into Lake Winnipeg in Canada. This can occur in ways that may be difficult for any U.S. state or international effort to achieve. Collective action problems exist for organizing PEG efforts just as they do for organizing voters in any one country, but the increasingly global glows of information, low costs of organizing, shared preferences of many people around the globe, and globalization of commerce are facilitating collective action on environmental issues.

- *Polarization*. The combination of polarization, sorting, and the democratic design is making it increasingly difficult for governments to adopt major new environmental statutes, to implement existing statutes in a consistent way, and to interpret existing statutes in ways that can address new problems. PEG cannot substitute for government action on any many environmental problems, but it can bypass legislative polarization. Senators from rural states and members of Congress from gerrymandered districts often respond to constituents who resist government environmental protection measures, but investors, lenders, insurers, and companies that have international or national markets cannot gerrymander their markets. On environmental issues and many others, they may feel pressure to respond to majority preferences in ways that politicians do not. PEG initiatives also can affect support for public and private governance.

This is just a brief overview of how PEG can address the core causes of environmental problems and the reasons why environmental problems are difficult to address. We will dive into the specifics in more detail in later chapters as we explore the PEG initiatives that have developed in each of the major areas of environmental law and policy, but this overview can help you avoid losing the forest for the trees and stimulate new applications of PEG as you study specific areas.

II. Does Private Environmental Governance Work?

Assessing the effects of PEG is a difficult task. Greenwashing is a major concern because companies often have incentives to announce that they are taking steps to protect the environment even if they are not making meaningful changes. But government gridlock on climate change and many other environmental issues is also a concern. Thus when asking whether PEG "works," we also have to ask, "compared to what?" Although it can be difficult to evaluate which PEG initiatives are having desirable effects, it is important to keep several core ideas in mind before we dive into greenwashing issues in greater depth in Chapter 6.

A. How Should We Assess the Performance of PEG?

At the outset, we cannot evaluate PEG without a standard to judge it against. As with any assessment, understanding whether PEG "works" requires identifying and applying criteria for assessing whether it is achieving the goals we might set for it. As we set these criteria, we should be cognizant of the fact that few public or private governance efforts have fully resolved environmental problems. Here are several questions we suggest keeping in mind:

- *What effects does the PEG initiative have on the desired environmental outcome?* Ideally we would assess whether any initiative, be it a private or public governance effort, is achieving the desired environmental conditions. For a non-point source water pollution effort, the desired conditions might be achieving water quality standards for the waters that receive agricultural runoff. For climate change, it might be achieving the atmospheric concentrations of GHGs necessary to achieve no more than a 1.5°C or 2°C global average temperature increase over pre-industrial levels. It is important, though, not to fall into the trap of asking whether any one PEG initiative will "solve" the climate problem or any other environmental problem. Very few government laws and policies can meet this standard, and we should not discard PEG initiatives when they also cannot do so. Instead, it is valuable to assess whether PEG initiatives are likely to be improving the desired environmental outcomes.

- *What effects does the PEG initiative have on the desired environmental behavior of the target?* In the absence of measuring environmental conditions, it is often more promising to measure whether the targets of PEG are changing behavior in desirable ways. For instance, have farmers adopted best management practices for non-point sources of water pollution? Have corporate buyers adopted and enforced contractual requirements for farmers to adopt best management practices? As to climate change, have companies accurately reported GHG emissions to the public? Have they adopted realistic, science-based plans to reduce emissions at a rate consistent with the 1.5°C or 2°C goals? Have they achieved targeted emissions reductions so far? These are the types of questions that should be answered in an assessment of whether PEG initiatives are achieving the desired behavior of firms.

- *How does the PEG initiative compare to other viable alternatives?* PEG initiatives, like public governance initiatives, should be judged against the viable alternatives. If they are judged only against ideal or perfect alternatives, initiatives that are feasible will not be pursued even if the ideal alternatives cannot be adopted.

- *Do the benefits of the PEG initiative outweigh the costs?* PEG initiatives can be assessed against a standard of Kaldor-Hicks efficiency (benefits outweigh the costs so that the winners could compensate the losers with something left over). In recent years, some conservative groups have argued that investor, lender, and company PEG actions are just forms of "woke capitalism" that are attempting to impose progressive social values on companies. We discuss this further in Chapter 6. Presumably this critique is based on the idea that companies should be value-free or that pursuing social goals will undermine the profitability of firms and the efficiency of the economy as a whole. The role that values should play in the management of a firm is beyond the scope of this Chapter, but a complete assessment of the success of a PEG initiative should certainly involve assessing the net economic effects of the initiative.

- *Are the outcomes and processes of the PEG initiative just?* PEG initiatives can be assessed against a justice standard as can environmental regulations. For instance, how might a PEG initiative requiring farmers to adopt best management practices to reduce non-point water source pollution affect the costs of compliance and the benefits of clean water distributed across different populations? Are disadvantaged farmers and communities included in the decisionmaking processes about the development and implementation of the standards? For climate change, what effects might a PEG initiative have on achieving intra- and intergenerational environmental justice? We discussed environmental justice issues in Chapter 2 and will return to justice issues in in other chapters, but it is important to remember that if PEG is performing governance functions it is appropriate to include justice as a criterion for its success.
- *What effects does the PEG initiative have on public governance?* As we discuss in more detail in Chapter 7, PEG initiatives can have positive or negative spillover effects on public governance—they can increase or decrease the likelihood that more comprehensive public governance initiatives will be adopted and implemented. The net effects of a PEG initiative should be taken into account, not only its effects in isolation. To understand the net effects of PEG we should understand the interactions between public and private governance. If some types of PEG initiatives and tools undermine government action, environmental advocates, managers and policymakers may want to steer the private sector away from them. If other areas fill gaps that government cannot fill or enhance the likelihood of government action, more resources should be devoted to them.

B. How Does PEG Stack up Against These Criteria?

It is not possible to provide a single assessment of PEG's effects across all of the subject matter areas where it has emerged in the last several decades. Research suggests that some PEG initiatives are associated with major, meaningful shifts in corporate behavior. For instance, despite a lack of government requirements, the percentage of the largest firms that are including environmental requirements in supply chain contracts has increased from 50% in the early 2000s to over 80% by 2020. On issues such as climate change, high levels of participation have occurred in NGO-corporate initiatives committing companies to purchase renewable power, many companies have made net zero carbon commitments, and many investors have adopted environmental, social and governance (ESG) strategies. Companies such as Walmart that are not typically associated with liberal environmentalism have worked with leading NGOs to take major steps to reduce carbon emissions.

Yet scathing reports by NGOs and think tanks suggest that in many cases companies have not implemented their goals or have set goals that only look good on the surface. Some companies are setting and achieving renewable power and other decarbonization goals while sending annual dues to trade associations in Washington that are lobbying to prevent the government from adopting the kinds of public laws that would enable the society as a whole to meet those goals. We will discuss the performance of PEG initiatives as we examine each major subject matter area in the rest of the book, and we suggest that you set aside assumptions and engage in critical thinking to assess the successes and failures of the PEG initiatives in these areas.

QUESTIONS AND DISCUSSION

1. X Corp is a publicly traded corporation with 10% of its stock owned by Blackrock. It has borrowed $100 million from Bank of America to fund its ongoing operations, and it has comprehensive general liability insurance from Acme, a member of the Net-Zero Insurance Alliance. X Corp's headquarters, building, and manufacturing facilities are located in Atlanta, Georgia, and it makes widgets, which it sells to Walmart and Target in the United States, and Unilever in Europe, as well as to several global companies in the industrial machinery sector. X Corp uses Maersk as its preferred firm for shipping widgets to customers around the world. The production of the widgets requires a great deal of sophistication, so many of X Corp's employees are recruited from top universities with strong computer science and data analytics programs. The processes X Corp uses to make its widgets results in higher emissions of carbon dioxide and hexavalent chromium than its competitors. Out of concern about possible pressure to reduce carbon dioxide and hexavalent chromium emissions in the United States, X Corp is studying whether to secure project finance funding to open a new widget manufacturing facility in Indonesia.

a. Assume you are the chief sustainability officer for X Corp. What arguments would you make to the CEO about why reducing carbon dioxide and hexavalent chromium emissions may be in X Corp's financial interest, even if state and federal environmental agencies do not require reductions? What data would you want to have to persuade the CEO?

b. Assume you are a lawyer working with an environmental advocacy group. The group has not been able to persuade federal and state environmental agencies to regulate X Corp's emissions, and the president of the group has asked you to develop a new strategy. What characteristics or drivers of X Corp's business suggest that a PEG initiative might be effective?

c. Which of the companies with a role in the production or distribution of widgets listed above do you think would be more likely or less likely to be interested in an adopt meaningful PEG initiatives, and why?

d. As you read the following chapters, return to this hypothetical to explore how PEG initiatives on climate change, toxics, and other topics draw on the type of drivers that influence companies with characteristics like X Corp.

2. One of the most difficult challenges for environmentalists and private sector managers who develop and implement PEG initiatives is to account for potential tradeoffs between intragenerational equity and intergenerational equity. For instance, if a PEG initiative that pushes the private sector to demand renewable power and facilitates renewable power commitments will bypass government gridlock on decarbonization of the electric grid, it will reduce climate change harms for a hundred generations or more, and many of those harms would disproportionately affect communities of color and economically disadvantaged communities around the world. At the same time, PEG renewable power initiatives may not have safeguards to ensure procedural justice through enabling broad participation in the development and implementation of the renewable power initiative. And they may raise the price of power, including for those communities and individuals in this generation who are least able to afford it. How should public and private environmental advocates and decisionmakers think about these tradeoffs between the interests of this generation and the interests of many future generations who are not at the table today but will be affected? Is this a false tradeoff? If it is a real tradeoff, how can we think in better ways about how to make the tradeoff?

3. The non-point pollution from runoff of pesticides and fertilizer from farms, commercial businesses, and households is a leading contributor to water pollution and governments at the national, state and local levels have had difficulty reducing this form of pollution. Develop a PEG initiative that draws on the motivations for action discussed in this Chapter to address this non-point source water pollution problem. How might investor pressure, corporate supply chain pressure, retail customer pressure and other drivers provide opportunities to create incentives for farmers, commercial businesses, and households to better use pesticides and fertilizers? How might these drivers bypass polarization and gridlock? What specific tools or instruments might be used?

4. Environmental advocates differ on whether resources devoted to PEG will increase or decrease the likelihood of successful government legislation or regulation to address environmental problems. In what ways might PEG enhance the ability to develop government law and policy? In what ways might PEG undermine government action? Does the interaction of private and public governance differ based on the environmental threat, the level of government that might otherwise act, or the type of PEG initiative that is pursued?

5. Research suggests that many consumers in the United States will not pay much for more environmentally preferable goods. If that is true, does that suggest that PEG initiatives are unlikely to affect corporate environmental actions? What else might motivate a company to act?

Chapter 5

THE LEGAL RULES OF THE ROAD

Imagine that you are the Chief Executive Officer of a publicly traded firm that sells consumer products. Your Board of Directors has agreed with your assessment that it is in the firm's best interest to make a public pledge both to achieve "net zero" emissions in the firm's operations and its supply chain by 2050, and to reduce the firm's other environmental impacts. And you also agree that it is the right thing to do for the environment. Some of the key ingredients for the firm's best selling products are under stress from extreme weather events and droughts, so you know it is time to be forward-thinking about protecting the inputs to the firm's products. You believe, based on research, that consumers are likely to be willing to pay a "green premium" for some of these more environmentally friendly products. And you know that your employees will be happy with this change, as they have signed petitions seeking a more environmentally conscious path for the firm.

This, of course, requires more than just a board vote. It will require the firm to change the formulation of some of its products like laundry detergent to replace some of the chemicals in your products with more environmentally friendly alternatives. It will require redesigning packaging to reduce plastic waste. These will both require some upfront research and development investments. And the net zero pledge will require the firm to purchase substantial amounts of renewable energy to power its operations moving forward. Some of these short-term costs to the firm may temporarily depress the stock price, even if they will pay out financially in the longer term or increase the firm's resilience in the face of future changes to the climate.

What if a frustrated shareholder sues the firm, claiming that the officers and directors failed to maximize the short-term value of the firm, as reflected in its stock price? Would that suit succeed? What are the officers' and managers' duties to the shareholders? What about other stakeholders of the firm like its customers and employees? Could all of the firms in this consumer products space decide collectively to take the same steps to stop using a particular ingredient or to require the use of recycled plastic in their packaging? Could they reach an agreement to develop an industry "code of conduct" on the formulation of common products or the use of renewable energy to power their facilities? And, finally, does the firm have any obligation to disclose the fact that it is concerned about future supplies of its product ingredients as a result of a changing climate?

While we think of these actions as within the scope of private environmental governance, it is important to recognize that the participants in PEG, especially those in the corporate space, operate within the duties and limitations defined by the law. In other words, the answers to these questions come from the background legal rules that govern corporations and other organizations, including state corporate law, antitrust law, and securities regulation. These laws provide the background legal rules governing the duties of firm officers and directors, how firms may permissibly interact in the marketplace, and what information they must disclose to investors to ensure the integrity of markets.

The field of administrative law sets out the "rules of the road" for what agencies can or cannot do when it comes to adopting public environmental regulations. This Chapter tackles the parallel question of what laws set the background "rules of the road" for private environmental governance. These background laws determine when managers may or must take environmental impacts into account in their business decisions, whether they have incentives or disincentives to do so, or whether they are prohibited from doing so. Statutes passed at the state level and state judicial decisions interpreting those statutes determine the legal duties that corporate directors owe to the firm's stakeholders, including its shareholders. Laws passed by Congress at the federal level—including securities regulation, antitrust law, bankruptcy law, and consumer protection laws that prohibit false advertising—all have an impact on what private actors can do as a matter of private environmental governance. Just as it is essential to know administrative law in order to understand public environmental laws and regulations, it is essential to understand how these background legal rules and frameworks affect private environmental governance.

I. How Law Interacts with Business Decisionmaking

Private environmental governance is all about actions by private actors, including business firms' directors and officers. So why is the law relevant at all? First, the law is relevant because it sets background rules that govern whether business managers are permitted to take specific actions—like prioritizing long-term sustainability over a short-term profit—or whether those actions are simply prohibited by law. Second, the law makes clear that certain types of environmental actions are required—such as securities regulations mandating the disclosure of certain environmental risks in public reporting to investors. Third, the law is relevant because it sets the rules governing how business firms interact within the marketplace. We might applaud a firm for including provisions requiring carbon emissions reductions in its contracts with suppliers, or two firms getting together to agree on catch limits within a fishery and taking steps to exclude others to conserve the fish population. These steps would potentially protect the environment, but under certain conditions they also might violate antitrust law. And finally, the law may provide incentives or disincentives to engage in private environmental governance.

Taken as a whole, the legal background rules for PEG can be categorized as follows: Laws can (1) provide safe harbors, (2) create incentives, (3) mandate, (4) prohibit, or (5) provide disincentives for business firms to engage in private environmental governance. The next sections of this Chapter provide some detail on how these five types of rules work in practice. Of course, the law (and the courts) are also essential for enabling organizations to enforce legal obligations, whether for environmental provisions in contracts (which we discuss in Chapters 8, 9, 10, and 11), for conservation easements (which we discuss in Chapter 12), or for many of the other PEG tools we discuss in this book. We discuss these background legal rules as they become relevant throughout the book.

A. Safe Harbors in Corporate Law

State corporate law governs the legal duties that exist among corporate managers, directors, and officers, and the many stakeholders of the firm, including its shareholders. It provides the architecture that influences how managers make decisions about the day-to-day operations of the firm and how the Board of Directors (directors) set the overall strategic choices for the firm. Some of these rules are mandatory. Others are "default" rules around which the parties can contract. It is worth noting that not all private firms engaging in private environmental governance are corporations—some may be partnerships, sole proprietorships, privately-held companies, or specialized entities like limited liability companies. But because the corporation is so common, and because such a substantial number of major firms that engage in PEG are publicly held corporations, we focus primarily on corporations here.

Corporations are creatures of state corporate law. Each state has its own statute, which is ultimately interpreted by state courts. Most state corporate laws provide that the corporation's business affairs must be managed under the direction of a Board of Directors. In practice, most actions on a day-to-day basis are taken by officers pursuant to authority that the Board of Directors delegates to them. The law provides that shareholders of the firm have certain rights, including to elect the directors, to approve amendments to the corporate charter and bylaws, to approve mergers or the sale of substantially all assets of the firm, and to approve the voluntary dissolution of the firm.

Most discussions of state corporate law begin with the state of Delaware. Why? Because Delaware is home to more than 1 million corporations and more than two-thirds of Fortune 500 firms. Therefore its state corporate laws and its Court of Chancery (which is the final arbiter of Delaware corporate law) play an important role in setting the legal rules that govern managers. It is well settled corporate law that firm directors owe a fiduciary duty to the corporation and its shareholders. This aspect of state corporate law thus operates as a mandate. However, the Business Judgment Rule insulates the decisions of firm managers and directors from challenges by shareholders about the correctness of a particular decision. Under this Rule, when managers or directors make a decision that they believe is in the best interest of the firm, and that decision is not tainted by fraud or self-dealing, courts will not second-guess the decision even if it fails to maximize short-term value for shareholders. The Business Judgment Rule, then, provides an important safe harbor for directors and managers who need to balance among competing interests in their decision making, including when they wish to take environmental considerations into account for the long-run interests of and financial sustainability of the firm.

Every state—not just Delaware—employs the Business Judgment Rule to avoid courts second-guessing the decisions of directors and officers in the day-to-day business affairs of the firm. One of the best-known cases in which the Business Judgment Rule was invoked was *Shlensky v. Wrigley*, in which a disgruntled shareholder sued the owner of the Chicago Cubs and Wrigley Field (and the Wrigley's Chewing Gum Company) for failing to install lights at Wrigley Field which would have permitted the playing of nighttime baseball games. The shareholder complained that the firm's directors were forsaking profits that all of the competing teams were earning from hosting night games. Mr. Wrigley countered that baseball was a daytime sport, and that installing lights would not only destroy the nature of the sport, but that they might lead to harm to the neighborhoods near the stadium. The court agreed with Wrigley, stating:

> The response which courts make to such applications is that it is not their function to resolve for corporations questions of policy and business management. The directors are chosen to pass upon such questions and their judgment unless shown to be tainted with fraud is accepted as final. The judgment of the directors of corporations enjoys the

> benefit of a presumption that it was formed in good faith and was designed to promote the best interests of the corporation they serve.[1]

Importantly, a safe harbor gives these decisionmakers only discretion—it does not mandate or even provide incentives for managers to take the environmental implications of their decisions into account. But it insulates those decisions from attack by shareholders. Many forms of PEG are likely to fall squarely within the Business Judgment Rule, in that they ultimately promote the long-term value of the corporation by reducing costs, reducing risks, promoting resilience, or enhancing the firm's reputation. Indeed, as the Delaware Chancery Court explained:

> It is not for this court to question rational judgments about how promoting non-stockholder interests—be it through making a charitable contribution, paying employees higher salaries and benefits, or more general norms like promoting a particular corporate culture—ultimately promote stockholder value.[2]

There is an important exception to the Business Judgment Rule in some states, however (including Delaware). The Rule does not apply in the limited context of takeovers, during which directors' decisions are subject to heightened scrutiny to take shareholder value into account. The reason for this exception is to limit discretion where the Board of Directors might seek to entrench its own interests. Thus, in this context, the shareholder value duty operates more like a mandate, or at the very least a disincentive to prioritize any values (including environmental values) other than wealth maximization in the short term.

Imagine the following scenario. A firm, Greens 'R Us, has long prided itself on its environmental performance. It takes care to use responsibly-sourced ingredients in its products, to reduce waste in plastic packaging, and to rely on renewable energy to power its facilities. It is even developing new products that are more efficient than existing ones, using less energy and producing less waste in the process. Perhaps Greens 'R Us becomes the target of a takeover bid by Doomsday, Inc. Doomsday, Inc.'s management and Board are driven purely by financial considerations, and see Greens 'R Us as an undervalued target that they can make more efficient by dropping some of its environmental goals. The officers and directors of Greens 'R Us must now decide whether to accept the terms of a takeover bid, or whether to fight. Their actions must be governed by their duties to

---

1 *Shlensky v. Wrigley*, 95 Ill. App. 2d 173, 237 N.E.2d 776 (Ill. App. 1968).

2 *eBay Domestic Holdings v. Newmark*, 16 A.3d 1 (Del. Ch. 2010); *Simeone v. The Walt Disney Company*, 2023 WL 4208481 (Del. Ch. June 27, 2023)

the firm under the law. In Delaware, in this scenario, the officers and directors of Greens 'R Us could be limited in their ability to take into account a desire to preserve the environmental reputation and practices of the firm going forward—unless that reputation and practices could be tied to a benefit to shareholders as required by the law.

However, Delaware and its shareholder-friendly approach is not the only game in town. More than forty states have adopted what are known as "constituency statutes." These statutes, which were adopted in response to a wave of takeovers in the 1980s beginning with the state of Pennsylvania, permit the directors of a corporation to take into account the interests of constituencies other than shareholders in their decision making. For example, the state of Pennsylvania's constituency statute provides:

> (a) General rule. In discharging the duties of their respective positions, the board of directors, committees of the board and individual directors of a business corporation may, in considering the best interests of the corporation, consider to the extent they deem appropriate:
>
> > (1) The effects of any action upon any or all groups affected by such action, including shareholders, employees, suppliers, customers and creditors of the corporation, and upon communities in which offices or other establishments of the corporation are located.
> >
> > (2) The short-term and long-term interests of the corporation, including benefits that may accrue to the corporation from its long-term plans and the possibility that these interests may be best served by the continued independence of the corporation.
> >
> > (3) The resources, intent and conduct (past, stated and potential) of any person seeking to acquire control of the corporation.
> >
> > (4) All other pertinent factors.
>
> (b) Consideration of interests and factors. The board of directors, committees of the board and individual directors shall not be required, in considering the best interests of the corporation or the effects of any action, to regard any corporate interest or the interests of any particular group affected by such action as a dominant or controlling interest or factor. The consideration of interests and factors in the manner described in this subsection and in subsection (a)

shall not constitute a violation of [the] section [of the Code] (relating to standard of care and justifiable reliance).[3]

Some of these statutes are drafted specifically to apply in the context of takeovers—specifically to override the common law limitation on the Business Judgment Rule. Some statutes—such as Pennsylvania's—have been drafted even more broadly to apply to decisions by managers and directors in other contexts beyond takeovers. In these other contexts, arguably the Business Judgment Rule already insulates these decisions from scrutiny; however, these statutes make that safe harbor even more clear.

B. Incentives in State Corporate Law

In addition to state constituency statutes that insulate managers and directors in ordinary corporations, many states have adopted innovations in the corporate form, including permitting firms to incorporate as "public benefit corporations." A public benefit corporation is a corporation that has a dual purpose—both the promotion of shareholder value/welfare *and* promotion of a social or environmental benefit. Patagonia, Plum Organics, and Kickstarter are all public benefit corporations. Each public benefit corporation is required under state law to pursue a "general public benefit" (the benefit may be social or environmental in nature) in addition to maximizing welfare for the corporation and its shareholders. In addition to this general benefit, most states require a public benefit corporation to declare in its corporate documents a *specific* social or environmental purpose or benefit to which the firm seeks to contribute. The laws then declare that the general public benefit and any specific public benefit are in the best interests of the corporation. Thus, the directors and managers of a public benefit corporation are insulated from liability when they pursue these benefits in their decision making. Maryland adopted the first public benefit corporation statute in 2010, and since then more than thirty states have adopted similar laws.

State public benefit corporation laws require transparency and accountability with respect to the pursuit of general public benefit and any specific public benefit. With respect to accountability, many of these statutes require that the firm make clear in its name that it is a public benefit corporation and include this information on key corporate documents. Finally, these laws generally provide for accountability by requiring the publication of an annual report on pursuit of the general and any specific benefit, and typically require that the corporation define its benefit according to a credible third-

---

3 PA Title 15, section 1715, Exercise of Powers Generally.

party standard. Many firms thus select the standards set by the non-profit B-Corp certification program.

Once a firm is incorporated as a public benefit corporation, its directors and officers are insulated in their decisionmaking when they pursue the general and specific public benefits that are part of their charge. Firms may also decide to opt out of the form, and can reincorporate as ordinary corporations. By spelling out these general and specific public benefits, firm managers arguably have a greater incentive than managers in an ordinary corporation to take those benefits into account. These statutes do not require a firm to achieve a social or environmental benefit, since a firm can always choose to opt out of the form.

Notably, Delaware has adopted its own Public Benefit Corporation statute. However, its rules differ from the Model Benefit Corporation statute and those of other states in several ways, including that firms must declare one or more specific benefits, and that firms are not required to pursue a general public benefit. In addition, public benefit corporations in Delaware are not required to publish annual reports on the pursuit of the specific benefits.

Where do public benefit corporation statutes fall on the matrix of mandates, safe harbors, and incentives? They are best understood as incentives rather than mandates—once a firm decides to incorporate as a public benefit corporation, it must pursue general and/or specific public benefit. However, a firm can also decide to leave this more specific corporate form without penalty. Accordingly, we think this form falls more on the side of providing incentives (reputational and otherwise) to pursue environmental protection rather than mandates.

It is worth noting that the non-profit organization B-Corp, a private certification organization, has played an important role in drafting and lobbying for the Model Benefit Corporation Statute, the model for many of the state benefit corporation laws. B-Corp separately offers a private certification scheme for business firms (whether or not they are formed as corporations), and it is important not to confuse a public benefit corporation (which is organized under a state's benefit corporation law) with a "B-corp"—the nickname for a corporation certified by B-Corp. In many cases, firms may choose to pursue both the public law incorporation and private certification.

C. Mandates in Federal Law

Different aspects of corporate and business law can impose legal obligations on business firms to take the environment into account. The clearest example of such a mandate exists in securities regulations that impose disclosure obligations on publicly traded firms.

The Securities Act of 1933 and the Securities Exchange Act of 1934 govern the sale of securities to the public. They seek to promote market integrity and to protect investors against the manipulation of stock prices, among other goals. Pursuant to these statutes, the Securities and Exchange Commission (SEC) has adopted numerous regulations, including Regulation S–K, which governs the disclosure of information to investors when securities are offered to the public, disclosures in advance of the annual shareholders' meeting, disclosures that must be made on a regular basis in quarterly (10–Q) and annual (10–K) reports, and disclosures that are required in the case of specific events like a merger.

Regulation S–K has long required publicly traded firms to disclose certain environmental matters, such as the cost of compliance with environmental laws (including material capital expenditures), any material legal proceedings involving the company (including environmental proceedings), material impacts of risk events (including environmental risks), and a general "management discussion and analysis" (called the "MD&A") of the firm's financial condition (including known future trends and "uncertainties that are reasonably likely to have a material effect on financial condition or operating performance"). In this context, a fact is "material" as defined by the Supreme Court, if there is a "substantial likelihood that the . . . . fact would have been viewed by the reasonable investor as having significantly altered the 'total mix' of information made available."[4] A serious debate exists over how broadly to understand materiality in the environmental and climate context; should the term be limited to only those facts that are financially material to a firm's bottom line, or should it also include environmentally material information even if it would not affect the firm's financial position in a significant way?

In 2010, the SEC issued Guidance to firms on its interpretation of how climate risk interacts with existing regulatory requirements. The SEC indicated that firms must disclose the impact of actual or potential legislation and regulations regarding climate change on the firm's operations and performance; the indirect consequences of climate-related regulations or business trends, such as, for example changes in demand for goods and services; and risks to the firm's performance and operations that arise out of the physical impacts of climate change such as extreme weather events.

---

[4] *TSC Industries v. Northway, Inc.*, 426 U.S. 438, 449 (1976); *see also Basic, Inc. v. Levinson*, 485 U.S. 224 (1988).

Notably, firm compliance with the 2010 Guidance was spotty, tending toward boilerplate language and a lack of quantitative information. Several studies showed that firms provided more data in their own sustainability reports or in response to investors demands such as through private non-governmental organizations like the CDP (formerly the Carbon Disclosure Project), which solicits annual reports from major firms on behalf of investors about their climate, water, and forest-related impacts (discussed in Chapter 8). While these PEG disclosure requests and platforms did lead to more environmental information in the marketplace, the multitude of different standards and platforms—from CDP to GRI, SASB, TCFD, and an alphabet soup of others—made it extremely difficult to benchmark or compare performance across firms.

In March 2022, the SEC issued a proposed regulation called the Enhancement and Standardization of Climate-Related Disclosures Rule. As of the date of writing, the SEC has not yet issued a final rule. The proposed rule would mandate that publicly-traded firms disclose climate-related risks and their actual or likely material impacts on the firm's business, strategy, and outlook. Firms would also be required to disclose governance of climate-related risks—for example, to identify how the Board of Directors engages in climate-specific oversight and risk management as well as processes for identifying, assessing, and managing those risks. In addition, the proposed regulation would require firms to disclose their Scope 1 and Scope 2 greenhouse gas emissions. Scope 1 emissions refer to direct, onsite emissions and Scope 2 emissions are those arising from purchased electricity, heat, and cooling. Larger firms would be required to disclose their Scope 3 emissions—arising indirectly from the firm's value chain—only if material, or if firms have set a Scope 3 emissions reduction target. Firms would also be required to disclose information about their climate-related metrics (such as whether the firm employs an internal carbon price) and targets set (such as whether the firm has committed to a science-based target to reduce emissions). If a firm has employed scenario analysis, the firm would be required to disclose all assumptions and financial impacts regarding how the firm would fare in different future states of the world.

Not surprisingly, the proposed rule has been criticized both for going too far and for not going far enough. On the "goes too far" side, the primary critique is that the SEC is not an environmental regulator and thus that the proposed rule strays beyond the SEC's core mandate without adequate authorization from Congress. On a more mundane level, critics contend that compliance with the rule would be costly, especially if Scope 3 disclosures are required; others contend that firms are already doing voluntary disclosures and that this proposed rule is thus not needed. On the "doesn't go far enough" side, critics wonder why the proposed rule is limited to climate risks, and does not include other environmental risks such as biodiversity loss or water scarcity. Other critics point out that more firms should be required to disclose Scope 3 emissions. And finally, it is worth pointing out that the SEC's disclosure rules only apply to publicly traded firms; thus, there are large segments of the economy such as private equity or other privately-held firms that are not subject to this proposed disclosure mandate.

While we do not yet know the text of the final rule, it is very clear that as soon as that rule is finalized it will be challenged in court. Thus, we can expect an extended period of uncertainty about the SEC's requirements for climate-related disclosures.

D. Prohibitions and Disincentives in Federal Law

Just as corporate and business law can mandate that firm managers take the environmental impacts of their actions into account, it can also *prohibit* or provide *disincentives* for certain forms of environmentally-focused decisionmaking. For example, antitrust law in the United States is not generally considered to be part of environmental law. But antitrust law has significant implications for private environmental governance because it structures the permissible forms of interaction among firms within the marketplace. Certain forms of agreements between or among firms—even with good faith intentions to protect the environment—may run afoul of antitrust law's prohibitions. For example, firms in the consumer products industry might want to agree that they should stop selling large boxes or bottles of detergent in favor of smaller, more concentrated formula, but fear being the "first mover" to sell what appears to be less product. Major automakers might desire to agree to sell vehicles that emit fewer particulates from their tailpipes, but fear being the "first mover" in their industry to sell a car that might have a higher sticker price to account for the new technology. Antitrust law in the United States would prohibit these firms from getting together to agree to change products (even if environmentally friendlier) and to raise prices to avoid this first-mover problem.

Perhaps the best example of how antitrust law operates in this space arises in the context of the tragedy of the commons. As we discussed in Chapter 2, the tragedy of the commons can arise when there is a resource common to all—like a fishery—without clear rules on how it is governed. Individual firms with access to the fishery have an incentive to fish as much as they can, as quickly as they can, in order to ensure that they, and not the other firms, reap all of the economic benefits of fishing. However, if every firm follows the rule "fish as much as you can as quickly as you can," then the fishery will ultimately collapse. No fish will remain to spawn and replenish the fishery, ultimately leading to the ruin of the fishery. Although the adjacent state (or states) could try to step in to limit catch, or otherwise create rules to ensure a sustainable fishery, fish swim across borders, and this issue has been notoriously difficult to govern by governments alone.

One option for private environmental governance to address this tragedy of the commons is for all of the business firms that participate in the fishery to get together to set limits on their catch. They could also enter into an agreement to limit the number of new "outsiders" that would be allowed to fish as well. They could raise prices for the remaining catch to ensure that their profit levels are not harmed by this long-term focused behavior. Indeed, Elinor Ostrom's work, which we referenced in Chapter 2, highlights "insider solutions" like these to address the tragedy of the commons. And the goal of such an agreement would be to promote conservation of the fish within the fishery—in other words, putting the environment first.

So what is the problem? Under U.S. antitrust law, private firms cannot enter into agreements to exclude other firms from an industry; nor can they enter into agreements to limit production, as such an agreement could lead to higher prices for consumers; nor can they fix prices at a certain level, even if the goal is to promote conservation. The goals of antitrust law are multi-faceted, but they largely focus on promoting market efficiency, protecting consumers from price increases by monopolies, and protecting smaller firms from larger firms that are more efficient or dominate in their markets.

At a glance, then, promoting competition within markets sounds at odds with the idea of promoting conservation within markets. Whether antitrust law operates as a clear prohibition or just a disincentive depends upon the facts of the agreement, and whether it includes some of the *per se* prohibited actions. But in both cases, it is important for business firms engaging in private environmental governance to be cognizant of these considerations.

To be sure, antitrust law does not always frustrate environmental protection. Indeed, before the Clean Air Act was adopted in 1972, the federal government sued the major automakers under antitrust law to break up a collusive agreement to keep pollution-control technology for cars (the catalytic converter) off the market in California. And there are many types of industry collaboration that the Supreme Court has said do not run afoul of antitrust law.

In practice, it is important to understand that antitrust law can operate either as a clear *prohibition*, or merely as a strong *disincentive*. Some kinds of agreements between firms—to fix prices, to engage in horizontal boycotts, or to limit output—are considered illegal *per se*. Antitrust law therefore operates as a clear *prohibition* on prioritizing environmental conservation through these methods. Other kinds of agreements are evaluated under the antitrust "rule of reason," which examines whether the restraint on trade is "merely regulating" and thus promoting competition, or whether it is actually suppressing competition. In evaluating a case under the rule of reason, a court would hear evidence on whether the agreement is increasing or decreasing prices and choices for consumers, as well as whether it is increasing or decreasing market output. If the fact-based inquiry shows an anticompetitive effect, then the action violates antitrust law, and the law acts as a *prohibition*. But even in those cases when no anticompetitive effect is demonstrated, the law arguably acts as a *disincentive*—chilling private firms from engaging in such activities out of a concern that they might be subject to litigation risk or penalties.

Indeed, this issue has arisen recently. As we discuss in greater detail below in Chapter 6, a number of states have adopted laws that limit financial institutions that are taking climate change (and other environmental, social, and governance factors) into account from doing business with their states. In addition, some of these states' attorneys general have sent civil investigative demands under state competition laws to firms that are participating in industry associations such as the Net Zero Insurance Alliance (NZIA), which was launched in 2021 as part of the Glasgow Financial Alliance for Net Zero under the auspices of the United Nations. NZIA provides a forum for global insurance firms to discuss best practices for climate risk. These civil investigative demands suggest that participation in the NZIA's target setting and other requirements would violate state and federal antitrust law. Perhaps out of an abundance of caution, multiple insurers, including major firms like Swiss Re, Munich Re and others, announced publicly that they were leaving the association. In July of 2023, the UN Environment Program issued a statement on the NZIA clarifying that each firm participating in the association "unilaterally and independently decides" on which steps it may take and whether it wishes to set or publish emissions reductions targets. It remains to be seen whether these investigative demands will lead to litigation or whether the NZIA and its sibling alliances for asset managers and asset owners will simply become loci of best practices going forward.

Although purely private agreements may run afoul of antitrust laws in some circumstances, there are other forms of private environmental governance that do not. Rather than having a purely private discussion among firms, a non-governmental organization or government actor could convene key industry players to adopt rules for a certification program, for example. This would not lead to the same kind of antitrust scrutiny as a purely private agreement among firms. The Supreme Court itself has pointed out, in a case called *Allied Tube & Conduit Corp. v. Indian Head, Inc.*, that private standards, based on the "merits of objective expert judgments and through procedures that prevent the standard-setting process from being biased by members with economic interests in stifling product competition. . . . can have significant procompetitive advantages."[5] In other words, the Court acknowledged that private standard setting can be procompetitive as well as anticompetitive—and this is certainly true in the environmental context.

As we delve deeper into the practical application of PEG in this book, keep in mind that PEG is not purely private. What firms can do in this space is both enabled and limited by public laws at the state and federal levels.

QUESTIONS AND DISCUSSION

1. Do you think that a corporation can have a "purpose" at all? Some corporate law scholars question whether a corporation can and should have a purpose. Why or why not?

2. Do you think that firms should be required to disclose only those climate-related risks that are financially material to the firm's bottom line, or those that are environmentally significant, even if not financially material?

3. Do you think that firms should be required to engage in mandatory climate-related risk disclosures such as those envisioned by the SEC, or do you think that voluntary disclosures are sufficient? Why or why not?

4. Does the SEC's mandate to ensure the integrity of markets include or exclude mandating the disclosure of environmental and climate risks?

5. The SEC's 2010 climate disclosure guidance and its draft disclosure rule focused on the *physical* risks of climate change and the *transition* risks. The physical risks include the effects on a company of sea level rise, heat waves, and reductions in crop yields among others. The transition risks include the effects on a company of transitioning to a decarbonized economy. Yet when the SEC provided examples of transition risks it focused largely on the financial risks posed by a carbon tax, carbon regulations, or other government measures. Do some PEG initiatives, such as supply chain requirements, or investor or lender pressure to decarbonize, pose material transition risks to some companies? If you were responsible for a company's climate risk disclosure, would you disclose these risks? Why or why not?

---

[5] 486 U.S. 492, 500–01 (1988).

6. Should the United States amend its antitrust laws to include a "conservation exception" or a more general exception for activities that enhance public welfare? What kinds of cooperation would you want to include in this conservation exception, and how would you ensure that firms do not abuse the exception?

Chapter 6

CRITICAL PERSPECTIVES ON PRIVATE ENVIRONMENTAL GOVERNANCE: GREENWASHING AND ANTI-ESG LAWS

This Chapter addresses a number of critical perspectives on private environmental governance. First, it discusses the charge that PEG is just corporate greenwashing rather than meaningful environmental action, and goes into depth about how both public law and private action can help to deter or ferret out misleading marketing claims. Second, it discusses recent backlash in a number of states against "ESG" or "woke" integration into business and financing strategies more broadly. The discussion of this backlash describes some of the laws that states have adopted requiring divestment of pension assets or cancelling of state contracts with firms that engage in ESG integration, in particular, with respect to climate change.

I. Greenwashing

When business firms adopt PEG to address environmental problems like climate change, biodiversity loss, water scarcity and toxic chemicals, it is essential to ask whether these private commitments are real or whether they are merely "greenwashing," burnishing their brand with no real intent to change behavior. PEG may be meaningless, or even harmful, if corporate claims of environmentally responsible behavior are bogus. Indeed, a major criticism of PEG stems from skepticism that the claims are real.

To give one concrete example, in the past several years, thousands of business firms globally have stated their intention to achieve "net zero" emissions by 2050, in line with the goals of the Paris Agreement. However, a recent study by the New Climate Institute reviewed the climate strategies of twenty-five major global firms, and concluded that the actual commitments firms had made were likely to reduce their emissions by only 40 percent, rather than 100 percent.[1] And some firms had not taken any meaningful actions beyond their vocal pledges.

There is no question that anyone—be it a firm or a government—making a public climate commitment should make that commitment

---

[1] THOMAS DAY ET AL., CORPORATE CLIMATE RESPONSIBILITY MONITOR: ASSESSING THE TRANSPARENCY AND INTEGRITY OF COMPANIES' EMISSION REDUCTION AND NET-ZERO TARGETS 5 (2022).

with integrity. We note as an aside that private companies are not the only entities that may not be completely fulfilling their climate commitments. Studies of the extent to which nations have fulfilled their commitments under the Paris Agreement suggest that countries are complying with their commitments at levels that are comparable to the levels that corporations are complying with their commitments, and many governments are struggling to regulate corporate emissions so the viable options may be limited. Thus while we focus on greenwashing by private firms in this Chapter, keep in mind that greenwashing applies to both companies *and* governments.

We also wish to point out that some scholarship questions whether greenwashing is always problematic. These scholars argue that even partially fulfilled commitments may make important contributions to climate mitigation by creating a sense among corporate managers that climate commitments are the norm. This may have positive spillover effects on the extent to which other companies make—and fulfill or partially fulfill—their own climate commitments. This does not suggest that greenwashing is good, only that lawyers, managers, and advocates will benefit by taking the same critical approach to thinking about greenwashing as they will from thinking about other environmental issues.

This Chapter delves into the issue of greenwashing, first identifying what greenwashing is and why firms might be motivated to engage in greenwashing. It then discusses the legal limits on greenwashing, focusing primarily on the Federal Trade Commission's authority to enforce laws governing deceptive practices affecting commerce, Securities and Exchange Commission (SEC) disclosure rules, and state laws that are designed to protect consumers from false or deceptive advertising. It then examines the ways in which PEG itself can address or limit greenwashing, primarily through the use of third-party certifications and disclosures.

A. Defining Greenwashing

A consumer products company advertises its disposable coffee pods as "recyclable" when they are technically capable of being recycled, but are not actually accepted by most local municipal recycling programs. A fossil fuel firm publishes a glossy advertisement touting its major investments in renewable energy when in fact those investments constitute less than one half of one percent of the firm's business. An investment firm publishes a commitment to achieve "net zero by 2050" in its investment portfolio but still holds shares in fossil fuel companies and does not vote those shares in favor of measures that would accelerate decarbonization. A major mining company changes its logo to the color green and includes images of trees and nature in its annual corporate sustainability report without any meaningful changes in policy. Are any of these actions greenwashing?

The term "greenwashing" refers to a broad set of deceptive marketing practices about the environmental impacts of a product, service, or an entity's own operations or impacts. Most commonly, the term refers to marketing claims by business firms that publicly misrepresent or exaggerate the positive environmental attributes of a product or service, while minimizing or ignoring the negative environmental attributes or impacts. But greenwashing is broader than this—it can also include public misrepresentations or deceptive communications about a firm's overall environmental strategy, operations, or impacts. And greenwashing behavior is not limited to business firms. Many scholars and commentators have pointed out that governments, individuals, and non-governmental organizations can *all* engage in greenwashing. However, because the focus of this text is PEG, we focus here on greenwashing in the business context.

One important note to keep in mind throughout this discussion is that the term "greenwashing" is a colloquial one that is used in common language—it is not a legal term like "fraud" or "battery" or "negligence." Whether members of the public might informally be troubled by a firm's advertisements or statements in corporate sustainability reports does not mean those advertisements are therefore subject to legal enforcement actions.

Before we can understand which forms of greenwashing might raise legal concerns, which public regulators have the authority to assess the integrity of green marketing claims, and whether PEG itself could act as an enforcement mechanism to prevent, deter, or ferret out greenwashing, it is essential to understand that greenwashing can take many forms. Accordingly, this section begins with a discussion of the different types of greenwashing which range from false statements to deceptive or misleading symbols, offering examples to help highlight the challenges that arise in addressing these claims. The next section will then discuss some of the reasons why firms might be tempted to engage in greenwashing, and the implications of greenwashing.

1. *False Product- and Firm-Level Claims*

The most straightforward type of greenwashing occurs when a firm makes a false statement in an advertisement for its products or services. Examples of such claims have included factual statements in advertisements that a firm's toilet paper was made of recycled materials, when in fact only the inner cardboard tube was made of recycled materials but the toilet paper itself was not. These have also included claims that products were vegan when they contained honey or milk-based ingredients, or that cookware was "earth-friendly" and "non-toxic" when in fact they contained chemicals that were known to be harmful to human health.

And not all greenwashing claims involve words—greenwashing can also include false symbols or images. That could mean that a firm displays a third-party certification on a product when it has not in fact earned the certification. Likewise, a false claim could involve a firm inventing a fake eco-label that it then displays on a product.

While product-based claims are the easiest cases, not all greenwashing occurs in product advertising. Some claims of greenwashing are about the environmental impact of the firm itself. Critics have argued that statements in firms' corporate sustainability reports, which are voluntary descriptions by firms of their environmental programs and achievements, or statements in overall "brand advertising" that do not focus on a specific product, can generate false impressions about the firm. These greenwashing claims focus more broadly on the firm's overall operations and impacts. Thus, a firm could engage in greenwashing by making false claims in a corporate sustainability report that it has achieved "net zero" or "carbon negative" emissions when the firm has not actually achieved this goal. Alternatively, a firm could claim in a sustainability report that it has achieved a certain degree of water efficiency in its beverages unit when in fact it has not achieved the stated level of water efficiency.

One major area in which claims of greenwashing have arisen relates to the use of carbon offsets by business firms to achieve their emissions reductions or net zero targets. Some portion of private GHG reduction commitments can be made through the onsite actions of the firm making the voluntary commitment to reduce its environmental footprint. For example, a firm can purchase renewable energy to power its facilities or enter into a long-term power purchase agreement for solar power. A utility bound by emissions regulations can make energy efficiency improvements in generating power or switch fuel sources from carbon-intensive sources like coal to zero carbon sources like wind or solar. A private firm can implement a limited carbon budget for business travel by employees or divest from carbon-intensive activities within its value chain. In some cases, however, emissions reductions within the firm's immediate footprint may be inadequate, too expensive, or require such substantial changes to its business model that it may be unable or unwilling to make such changes to achieve voluntary net zero commitments.

According to the accounting and consulting firm Accenture, as of late 2022, more than one third of the world's largest companies have made net zero commitments, but more than ninety percent of those firms will not achieve their goals without significantly increasing the pace of emissions reductions with intermediate targets by 2030.[2] How is it possible to reduce emissions to net zero along this timetable? That is where carbon offsets (or credits) come in.

One carbon credit represents the reduction of one metric ton of carbon dioxide equivalent somewhere in the world. An entity may then use this credit to *offset* one ton of emissions from its overall emissions balance, leading to an accounting reduction. While private firms making net zero commitments pursuant to a third-party certification program like the Science-Based Targets Initiative (discussed further below) are limited in the amount of emissions reductions that can come from offsetting, many private firms making purely voluntary emissions reductions pledges face no limits on the percentage of reductions that can be met through offsets. Offsets are usually project-based, and can be generated from projects that include afforestation/reforestation projects (planting trees or preventing the destruction of forests), carbon capture and storage (CCS), shifts in agricultural practices, methane capture from waste, and renewable energy generation, among others.

Despite their ability to reduce or remove greenhouse gasses from the atmosphere, carbon offsets are controversial. First, there is controversy as to their legitimacy: namely, whether firms should be permitted at all to achieve "net zero" goals through purchasing offsets as opposed to reducing their own emissions. Second, there is controversy over how to ensure the integrity of offsets, to ensure that they meet the criteria of additionality, permanence, no leakage, and no double-counting. Third, there is a debate over what types of offset projects should qualify: those that avoid or reduce emissions or also those that remove emissions already present in the atmosphere.

Arguably, the biggest concerns about greenwashing arise on the second point—whether they are actually reducing emissions as pledged by their purveyor or their purchaser. Some offsets will very likely reduce emissions, such as offsets that pay for new systems to capture methane emissions that would have otherwise leaked from landfills. But what if a firm's net-zero commitment depends upon the planting of trees? Those trees are subject to substantial wildfire risk, and thus may not be able sequester the necessary amounts of carbon on a long-term or permanent basis? What if the country in which the trees are being planted is simultaneously counting the carbon credits

---

2 ACCENTURE, ACCELERATING GLOBAL COMPANIES TOWARD NET ZERO BY 2050 (2022).

against its national carbon budget, so that the private firm purchasing the credit and the nation are both counting the single tree in two account balances? What if the offset results from a pledge to prevent forests from being cleared when there was no real threat of deforestation in the first place?

And if the carbon credit is not actually removing carbon from the atmosphere, but is instead simply emitting fewer tons of carbon than an alternative activity (e.g., burning national gas instead of coal), should this generate an offset? What if the trees would have been planted anyway, even in the absence of the carbon market, thus raising the concern that the carbon removals were not "additional"? You can see how these questions become both fact-intensive inquiries and complex. But at the end of the day, if a firm is making a pledge to reduce or net out its emissions that relies on purchasing offsets, and the carbon-reduction projects do not deliver as promised, then arguably the net-zero commitment is subject to the charge of greenwashing.

To summarize, the easiest category of greenwashing to understand and to police is when a business firm makes a factual claim—one that can be verified as true or false—and the claim is demonstrably false. The Federal Trade Commission has pursued such claims for directly false factual assertions, for example, against both Engineered Plastics Systems and American Plastic Lumber, Inc.. Each of these firms had made claims about the percentage of recycled content of its "plastic lumber" products such as benches and picnic tables. The FTC determined that products were made with far less recycled content than was claimed in the advertisements. Delta has been sued by passengers for using allegedly non-additional offsets to reduce its overall GHG emissions.

Demonstrating truth and falsity may become more complicated for firm-level greenwashing, as you can see from the example of carbon offsets.

2. *Deceptive or Misleading Claims and Images*

Not all claims in advertisements or corporate sustainability reports are factual claims that can easily be verified as true or false, however. A far broader category of marketing practices that fit under the umbrella of greenwashing includes claims or images that are deceptive or misleading. These claims may be factual in nature—or not. They may even include claims that are technically true, but that in the larger context are deceptive or misleading because they create a mistaken impression in the minds of consumers about the environmental benefits or positive environmental attributes of a product, service or the firm itself.

For example, many products made of plastic are marked with a "chasing arrows" recycling symbol, formed by three arrows in the shape of a triangle. Consumers understand the chasing arrows symbol to mean that the product can be recycled, and therefore, that they should deposit the product into a recycling bin at the end of its useful life, rather than into the trash. It may in fact be true that the plastic resin in the product is technologically capable of being recycled somewhere in the world. However, many recycling programs in municipalities do not actually have the capacity to recycle all different types of plastic resins. Accordingly, the state of California has recently adopted a law that prohibits the use of the chasing arrows symbol on plastic packaging unless the firm using the symbol can demonstrate that the product can actually be accepted for recycling in most communities in California, and that the plastic that is generated from the recycling process is actually reused as feedstock for new products. The state of New York is currently considering a similar bill. Thus, a plastic yogurt container may be technically capable of being recycled, but if the symbol appears on the product in California and it can only be recycled in Massachusetts, then the use of the chasing arrows symbol is misleading and subjects the firm to legal liability and penalties.

Other environmental claims in advertisements can be technically true but misleading in other ways. For example, a firm may include a claim in its advertisements that its product is "free of chlorofluorocarbons (CFCs)" despite the fact that CFCs have been banned in the United States since the late 1980s. *All* products are therefore CFC-free. But a consumer who isn't up to speed on the details of the Montreal Protocol on Ozone-Depleting Substances (i.e., almost all consumers) might not know this fact. She might assume that of two competing products on the shelf, the one that says it is "CFC-free" is better for the environment. She might therefore choose to purchase that product, even paying a price premium when, in fact, the two products are identical along this dimension.

Other examples of deceptive advertising include claims by investment firms that their investment funds are "green" or "socially responsible." However, in the investment industry, there are many potential ways for a fund to be cognizant of environmental risks or impacts (or other social or governance factors, if we are considering the broader "ESG investment" movement). Some funds may exclude certain types of stocks from a portfolio, such as upstream oil and gas firms. Other funds may continue to invest in oil and gas firms, but use their influence as investors to push for a greater focus on decarbonization. Other funds may invest actively in firms that seek to reduce or avoid emissions, such as renewable energy generation, carbon capture and sequestration technologies, or electric vehicle production. But because to date there have been no clear rules on what a "green" investment fund is, several studies have shown that funds claiming to be "green" often continue to invest in fossil fuel firms or coal companies.

It is ambiguous as a factual matter whether this is deceptive or misleading, as some might argue that continuing to hold shares in such firms while working actively to decarbonize their business operations is not greenwashing. This, too, is an area that has drawn the attention of regulators including within the European Union and the United States through the Securities and Exchange Commission, each of which have issued rules or proposed rules to require firms making claims about their investment funds "greenness" to back these claims up with more transparent investment criteria about how to categorize different types of funds data.

There are, however, more complex examples of misleading or deceptive claims in advertisements. A good example is the issue of whether electric hand driers or paper towels in restrooms are better for the environment. The environmental comparison is actually quite complicated. When a manufacturer of electric hand driers claims that its product is environmentally preferable because it "generates no paper waste," the fact that it does not generate such waste is technically a true statement. However, the factors that must be compared are not just about paper waste—they also include the upstream environmental impacts of the manufacture of the electric drier versus the upstream environmental impacts of quantity of paper towels it might replace over its useful life, as well as the emissions generated from the electricity needed to power the electric drier. These emissions may depend upon whether the power generated locally relies on fossil fuels or on renewable sources. So an advertisement that focuses only on one aspect of this environmental comparison may be misleading or deceptive if the overall environmental impact of the hand drier is actually worse, considering the entire lifecycle of each product.

This example raises an important issue about what evidence might be required to substantiate an environmental marketing claim. If a firm wants to claim that its product is "better" for the environment, should it be required to conduct a full lifecycle analysis? As you can see from this example, some cases of misleadingness or deception may be easier to police than others.

Deceptive and misleading claims can also arise at the level of the firm as well. For example, a firm might highlight its investments in renewable energy in a corporate sustainability report, but these investments may form a tiny percentage of the firm's overall business, which is focused on fossil fuel extraction. Or a firm might highlight a reduction in the intensity of its overall water use (meaning the water used per product unit)—when its absolute water use has increased due to an increase in the number of products/units produced. Each of these statements might be technically true, but could be deceptive or misleading to a consumer, investor, or member of the general public.

In contrast to some of these forms of deceptive or misleading environmental marketing claims, some advertisements are simply seeking to create a positive overall impression of a firm or its products and services by using flowery or vague language. This is arguably the point of many marketing campaigns. Examples of such claims include words like "green," "natural," or "earth-friendly." Other examples may include image advertising, such as the use of the color green, images of nature scenes within an advertisement or of children frolicking in a field of flowers. It is hard to categorize such imagery or flowery language as "true" or "false," but in certain contexts—for example, such images in an advertisement for a mining company—they may create a more positive impression of the firm's environmental record or attributes than is warranted.

One example of fanciful imagery that has sparked claims of greenwashing includes BP's (formerly British Petroleum's) adoption of a green and yellow "helios" logo. The firm adopted this new logo as part of a strategic campaign in 2000 to highlight that all energy ultimately comes from the sun. This symbol cannot be verified as true or false—however, some critics have argued that it represents an effort to mislead the public about the firm's environmental record, and to distract from environmental disasters like the BP Oil Spill in the Gulf of Mexico. Other examples of fanciful image-based advertisements that have drawn public ire include Mazda's advertisement, in concert with the producers of the film "Dr. Seuss's The Lorax," that showed a Mazda CX-5 driving through "Truffula Valley" with the statement that the car received the "Truffula Tree certified seal of approval." Unlike a false certification claim that could arguably mislead the public about whether it is real, it is not likely that any adult consumer would be fooled by a claim of the "Truffula Tree" certification. It is not likely to rise to the level of a legally actionable claim. Indeed, use of this imagery is mere fancy. But it nonetheless falls under the umbrella of greenwashing, as firms using fanciful imagery may be seeking to create a more positive impression of their environmental performance than is warranted.

B. Why Firms Engage in Greenwashing

Why do firms engage in greenwashing in the first place? Empirical research has demonstrated that when a firm markets its corporate or social environmental responsibility efforts, this can influence consumer perceptions about the quality of the firm's goods and services, as well as about the firm overall, in ways that influence purchasing decisions. Empirical research has also demonstrated that many employees seek employment with firms with stronger environmental performance. In addition, claims by firms that they are engaging in private environmental governance or otherwise limiting their environmental impacts can influence perceptions about not only individual firms but the industry as a whole is perceived by the public, including investors, consumers, and regulators, with implications for the public's appetite for public regulations on the same subject matter. This Part discusses the most important reasons why firms engage in greenwashing.

1. Influencing Consumers and Other Stakeholders

Business firms take a number of different steps to gain legitimacy in the views of firm stakeholders. These can include actions that are real, actions that are merely window-dressing, or something in between. In other words, if there are incentives to be viewed as environmentally aware, firms will seek to be perceived as environmentally aware. Empirical studies have demonstrated that firms with weak environmental performance that nonetheless market themselves as having strong environmental performance (greenwashing) gain a reputational benefit. While they are not perceived to have as good environmental performance as those organizations that actually perform well environmentally, weak environmental performers that tout their environmental credentials are perceived to be better on that dimension than weak environmental performers that remain silent on the issue. In other words, even for polluting firms, highlighting the environmental benefits of the firm's goods, services or operations appears to be better than remaining silent.

What is the mechanism that yields this reputational benefit? Research in this area categorizes the benefit as a "halo effect." The "halo effect" is a psychological phenomenon that when an individual perceives one aspect of a firm's products, services or operations to be positive along a certain dimension (such as environmentally beneficial), they are more likely to extrapolate that positive impression or "halo" to other aspects of the firm's products, services, or operations along the same dimension, even in the absence of evidence. To give a concrete example, if I were to learn that a firm used renewable energy to power its operations in one of its manufacturing facilities, I would be inclined to believe that the firm's other manufacturing facilities were equally environmentally beneficial, even in the absence of any direct evidence to that effect.

The halo effect has been studied in many contexts. For example, one study demonstrated that when consumers learned that a firm engaged in charitable giving or a corporate social responsibility program, they perceived the firm's products to be of higher quality than when they learned nothing about the firm's beneficence. This was true even when the products were totally unrelated to the subject of the charitable giving or CSR program—such as a tooth whitening product or hair-regrowth serum. There is an important limitation, which is that when consumers perceive the engagement in a corporate social responsibility program to be for selfish or strategic reasons, rather than out of benevolence, the halo effect does not necessarily arise. Thus, when consumers know it is fake or greenwashing, the reputational benefit does not come about. However, studies have shown that even when consumers know that positive environmental marketing is not *entirely* true, the mere fact that an organization has cared enough to speak about environmental performance creates some minor reputational benefit. This suggests that firms are more likely to highlight aspects of their environmental performance that are true (even if small) rather than to make outright false statements.

Why does the halo effect matter? It can drive consumer choices within the marketplace. If Firm A highlights its use of renewable energy and Firm B remains silent, I might perceive even Firm A's unrelated products to be of higher quality and choose to purchase them in the marketplace over those of Firm B.

It is worth noting that consumers of a firm's products and services may not be limited to retail (individual) consumers. Business-to-business relationships may likewise depend upon the environmental qualities of the products and services produced by a firm. As we discuss in Chapters 8 and 10, many firms specifically seek out raw materials and products within their supply chains that have environmental qualities or characteristics. For example, a company renovating its offices might seek a carpeting or flooring solution with a lower-than-average carbon footprint or one that is made of recycled materials. A food and beverage conglomerate might seek to partner with ingredient suppliers who engage in regenerative agricultural practices and sequester carbon in the soils by planting cover crops. Greenwashing can likewise distort this business-to-business market and supply chain contracting.

In addition, stakeholders of the firm other than consumers may care a great deal about the organization's environmental practices. For example, studies have shown that certain employees prefer to work for organizations that take their environmental impacts seriously, and indeed, are willing to accept lower salaries to work for an environmentally-minded firms. So in addition to influencing consumer choices, greenwashing could influence the employment-related decisions of employees and potential employees who choose to work for Firm A over Firm B. Studies also show that firms often need local community support to build or expand a data center, office, or factory, and they manage their environmental reputation to build good will with community stakeholders.

2. *Policy Spillovers*

A second important implication of environmental marketing is that it may affect public attitudes about whether public law or regulation is needed to address a particular environmental problem. Scholars have referred to this impact as "policy spillover" and importantly, spillovers can be either positive or negative.

Negative spillovers occur when members of the public learn that private firms are engaging in private environmental governance to address a problem and conclude the public laws or regulations are not needed on the same subject matter. In other words "the private sector is already managing the problem." For example, one study demonstrated that when members of the public learned that all firms in an industry had adopted standards to use recycled materials in their products (as compared to only half of the firms in the industry), the participants were less likely to support public laws or regulation on the subject of recycling. Often, there is an assumption that any policy spillovers from private environmental governance are likely to be negative.

However, research has also shown that policy spillovers can be positive. In other words, upon learning that business firms have adopted private environmental governance, in some circumstances, members of the public may actually be more inclined to support public laws or regulations on the same subject matter. One study recently tested whether ideological views served as a moderating factor in the direction of policy spillovers, concluding that members of the public who identify as conservative were actually more likely to support public policies on certain environmental issues when they learned that major corporations were already adopting private governance on the issue. Specifically, the study tested whether there were differences in support for public policies on cage-free eggs when participants learned that either the state of California or McDonald's was adopting a policy of purchasing only cage-free eggs. Interestingly, while liberals were generally supportive of public policies requiring cage-free eggs, conservatives were not—unless they learned that McDonald's had adopted a supply chain policy of only purchasing cage-free eggs. The authors hypothesized that conservatives found the source—a major corporation—to be "credible" on the issue in a way that the state of California was not (just full of tree-huggers), and that conservatives were more likely to perceive the issue as a real problem if a corporation were concerned about it. Another recent study found that the positive and negative effects of private efforts essentially cancel each other out, leaving no economically significant spillover or crowding out effects.

It is of course worth noting that in the past few years there has been a significant backlash by some conservative politicians and commentators against corporate actions that are perceived to be "woke" or taking into account environmental or social factors like climate change. Accordingly, if this study were repeated now, it is possible that the effect on conservatives of learning about a hypothetical McDonald's policy on cage-free eggs might likewise be different.

C. Legal Rules to Address Greenwashing

Some scholars have identified yet another reason why firms engage in greenwashing—the lack of clear rules and inconsistent enforcement of existing rules. This Part briefly surveys several of the key sources of public law to address greenwashing, including at the federal and state levels. We note that other nations have public law rules to address greenwashing, including the recent EU Taxonomy and Sustainable Finance Disclosure Regulation, but we focus here primarily on domestic laws in the United States.

Most importantly, we divide these legal rules into two categories—ex post enforcement actions (such as by the Federal Trade Commission or by the states under state false advertising laws) and ex ante disclosure rules (such as the SEC's climate-related disclosure requirements). These two different categories of legal rules serve complementary purposes. While ex post enforcement actions such as by the FTC or the states under state false advertising laws serve to address specific claims made by firms that can be demonstrated to be false or misleading, ex ante disclosure rules arguably aim to deter or prevent greenwashing by increasing the amount of factual and accurate information available to members of the public. Disclosure rules likewise do not require courts or regulators to make determinations as to whether a specific claim is false or misleading in a given circumstance, which as we see above, can be challenging and contested as a legal matter.

1. The Federal Trade Commission

The primary regulator at the federal level in the United States for claims of false, misleading, or deceptive advertising is the Federal Trade Commission (FTC). The FTC is authorized under the Federal Trade Commission Act, which was adopted in 1914 to prohibit "unfair methods of competition" that affect commerce, including false or deceptive advertising claims. The Act broadly prohibits the use of "unfair or deceptive acts or practices in or affecting commerce," and defines "unfair methods of competition" to include false or deceptive advertising claims. The goal of the statute is to protect consumers.

To establish a violation of the Act in the context of a deceptive marketing claim, the FTC has interpreted the Act to require three showings: first, that the defendant made a "representation, omission or practice;" second, that the representation, omission, or practice was likely to mislead a "consumer acting reasonably in the circumstances;" and third, that the representation was "material."[3]

As noted above in the general discussion, a representation, omission or practice could include the use of a statement or an image, a certification or label, or a test or demonstration that aims to verify an environmental marketing claim.

With respect to demonstrating that a claim is "likely to mislead" the FTC is not required to put forward evidence that any consumers were actually misled in fact, but rather than the claim has the potential to mislead or the "capacity" to deceive. And the defendant's lack of intention to deceive is not relevant to the inquiry. For example, a court upheld the FTC's conclusion that an advertisement by Montgomery Ward & Co. was misleading based on its "guarantee" in an advertisement, when there was a discrepancy between the advertisement and the actual guarantee certificates.[4] There was no evidence that a single customer had made a claim based on the advertised guarantee that was denied under the actual guarantee policy; the discrepancy alone was sufficient to establish that the statement was likely to mislead an ordinary consumer.

And finally, with respect to materiality, the FTC has defined the term to mean "whether the act or practice is likely to affect the consumer's conduct or decision with regard to a product or service"—in other words, whether the consumer would have made a different choice in the marketplace in the absence of the misleading information.

Starting in 1992, the FTC has published the Green Guides, which lay out the Commission's views on environmental marketing claims and how the broader FTC Act applies to such claims. These Guides, which are not binding regulations, but rather the FTC's interpretations of "how reasonable consumers likely interpret" various marketing claims, have been updated several times, most recently in 2012.

---

[3] Federal Trade Commission Policy Statement (Oct. 14, 1983), https://www.ftc.gov/system/files/documents/public_statements/410531/831014deceptionstmt.pdf.

[4] *Montgomery Ward & Co. v. FTC*, 379 F.2d 666 (7th Cir. 1967).

The Guides make clear that the FTC expects the claimant to possess evidence that any claims made in advertisements are supported by a "reasonable basis," which might include scientific studies, depending upon the claims made in the advertisements. The Guides further make clear that advertisers ought to avoid certain vague statements or claims of general environmental benefit because they may falsely convey that a product has no negative environmental impacts. Finally, there are specific guidelines providing for claims such as those regarding the use of renewable energy, biodegradability, recyclability, or whether a product is "free of" a substance, among other claims.

2. State Laws

Many states have followed the FTC's lead to adopt general laws prohibiting false or deceptive claims in advertising. Other states, led by California, have adopted even more specific laws to address specific forms of false advertising and even false or deceptive environmental marketing claims. For example, California not only has a general law prohibiting unfair competition, but also a false advertising law more specifically, and even more specifically, a prohibition on using the "chasing arrows" symbol on a product that cannot actually be recycled in the local area. Other states have likewise adopted specific prohibitions on false and deceptive advertising claims. In many cases, not only can the state Attorney General enforce these laws, but they also provide a private right of action to consumers who claim to have been misled by advertisements.

3. The Securities and Exchange Commission

In addition to laws specifically targeting false or deceptive advertising claims, federal securities laws provide both a public and private right of action for "material misstatements or omissions" by firms that offer securities to the public. Both the SEC and members of the investing public can enforce these provisions.

Under the Securities Exchange Act of 1934, it is unlawful for a person to use a "manipulative or deceptive device" in connection with the purchase or sale of securities. Under this statute, the SEC has promulgated Rule 10b–5, which prohibits an issuer from making "any untrue statement of material fact or. . . omit[ting] . . . a material fact" that would be necessary to make any statement made not misleading under the circumstances.[5] The purpose of these laws is to ensure transparency and market integrity.

---

[5] 17 C.F.R. § 140.10b–5(a) (2021).

Although Rule 10b–5 in theory offers a remedy for greenwashing claims by issuers of securities, there are some important limitations. First, consistent with other constitutional limitations, broad "expressions of opinion" rather than fact are not actionable under Rule 10b–5. And claims that are so vague as to be meaningless or "puffery" are likewise not actionable as false or misleading. For example, when Ford Motor Company made public statements about its commitment to safety, and its tires were subsequently recalled—clearly demonstrating a safety issue—a court rejected claims that broad and vague statements like "Ford is a worldwide leader in automotive safety" were misleading under Rule 10b–5. The court concluded that such general claims were either "mere corporate puffery or hyperbole" that a reasonable investor would not view as material to any investment decision.[6] Likewise, statements by an executive that accidents were the result of driver error were found by the court to constitute statements of opinion rather than of fact.

Despite the limitations of Rule 10b–5 enforcement actions to police claims of greenwashing, the SEC has other arrows in its quiver. The securities laws also require issuers to make periodic public reports of information to investors. Specifically, Regulation S–K requires mandatory annual and quarterly reports—on form 10Ks and 10Qs, respectively, as well as in the case of a specific event like a merger on Form 8K. The purpose of these reports is to promote market integrity and protect against manipulation of stock prices. Information that is material to investors must be disclosed—namely that information that would affect decisions to purchase, hold or sell securities.

Since the 1980s, the SEC has required certain material environmental information to be included in these disclosures, including such information as the cost of compliance with environmental laws and the material impacts of environmental risk events, as well as material environmental legal proceedings. In 2010, the SEC issued guidance clarifying its view that existing regulations required the disclosure of certain climate-related risks. These include the impact of actual or potential climate-related legislation or regulation, risks such as changes in demand for goods and services, or physical risks that could affect operations. This guidance was spottily enforced, however, and many of the disclosures made during the time it remained in force tended to be boilerplate disclosures saying very little of substance.

In 2022, the SEC published a proposed regulation on Enhancement and Standardization of Climate-Related Disclosures, which would require firms to include both quantitative and non-

---

6 *In re Ford Motor Co. Securities Litigation,* 381 F.3d 563, 566 (6th Cir. 2004).

quantitative information about climate risk in its periodic reports. The status of the proposed regulation will be uncertain for some time, which will leave some aspects of climate-related disclosure in doubt. However, the broad requirement to disclose material risks to investors will drive a substantial amount of disclosure, as will pressure on firms to participate in the private disclosure systems we discuss below and in Chapter 8.

D. PEG to Address Greenwashing

In addition to these public laws and regulations that can police claims of greenwashing, private environmental governance itself offers several tools to address claims of greenwashing—whether or not they rise to the level of legally actionable claims. The primary forms of PEG that may be able to ensure the credibility of environmental and climate-related private commitments include: third party certifications and partnerships with credible NGOs, public naming and shaming, and shareholder actions such as in the nascent "say on climate" approach or through shareholder resolutions.

In the first instance, third-party certifications can serve as a basis for ensuring the validity or integrity of private environmental governance initiatives. We discuss many of these in detail in Chapter 8, such as SBTi, SASB, GRI, CDP and Climate Action 100+, all of which play a role in encouraging, structuring, and policing corporate climate claims. For example, while any firm could make a general "net zero" pledge, the Science-Based Targets Initiative (SBTi) has defined what constitutes a "science-based" target, and requires firms that seek to use its certification to meet certain stringent standards. Firms must commit to set such a target, work with SBTi to develop a target that meets the SBTi's criteria, submit the proposed target to SBTi for validation, announce the target to stakeholders publicly, and track and disclose progress toward the target annually. SBTi also requires that firms using its certification actually reduce emissions by 90 percent before carbon offsets may be used to reduce the final 10 percent of emissions. Firms that have gone through this process are recognized on the SBTi website as "committed" as well as by other related partner organizations (CDP, WWP, WRI and the UN Global Compact) that participated in developing the science-based standards and metrics. We note that in 2022, the federal government's Federal Acquisition Regulatory Council proposed the *Federal Supplier Climate Risks and Resilience Rule* which would require major federal contractors to publicly disclosure their GHG emissions and climate-related financial risks, and to set science-based emission-reduction targets. The specifics of the required disclosures depend upon the value of annual contracts with higher standards imposed on larger contractors.

In other contexts such as forests and fisheries, third-party NGOs like MSC and FSC have some ability to establish whether voluntary environmental claims and pledges are credible, since they police the use of their labels for fisheries and forests before granting their third-party certifications. While third-party certifications hold great promise to ensure the credibility of private commitments, its worth noting that the profusion of private standards and lack of clarity about which standards are meaningful is a real problem that may hinder the effectiveness of third-party certifications in this regard. It is also worth pointing out that certification provides an endorsement that a company's claim is accurate, but it does not necessarily make clear that the claim is meaningful or not otherwise greenwashing some other aspect of a firm's environmental footprint.

Naming and shaming is a second method of private governance to address claims of greenwashing. As we discuss in detail in Chapters 8 and 10, naming and shaming initiatives use climate- or environmental-related information to create moral or normative pressure for emissions reductions, often by affecting companies' reputation. Reputation is critical to consumer-facing companies with recognizable brand names, so they spend large sums creating positive reputations and defending against reputational attacks. They also invest heavily in developing positive brands for their products.

A third source within PEG that has the power to ensure the credibility of private climate and environmental commitments is embodied in the broad category of shareholder initiatives. One prominent initiative in this regard is "Say on Climate," which aims to push companies to publish their climate transition plans and to be accountable to shareholders on an annual basis through a vote on these climate transition plans. Major companies like Unilever, Moody's, Royal Dutch Shell, Glencore, Rio Tinto, Canadian National Railway, National Grid, Nestle, S&P Global, Total, and others have voluntarily adopted a commitment to the Say on Climate Campaign. And major asset managers and asset owners have stated publicly their support for this initiative. A second category of shareholder initiatives includes proposed shareholder resolutions—which are often non-binding—but which aim to focus company attention on particular environmental or climate-related issues. NGOs like As You Sow and the Sierra Club, individual filers, and major investment firms have filed resolutions seeking greater transparency on GHG emissions, water use, plastic pollution, methane measurement.

II. Anti-ESG Laws

A second major critique of PEG comes from those who think it goes too far or otherwise is outside the boundaries of what business firms and financial institutions should be considering in their decision making, risk management, and other aspects of strategy. These critiques have taken shape as a panoply of state anti-ESG laws, frequently singling out those financial firms that either have made climate commitments (to reduce emissions to net zero by 2050, to participate in an association such as the Net Zero Asset Managers Alliance under the Glasgow Financial Alliance for Net Zero), or that have made public statements that they are declining to invest in new fossil fuel projects of certain types (Arctic exploration, unabated coal-fired power plants). The state laws require either divestment of pension assets from such firms or make clear that the state and its agencies cannot do business with such firms. We categorize these laws below. Notably, there has been a backlash against this anti-ESG backlash; some state legislators have rejected these types of restrictions.

These state laws appear on their face simply to be echoing Milton Friedman's argument (discussed above in Chapter 2) that the purpose of a firm is to seek profits, rather than to pursue any other purpose (such as social good). However, to the extent that either the physical or transition risks associated with climate change could materially affect the financial position of the firm, its assets or investments, or the products and services it offers, even Milton Friedman would have to admit that firm managers have discretion to these factors into account in their strategic decision making.

In Chapter 5 we discussed how the business judgment rule affords firm managers a significant sphere of discretion to take into account those factors that managers deem relevant to business decisions. Under the business judgment rule, courts will not second-guess firm managers' decisions to weigh particular factors in their decision making, unless such decisions were tainted by a conflict of interest or some form of self-dealing. Under this governing law, managers of a firm who determine that financial risks related to climate change are material to the value of an asset—for example, homes in Florida whose mortgages have been bundled into a securitized asset and that face flood risk or the long-term risk of sea-level rise—can take that assessment into account in their decision making about whether to purchase, hold, or sell the asset. Asset managers may likewise determine that the risk of regulation of emissions from unabated coal-fired power plants is high (see, for example the EPA's recent proposed regulations on greenhouse gas emissions from stationary sources) and choose not to invest in new coal-fired power plants. Or they may determine that corporate supply chain commitments will reduce the profitability of a company by reducing the demand for the company's products. Similarly, a financial firm that manages investment funds may take these financial considerations into account. Each of these decisions involves the application of business managers' discretion to determine whether risks or opportunities related to climate change may affect the short- or long-term value of assets or investments.

Some of these anti-ESG laws turn the business judgment rule on its head by expressly prohibiting the consideration of "environmental" or "social" factors, and deeming them categorically not financially material. Other anti-ESG laws take a slightly more limited approach and may be more bluster than bite.

For example, in 2021, Texas SB 13 came into effect. The statute has two primary components. The first prohibits certain listed state agencies, including various pension fund managers such as the Employees Retirement System of Texas, the Teacher Retirement System of Texas, among others, from doing business with financial companies that "boycott energy companies." The term "boycott energy companies" is defined in the law to mean:

> without an ordinary business purpose, refusing to deal with, terminating business activities with, or otherwise taking any action that is intended to penalize, inflict economic harm on, or limit commercial relations with a company because the company:
>
> > (A) engages in the exploration, production, utilization, transportation, sale, or manufacturing of fossil fuel-based energy and does not commit or pledge to meet environmental standards beyond applicable federal and state law; or
> >
> > (B) does business with a company described by Paragraph (A).[7]

The law provides a process by which the state Comptroller prepares an initial list of financial institutions that qualify for this provision based on public information, and then gives those companies notice and an opportunity to verify that they do not in fact boycott energy companies under the definition in the text. The law further obligates the state officials managing these pension funds to sell, divest, or withdraw all publicly traded securities of such companies.

---

[7] SB 13, § 809.001(7).

While the law makes clear that divestment from such "boycotters" is the goal, there are several important exceptions that arguably (as a matter of statutory interpretation) swallow the rule. First is the language "without an ordinary business purpose," in the definition of boycott above. Any firm taking these climate or environmental-related risk factors into account arguably has a business purpose for doing so. Second is the express exception that if there is "clear and convincing evidence" that the state entity "has suffered or will suffer a loss in the hypothetical value of all assets under management by the state entity" as a result of the mandate to sell or divest from the listed firms.[8] There are other exceptions as well. These exceptions appear to blunt the force of the law on its face.

The second provision of the statute provides that no state or municipal agency may "enter into a contract" with a value of $100,000 or more with a financial company unless the company verifies that it "does not boycott energy companies" and "will not boycott energy companies during the term of the contract."[9] This prohibition on contracting contains similar exceptions when the state or municipal entity concludes that compliance with the prohibition would be "inconsistent with the governmental entity's constitutional or statutory duties."[10] Notably, this provision would affect municipal and state bond underwriting—an important aspect of how government entities raise funds for necessary projects. A number of other states have adopted similar laws either requiring pension divestment or prohibiting state contracting with financial institutions that are alleged to "boycott" energy companies.

Notably, as a factual matter, several economists conducted a study after Texas SB 13 and a counterpart provision related to the boycott of firearms manufacture that came into effect at the same time. They found that the Texas laws raised the cost of capital for the states enacting them. In the eight months following the adoption of the Texas laws, the five largest municipal bond writers exited the Texas market. The study concluded that this exit and resulting diminution in competition from these major players increased the state's borrowing costs between approximately $300–$500 million in additional interest payments.[11] A subsequent study of other similar state laws found that other states would likewise face increased interest payments and borrowing costs.

---

8 Id. § 809.056.

9 Id. § 2274.002.

10 Id. § 2274.002(c)

11 Daniel G. Garrett & Ivan T. Ivanov, Gas, Guns, and Governments: Financial Costs of Anti-ESG Policies (Feb. 14, 2023), available at https://ssrn.com/abstract=4123366.

A second category of laws, recently adopted by the Florida legislature to become effective on July 1, 2023, expressly prohibits the consideration of any "social, political, or ideological interests" by financial officials acting on behalf of the state in a number of capacities, including in pension and retirement investments, as well as in other types of organizations like citizen support organizations.[12] More specifically, it defines the term "pecuniary factor" as a factor that the relevant official "prudently determines is expected to have a material effect on the risk or returns of an investment based on appropriate investment horizons consistent with applicable investment objectives and funding policy. The term does not include the consideration of the furtherance of any social, political, or ideological interests."[13] The new law then mandates that—notwithstanding any other law—the state official "must make decisions based solely on pecuniary factors and may not subordinate the interests of the people of this state to other objectives, including sacrificing investment return or undertaking additional investment risk to promote any nonpecuniary factor."[14] Similar language applies to multiple types of state organizations, as well as to voting of proxies.

In addition, the new Florida statute creates Florida Statutes Section 215.681, which prohibits the issuance of ESG bonds by the state or any political subdivision within the state that has the power to issue bonds. This list includes municipalities, higher educational financing authorities, water and sewer districts, industrial development authorities, port and transit authorities, and others. The statute defines ESG Bonds as "any bonds that have been designated or labeled as bonds that will be used to finance a project with an ESG purpose, including, but not limited to, green bonds, Certified Climate Bonds, GreenStar designated bonds, and other environmental bonds marketed as promoting a generalized or global environmental objective; social bonds marketed as promoting a social objective; and sustainability bonds and sustainable development goal bonds marketed as promoting both environmental and social objectives. The term includes those bonds self-designated by the issuer as ESG-labeled bonds and those designated as ESG-labeled bonds by a third-party verifier."[15] In addition to prohibiting the issuance of such bonds, the statute prohibits the expenditure of public funds to pay a third party with respect to the designation of such bonds, and the entry into contracts with a rating agency "whose ESG scores for such issuer will have a direct, negative impact on the

---

[12] Florida Statutes, § 17.57(1)(a).

[13] Id.

[14] Id. § 17.57(1)(c).

[15] Id. § 215.681(c).

issuer's bond ratings." Thus, the law not only directs behavior by state and local officials; it further seeks to deprive ratings agencies (which take ESG scores into account) of state and local business.

Third, the new Florida statute states that "qualified public depository" institutions such as banks, savings banks and savings associations may make determinations about the "provision of services or the denial of services based on an analysis of risk factors unique to each customer or member."[16] It states that such institutions do "not engage in the unsafe and unsound practice of denying or canceling its services to a person, or otherwise discriminating against a person in making available such services or in the terms or conditions or such services" on the basis of a number of factors including the person's political affiliations, beliefs, or speech, as well as "any factor if it is not a quantitative, impartial, and risk-based standard, including any such factor related to the person's business sector,"[17] the use of rating based on a "social credit score," that is in turn based on the person's engagement in different industries like gun manufacturing or exploration, production, or sale of fossil fuels, or the person's "failure to meet or commit to meet, or expected failure to meet" environmental or social standards, benchmarks, or disclosures, so long as the person is in compliance with applicable law.[18] The law requires an attestation of compliance with these requirements in order to avoid certain penalties, up to and including the inability to continue to serve as a qualified public depository within the state.

Fourth, the Florida statute prohibits the consideration of social, political, or ideological interests in government contracts both at the state level and for political subdivisions of the state.[19] Similar provisions are adopted within the statute for state licensing requirements.[20] Similar provisions apply to vendor contracts with school districts, colleges and universities within the state system.[21]

Each of these state laws raises distinct legal issues, and in at least one case banks have challenged them. In Kentucky, the state attorney general has issued both subpoenas and civil investigative demands to major U.S. banks, raising concerns about the financial institutions' participation in the U.N.-sponsored Net Zero Banking Alliance. In 2023, the Kentucky Bankers Association filed a lawsuit challenging the attorney general's demands, arguing that these

---

16 Id. § 280.02(26)(e).

17 Id. § 280.02(26)(f).

18 Id.

19 Florida Statutes, § 287.05701.

20 Florida Statutes, § 560.1115.

21 Florida Statutes § 1010.04.

demands violated their First Amendment rights of freedom of speech and association, as well as challenging the demands as overbroad. In addition, Ceres, an NGO that mobilizes investor support for decarbonization, has organized a "Freedom to Invest" initiative that has pushed back against the more than 140 anti-ESG bills introduced in state legislatures.

Time will tell the extent to which others will challenge these laws and whether those challenges will be successful. And it is possible as well that if additional research demonstrates large costs to taxpayers of enacting such measures, the states will be more circumspect about keeping them on the books. But this is an important area to watch.

QUESTIONS AND DISCUSSION

1. Do you think that public legislation or regulation is strong enough to address concerns about greenwashing? How would you update or amend laws to make sure that environmental marketing claims are made with integrity?

2. Do you think that public legislation and regulation or private tools are preferable to address claims of greenwashing? Why?

3. Is greenwashing always bad? Are there any situations in which you would be concerned about robust enforcement of anti-greenwashing laws?

4. Your major company's competitors have all announced net zero by 2050 targets. Your CEO comes to you to say "we can't look bad by comparison—let's announce a target." What do you do?

5. You are the general counsel of BigCo. The marketing department has given you the following four proposed advertisements. What do you advise? How would you compare each of the options?

   a. BigCo. believes in a green future.

   b. BigCo. has committed to achieving net zero emissions by 2050.

   c. BigCo. Has committed to achieving net zero emissions by 2050 and is working with the Science-Based Targets Initiative to set concrete goals to get there.

   d. Say nothing about your environmental programs. You do not wish to be targeted by those who will say either that you haven't done enough/are greenwashing or that you have gone too far and are discriminating against fossil fuel companies.

Part II

PEG IN ACTION: CLIMATE AND ENERGY

Chapter 7

CLIMATE CHANGE: RISKS, SOURCES, AND MOTIVATIONS

PEG initiatives have played an important and growing role in reducing greenhouse gas (GHG) emissions, so it is appropriate that climate change is the first environmental problem we address in this book.

When government policymakers tackle pollution problems, they typically focus on what to regulate, how much to regulate, where to regulate, and how to regulate. In a top-down system with a comprehensive federal climate statute, an agency such as EPA has the responsibility to develop top-down answers to each of these questions. But climate change has been described as "the mother of all collective action problems" and no government authority—international, national or subnational governments—has developed adequate responses. GHG emissions continue to rise.

In contrast to the traditional top-down approach of environmental law, PEG climate initiatives have emerged bottom-up, with no individual policymaker or group of policymakers developing an overall strategy and guiding resources to the most important problems. This ad hoc approach makes comprehensive answers to the what, how much, where, and how questions elusive for PEG climate initiatives. But it also makes understanding the role of PEG in addressing climate change a dynamic, exciting, and rewarding topic. A system of PEG climate initiatives has emerged that uses the same types of tools as public governance, filling important gaps in government responses to climate change and expanding the options available to many environmental lawyers, managers, and advocates.

We explore private climate governance over the next three chapters. This chapter begins by explaining climate change basics—the climate science, the types and sources of greenhouse gas (GHG) emissions, and the impacts of climate change. The chapter then lays the foundation for our exploration of PEG climate mitigation initiatives by discussing the motivations or drivers of private sector decarbonization and the interactions between public and private climate governance. We turn in Chapters 8 and 9 to the governance tools deployed by PEG climate initiatives. Along the way, we identify the reasons why PEG is addressing many of the mismatched boundary, collective action and other problems that make climate change the most challenging environmental threat.

I. Climate Change Risks

Climate change has become the top environmental priority for many governments, advocacy groups, and companies because it threatens the very stability of the natural, social, economic, and political systems that human societies rely upon. Even with our best efforts, some climate impacts are essentially irreversible. Unfortunately, climate change has also become a polarizing issue. Climate change often ranks low on the list of voters' priorities yet high on the list of the most polarized issues in the United States and some other countries, and misinformation is widespread. To make sound judgments about the risks and the tradeoffs necessary to respond to climate risks and to understand the role of PEG, we need to know the facts—the basic science and the likely causes and effects of climate change.

A. Greenhouse Gases

There is nothing mysterious or uncertain about the basic greenhouse effect. Understanding it only requires a straightforward application of the same principles of heat flow used by engineers every day to design practical technologies. In short, more of the sun's energy is being trapped by the Earth's atmosphere than is released into space, causing the globe to warm and disrupting the climate.

The most important human-made (or "anthropogenic") GHGs contributing to this warming are carbon dioxide (CO_2), methane (CH_4), nitrous oxide (NO_x), and several fluorinated gases. For simplicity, we often refer to these gases as "carbon emissions" although not all of these gases include carbon. These gases only account for about 3% of the earth's atmosphere, but they trap large amounts of heat that the earth radiates after absorbing the warmth of the sun's heat. GHG concentrations have been rising over the last century, particularly rapidly in the last few decades. For instance, the pre-industrial concentration of CO_2 was 280 parts per million or ppm (imagine a jar of outdoor air that contains one million molecules, of which 280 molecules are CO_2). Concentrations in recent years have exceeded 420 ppm and may exceed 450 ppm by 2050. Since the 19th century industrial revolution, the fossil fuel-based economy has been burning oil, gas and coal for energy. This releases GHGs that natural processes transferred from the atmosphere to organic matter in prehistoric times (and that transformed over millions of years into today's fossil fuel deposits). Deforestation and agricultural practices are releasing GHGs as well.

Some GHGs contribute more to warming the atmosphere than others. Carbon dioxide accounts for roughly 80% of global warming from GHGs, and methane is second with roughly 10%. Some GHGs are emitted in small amounts but are very potent, more than 1,000 times as potent as CO_2. To provide a simple way to assess GHGs, scientists start with the global warming potential of CO_2 (how much energy a molecule of CO_2 in the atmosphere absorbs) and then evaluate other GHGs based on their warming potential as compared to CO_2. This is expressed as CO_2-equivalent or CO_2e. If CO_2 has a global warming potential of 1, for example, then methane has a global warming potential of 27 (i.e., a molecule of methane in the atmosphere contributes 27 times more warming than a molecule of CO_2). You will see these terms in government, NGO, and corporate climate reports, and in contracts, investment policies, judicial opinions, and other documents.

GHGs are not inherently problematic. Indeed, they are essential for a habitable planet. Without them, Earth would not trap enough of the sun's energy and would be a frozen chunk of dirt and stone. Over the Earth's history, GHG concentrations have changed over long periods as has the climate. But humans have affected this process by releasing GHGs from fossil fuel burning, agriculture, and other sources. And although oceans and forests absorb large amounts of CO_2 from the atmosphere, many GHGs are long-lived. A substantial amount of GHGs emitted today will continue warming the planet for centuries.

The warming effects of CO_2 have been known and widely acknowledged for more than a century. Policy disputes about climate change arise over how severe the effects will be, what steps should be taken to reduce GHG emissions, and how to adapt to a changing climate. For many years, discussions about climate change focused on the science and were not polarizing. For instance, in 1979 a nonpartisan panel of experts issued one of the earliest assessments of the science of climate change. The panel found that although considerable scientific uncertainties existed about the details, there was "no reason to doubt that climate changes will result" from burning fossil fuels and "no reason to believe that these changes will be negligible." In the face of these conclusions, and given the largely irreversible nature of climate change, the panel concluded that "[a] wait and see policy may mean waiting until it is too late." During the 2000 presidential campaign, both Al Gore *and* George W. Bush ran on pledges to address climate change. It was not a Red/Blue issue.

The Paris Agreement is a 2015 international climate agreement that identified global goals for limiting GHG concentrations in the atmosphere and required nationally determined contributions (NDCs) for emissions reductions by most countries. The Agreement's stated goal is to limit global warming to well below 2°C, with an aspiration of limiting it to no more than 1.5°C. Anthropogenic (human-caused) GHG emissions—the principal driver of climate

emissions data, though, and these standard categories can unnecessarily narrow the focus of climate mitigation initiatives.

For instance, in the standard framing of sources, households (called the "residential" category) only contribute roughly 6% of the U.S. total. If that seems low to you, you are onto something: in this view of the data, the GHG emissions from your household electricity use are assigned to the electric utility sector and the emissions from your driving are assigned to the transportation sector. As you can see from this discussion, framing emissions in these different ways represents a choice to attribute emissions to the producer of a product, not the user. If we assign the home electricity use and personal transportation by individuals to the household sector, though, the total is now roughly one-third of all U.S. GHG emissions, so the importance of our household decisions is clear.

If the source of these emissions is considered to be the utilities that supply electricity, the public governance tools involve regulating utilities via a carbon tax or regulations reducing utility plant emissions. PEG utility sector initiatives could target fossil fuel-fired plants or promote renewables. If the overall goal is framed as reducing *household* GHG emissions, though, new governance tools come into focus. When the businesses and households that create demand for electricity are also considered sources, efforts that reduce energy use through weatherizing buildings and installation of more efficient heating and cooling systems become governance options.

In some cases, these types of PEG demand-side emissions reductions initiatives may be more feasible than the typical supply-side carbon taxes or GHG regulations, so keep in mind the importance of source framing as we examine how PEG climate initiatives are filling gaps in public governance.

Climate Literacy

Understanding core concepts and terms is essential for lawyers, managers and advocates working on climate change mitigation projects, whether via climate litigation, transactions that involve climate issues, advocacy campaigns, or other PEG initiatives. These are briefly set out below:

- ☐ Six gases covered by the Kyoto Protocol: carbon dioxide (CO_2); methane (CH_4); nitrous oxide (N_2O); hydrofluorocarbons (HFCs); perfluorocarbons (PFCs); sulphur hexafluoride (SF_6).
- ☐ Units of measurement: metric tons are the common unit of measurement for GHGs and are sometimes referred to as "long tons." A metric ton is 2,205

pounds, as compared to a short ton, which is 2,000 pounds.

- ☐ CO_2 v. Carbon v. CO_2-e: Carbon dioxide v. the mass of carbon in GHGs v. the carbon dioxide equivalent of a GHG
- ☐ 1 ton CO_2 = .2729 ton Carbon
- ☐ A metric ton of CO_2-e is a ton of CO_2 or any other GHG with an equivalent global warming potential (GWP).
- ☐ GWP is "[a] factor describing the radiative forcing impact (degree of harm to the atmosphere) of one unit of a given GHG relative to one unit of CO_2)." (CDP 2008/GHG Protocol).
- ☐ Climate Sensitivity: the temperature at a doubling of pre-industrial atmospheric concentrations.
- ☐ Flows v. stocks: Flows are ongoing emissions, often reported on an annual basis, and stocks are the total amount in the atmosphere.
- ☐ Fossil fuel-only v. fossil fuel plus land use: Fossil fuel-only emissions are only those GHG emissions that arise from burning fossil fuels, whereas fossil fuels plus land use also includes GHG emissions arising from agriculture, deforestation, and other land use practices.
- ☐ National total emissions v. per capita emissions: The national total emissions are all GHG emissions from within the national boundary whereas per capita emissions are the total national emissions divided by the population of the country.
- ☐ National total emissions v. GHG intensity: The national total emissions are all GHG emissions from within the national boundary whereas GHG intensity is all GHG emissions divided by another measure of economic productivity such as Gross Domestic Product.
- ☐ Baselines: The benchmark against which emissions commitments are measured. The Kyoto Protocol assigned emissions responsibilities based on 1990 emissions levels, but many national commitments in the Paris Agreement are based on 2005 or later year baselines. Emissions for many countries increased

after 1990, so later baselines result in lower emissions reduction commitments.

II. Direct and Indirect Effects

To understand why many advocacy groups, investors, lenders, and companies are motivated to respond to the climate threat, it is important to review the direct physical effects of climate change and the indirect social, political, and economic effects.

A. Physical Effects

The physical effects of climate change are occurring now and will get worse in the future. Global warming increases the energy in the atmosphere and, therefore, the climate system. As a result, climate change is driving more powerful storms, deeper droughts and more intense heat waves.

Government climate science reports by the IPCC and the US Global Change Research Program (GCRP) explore climate impacts in more detail. The most important direct threats include the following:

- **Rising Sea Levels**, which in the near term will cause beach erosion, flooding, loss of many marshes and wetlands, and increased salinity in coastal aquifers and estuarine systems, along with long term threats to coastal cities;
- **Acidification of Oceans**, which in the near term will affect coastal communities and economies by damaging the coral reefs that provide fish habitat, generate tourism, protect shorelines from erosion, and support biodiversity, along with long term threats to major fisheries;
- **Extreme Weather**, including floods, droughts, heat waves, and other events, which are increasing in severity and frequency now and will continue to do so in the long run;
- **Desertification**, which arises from the combination of drought, deforestation, and poorly managed agriculture, and which will continue in the long run.

B. Social, Political, and Economic Effects

The indirect social, political, and economic effects of climate change pose additional serious challenges. Feedback effects can occur when economic disruptions lead to social disruptions that lead to political disruptions that reinforce the economic and social disruptions. The social, political, and economic effects include:[2]

- **Migration** of large numbers of people may occur in response to food shortages, droughts, flooding, and economic disruptions;
- **Food Shortages** may arise from droughts, flooding, and other changes in weather and climate patterns;
- **Economic Costs** may increase for some sectors, such as when sea level rise or extreme weather events require relocation of facilities or increase insurance premiums for coastal or other affected properties;
- **Habitation Shifts** may occur for some areas of the world, such as for communities located in areas subject to desertification or flooding;
- **Conflict** may increase as resources become scarce and as heat waves, water supplies and agricultural areas change;
- **Political Instability** may occur as the physical, social, and economic disruptions arising from climate change undermine the legitimacy of existing governments and the ability to peacefully allocate resources and transfer power.

These social, political, and economic effects pose company-specific and economy-wide risks. As the U.S. Securities and Exchange Commission (SEC) has noted, "[i]n addition to the physical risks associated with the climate, issuers and investors may also face risks associated with a potential transition to a less carbon intensive economy."[3] The U.S. Commodity Futures Trading Commission (CFTC) has reached similar conclusions: "Climate risks may also exacerbate financial system vulnerabilities that have little to do with climate change, such as historically high levels of corporate leverage."[4] A 2021 Financial Stability Review by the European Central Bank noted that "[f]rom a systemic perspective, insufficient and potentially diminishing insurability of climate-related risks and

---

[2] See THE SHAREHOLDER COMMONS, CLOSING THE ENGAGEMENT GAP: TWO NEW CASE STUDIES ON CLIMATE CHANGE & AMR (2022).

[3] U.S. Securities & Exchange Commission, The Enhancement and Standardization of Climate-Related Disclosures for Investors, 87 Fed. Reg. 21334 (proposed Apr. 11, 2022).

[4] MARKET RISK ADVISORY COMMITTEE, U.S. COMMODITY FUTURES TRADING COMMISSION, MANAGING CLIMATE RISK IN THE U.S. FINANCIAL SYSTEM: REPORT OF THE CLIMATE-RELATED MARKET RISK SUBCOMMITTEE (Sept. 2020).

associated risk pooling could also significantly amplify future economic losses."[5]

Attributing disaster costs to climate change is difficult, but overall trends are concerning. In the U.S., the SEC has noted that California wildfires have become more frequent and more intense in recent years, and wildfires may pose material risks for property owners including wineries, farmers, and others. The SEC also has noted that wildfires have affected insurance markets by inducing some insurance companies to withdraw from wildfire-prone areas. When insurance against the potential exposure to damage, loss, and legal liability from wildfires is unavailable or is extremely expensive, investors may be reluctant to invest. On a global level, Munich Re, a global reinsurance company, calculated that $210 billion in global losses occurred in 2020 from natural disasters. Munich Re has noted that large losses of this type are consistent with the effect on financial risks of long-term increases in atmospheric and oceanic temperature.

A wide range of social and political effects are also likely. The Brookings Institute has noted that by affecting storms and other disasters, climate change will increase large-scale human migration, including increasing stress on the United States border as climate change degrades living conditions in Central America. Similarly, climate change will increase competition among nations for water, food, and other resources, and it will increase the severity and frequency of disease outbreaks. In addition to human suffering, these kinds of events will place increasing stress on government budgets and political processes.

We end our discussion of climate risks where we began: with the fact that substantial amounts of CO_2 will remain in the atmosphere for centuries absent development and deployment of new carbon removal and storage technologies at large scale. This means that climate harms will not only have a disproportionate effect on the most disadvantaged populations in the current generation, but also on the descendants of the most disadvantaged populations for tens or hundreds of generations. So climate change not only creates risks to the current generation, it creates risks to many generations that do not have a seat at the table in today's climate conversations. We will return to the justice implications of climate change, and how PEG initiatives are responding, in Chapter 9.

III. Private Environmental Governance Climate Actions: Motivations and Persuasion

For public governance, the regulatory structure follows a well-worn path: the constitution structures the branches of government

---

[5] EUROPEAN CENTRAL BANK, FINANCIAL STABILITY REVIEW 2021 (Nov. 2021).

and allocates authority among them, the legislative branch adopts legislation, the executive branch implements legislation through regulations, policies, programs, and enforcement actions, and courts hear disputes about the regulations and their enforcement. In contrast, on the surface PEG initiatives seem to include a bewildering array of private actors and actions. On closer inspection, though, PEG climate initiatives use the same tools as government climate mitigation efforts (persuasion, prescriptive requirements, payments and penalties, property rights, and insurance), and we identify those tools in Chapters 8 and 9.

But why are PEG initiatives effective? When are they likely to fail? In other words, why do private organizations engage in climate mitigation beyond what governments require?

To understand the opportunities and limits of PEG climate initiatives, it is important to focus on the motivations of the companies and other organizations that participate in these initiatives. Once we understand what drives PEG climate actions we can explore how the most important PEG climate initiatives use these tools, when we should worry about greenwashing, and where new opportunities may arise. PEG climate initiatives do not have isolated effects—they often interact with other public and private initiatives and sometimes create feedback loops—but they can be understood by a close examination of the business case for climate change mitigation.

A. Business Case

In some situations, the business case will be enough to motivate companies to commit to and achieve climate mitigation goals. The business case that an environmental advocate might make to company executives or that company executives might make to their board of directors about why reductions are in the company's interest can be thought of as arising in two steps: *existing incentives* that encourage action even absent PEG initiatives and *new incentives* that are created by PEG climate initiatives.

1. *Step One: Existing Incentives*

a. Efficiency

Efficiency is an important incentive that exists even absent PEG initiatives. Companies can become more profitable by increasing revenues or by reducing costs. GHG emissions often arise from inefficient energy or other resource use, and greater efficiency can lead to lower costs and emissions. A corporate manager with perfect information and sufficient resources would invest in efficiency opportunities that produce greater returns than other investments, but in some cases there is an efficiency gap—a gap between the efficiency that is in a company's economic interest and what it achieves in practice. PEG climate initiatives often call attention to that gap and help companies close it. We discuss the role that carbon labeling plays in driving efficiency below. An example of an initiative designed to increase efficiency through the development and uptake of new technologies is the Low Carbon Technology Partnerships (LCTPi). The LCTPi is a public-private hybrid led by the World Business Council for Sustainable Development (WBCSD), and it is designed to accelerate the development and uptake of low-carbon technologies in specific industry sectors to meet the 2°C Paris Agreement goal.

b. Anticipation of Future GHG Restrictions

Another motivation for GHG reductions that exists even absent current PEG climate initiatives is anticipation of future GHG requirements. Company executives may anticipate future government climate regulations or a carbon tax, and they may attempt to position the company to reduce the costs of compliance and find new market opportunities. It's hard to know how much GHG reduction activity results from efforts to anticipate future government regulations, but the topic comes up frequently when businesses explain their climate actions.

PEG initiatives also can affect this driver by becoming the anticipated "regulator." When companies anticipate future regulation, typically government will be the source of the regulatory risk. But PEG initiatives also can play this role. For instance, a company may anticipate future supply chain contracting requirements from its corporate customers, and it may try to position itself in advance to have a competitive advantage when the corporate customers adopt supply chain requirements. In the example we used in Chapter 1, Walmart felt pressure to reduce its carbon footprint, and the light bulb manufacturer that provided low-cost, attractive LED bulbs in response to Walmart's demands was able to vastly expand its sales. Companies that did not anticipate the Walmart LED requirements missed the opportunity.

c. Public Climate Change Preferences

The third incentive is closely related to the second. Public support for climate change mitigation creates pressure on the private sector for GHG emissions reductions in many ways. Well over half of the U.S. population has supported climate mitigation for the last decade or more, and support is even higher in Europe and some Asian countries. These public preferences for climate mitigation create pressure on companies even absent PEG climate initiatives, although

PEG initiatives often seek to harness support through naming and shaming, boycotts, employee campaigns, and other initiatives.

2. *Step Two: New Incentives*

The business case for climate action includes not only identifying incentives that already exist even without PEG climate initiatives—such as efficiency, anticipation of future regulation, and responding to public preferences—but also new incentives created by PEG climate initiatives. These incentives include financial gains from enhanced reputation, increased employee recruitment and retention, increased sales from retail customers, increased sales from corporate customers, greater access to capital and lower capital costs and other financial incentives from investors and lenders, and lower insurance costs. These initiatives use all of the tools that we discussed in Chapter 2: persuasion, payments and penalties, prescriptive requirements, property rights, and insurance. We discuss in detail these initiatives and tools through specific examples in Chapters 8 and 9, but first we address a common concern about PEG climate initiatives by examining the interactions between public and private governance.

IV. Public-Private Interactions

The effects of *private* climate initiatives on climate mitigation depend not only on whether they achieve large emissions reductions, but also on how they affect *public* climate initiatives. As we discussed in Chapter 6, if you follow debates about climate change mitigation in the media, it is easy to assume that corporate PEG initiatives are simply designed to greenwash or undermine government action. But the interactions between public and private governance are complex and can increase or decrease the adoption and success of government measures. Corporations have many incentives to engage in climate mitigation, and critical thinking is needed to understand the wide range of possible public-private interactions on climate change.

A. Spillover Effects

The term "spillover" refers to the effect that taking one action has on the likelihood or effect of a second action. Spillover effects occur at the individual and organizational levels and can occur for actions and for policy support. For instance, negative policy spillover occurs at the organizational level when an advocacy group focuses on an initiative that targets corporate climate actions rather than on government actions, making its government advocacy less effective. Negative policy spillover also could occur if learning about PEG initiatives convinces the public or policymakers that the market can solve the climate problem on its own, leading to reduced support for a government action. Princeton psychologist Elke Weber has noted that farmers who take climate mitigation steps exhibit what she calls a single action bias: They become less supportive of climate mitigation, even though the likelihood of climate effects did not change because of their actions.

Negative spillover effects at the policy level will only occur if PEG initiatives displace government actions that are otherwise feasible. In Chapter 2 we noted that efforts to adopt a carbon tax and many other government climate policies face difficult barriers. These barriers reduce the likelihood that PEG initiatives will displace major federal climate measures that would have been feasible in the absence of the PEG initiatives.

Positive spillover effects also could arise from PEG initiatives. The environmental advocacy group EDF describes its PEG programs as demonstrating proof of concept—using corporate collaborations to demonstrate what can be done by other companies and governments. Positive spillover also can occur indirectly if PEG initiatives create new constituencies that support mitigation. For instance, businesses that invest in GHG reductions may lobby to ensure that government levels the playing field by requiring others to reduce emissions as well. Another positive effect may arise if PEG initiatives induce companies to achieve efficiencies or invest in technologies that lower the costs of GHG emissions reductions and thus reduce their incentives to resist government requirements. At the individual level, research suggests that learning about PEG climate initiatives reduces resistance to government climate measures among moderates and conservatives (sometimes called solution aversion).

Finally, some PEG climate initiatives are expressly designed to increase government action. An example is "We Are Still In", an organization formed by the World Wildlife Fund and other organizations formed after the Trump administration announced the U.S. would withdraw from the Paris Agreement. We Are Still In was designed to show that numerous companies, universities, and state and local governments supported—and planned to achieve on their own—the emissions trajectory required to achieve the goals of the Paris Agreement even if the United States did withdraw from the Agreement. Another private organization that has promoted government action is America's Climate Pledge, which has collected climate commitments from hundreds of private and public organizations. Similarly, Ceres has formed the Business for Innovative Climate and Energy Policy (BICEP) Network to advocate for climate-friendly government policies, and several environmental advocacy groups have formed the Clean Energy Buyers Coalition (CEBA), an organization that draws on the influence of hundreds of corporate clean energy buyers to advocate for low carbon power with state legislatures and public utilities commissions.

Climate Voice is a novel example of a PEG initiative that is explicitly designed to increase support for government climate mitigation and that focuses on employees. Many companies have made climate commitments but also lobby against government action or pay annual dues to organizations that lobby against government action. Climate Voice has responded by focusing on corporate employees' preferences for climate mitigation. Formed by Bill Weil, a former Google and Facebook executive, Climate Voice motivates employees to push their employers to align their lobbying with their corporate climate commitments. A famous analysis by Albert O. Hirschman suggests that individuals in organizations have three options when confronted with a situation they dislike: exit, voice, and loyalty. By exit, Hirschman means that employees can leave their company to work for another employer. By loyalty, he means that they can simply go along with corporate policy. Using the motto "when employees speak, companies act," Climate Voice has conducted a series of campaigns to encourage high tech employees to pursue the "voice" option by pushing their employers to stop lobbying against government climate measures.

B. Government Responses

Government responses to PEG climate initiatives have ranged from hostile to supportive. As we mentioned in Chapter 1, during the Trump administration the Comptroller of the Currency and legislators attempted to discourage banks from using climate policies to reduce lending for fossil fuel-heavy projects, such as oil and gas leasing on federal lands in Alaska. The Department of Labor also sought to prevent managers of pension funds from accounting for climate change in pension fund decisions. More recently, as we discuss in Chapter 6, Texas, Florida, West Virginia and other states have adopted state laws and policies to discourage ESG investing.

Governments also have promoted PEG climate initiatives. The United Nations has encouraged private sector climate action through the Non-state Actor Zone for Climate Action (commonly referred to as "NAZCA"), the Principles for Responsible Investing, and numerous other programs. Organizations that target the financial sector such as the Taskforce on Climate-related Financial Disclosures (referred to as the "TCFD") have received support from international and national government agencies. The U.S. State Department has launched programs that support international and domestic public-private climate efforts such as the Clean Energy Demand Initiative, which connects countries with companies to foster global development of clean energy sources. The State Department also works with the World Economic Forum to support the First Movers Coalition, a public-private partnership that is attempting to jump start the global demand for low-carbon technologies.

Federal programs such as Energy Star labeling, EPA mandatory GHG reporting requirements for large stationary sources, and the Annual Inventory of Greenhouse Gases and Sinks provide emissions information that drives private sector climate actions. The federal Inflation Reduction Act commits billions of dollars for subsidizing private sector manufacturing and promotion of renewable power, electric transmission, and consumer items ranging from electric vehicles to home heat pumps. Major federal, state and local procurement programs are creating supply chain pressure for decarbonization that is likely to not only reduce the carbon emissions from government procurement, but also accelerate private supply chain contracting initiatives. California has taken many steps to promote private sector climate action, including reaching agreements with major vehicle manufacturers that commit the manufacturers to transition to electric cars and trucks not just in California, but throughout the United States.

QUESTIONS AND DISCUSSION

1. Assume you are representing an environmental advocacy group in a negotiation with a company about its forthcoming climate commitment. Your client is worried that the company is trying to use the terms in the agreement to reduce the GHG emissions reductions that it will have to make. Specifically, the company has proposed to commit to reduce "Scope 1 and Scope 2 fossil fuel-based carbon dioxide emissions from a 2023 baseline." The company makes retail consumer food products and purchases raw materials from suppliers that have been linked to tropical deforestation. It has been slowly increasing GHG emissions over the last 100 years. The company's competitors have higher current emissions but are all new companies formed in the last ten years. The company plans to double global sales in the next five years. How would you frame the company's emissions in the negotiations if your goal is to obtain the strongest possible commitment?

a. Total company emissions v. emissions intensity

b. Carbon dioxide v. all six Kyoto GHGs

c. Fossil fuel-based emissions v. all emissions (including emissions from land use)

d. Scope 1 and 2 emissions v. Scope 1, 2 and 3 emissions

e. Emissions flows v. stocks

f. Emissions reductions from a 1990 baseline v. a 2020 baseline

g. Emissions from the company alone v. emissions from the company and its suppliers

2. Do your answers to Question 1 differ if the company does not buy raw materials from suppliers linked to deforestation? Or if the company does not have corporate suppliers? Or if the company has been in business for 100 years but has been reducing emissions every year? Or if the company is one of the competitors formed in the last ten years?

3. Assume you are advising a company on the purchase of new materials for its production processes. The company has made a strong commitment to reduce GHG emissions, but has not yet decided whether to disclose its Scope 3 emissions. There are several choices of suppliers, but the two best from your perspective are a large multinational firm that already calculates its GHG emissions and that happens to sell the raw materials you need, and a local business that sells the raw materials you need at a comparable price, but that does not calculate its GHG emissions. Which of these suppliers would you prefer and why?

4. The discussion of climate risks in this Chapter draws from an analysis of climate risks by The Shareholder Commons, a non-profit group that is leveraging shareholder concerns about climate change to develop private standards for corporate conduct enforced by investors rather than governments. The IPCC has published numerous expert reports identifying the increases in heat waves, droughts, and other climate risks. Based on the discussion in this Chapter, what is the additional value for business managers of reports by groups such as The Shareholder Commons? What risks do these types of reports identify that might drive decision-making by investors, lenders, and company managers?

5. Of the direct and indirect climate change risks, which are most likely to motivate companies and investors to participate in PEG climate initiatives to account for the environmental, social and governance aspects of a business?

6. As we discuss in Chapter 6, PEG initiatives that draw on investor and corporate efforts to decarbonize or adopt ESG strategies have been criticized as "woke capitalism." What is the basis of this critique? Is it inappropriate or illegal for a corporate or investment fund manager to account for the environmental, social, and governance aspects of a business?

Chapter 8

CLIMATE CHANGE MITIGATION

We focused in Chapter 7 on climate risks, the types and sources of GHG emissions, and motivations for corporations to participate in PEG initiatives. Remember that a business may be motivated to reduce GHG emissions even absent PEG climate initiatives because of the financial benefits from identifying existing efficiencies, anticipating changes in regulatory requirements, and aligning its public profile with widespread public preferences for climate change mitigation. PEG climate initiatives draw on these existing incentives. PEG climate initiatives also create new motivations for businesses to act by using the governance tools we discuss in this Chapter—persuasion, payments and penalties, prescriptive requirements, property rights, and insurance—and by mobilizing investors, lenders, insurers, corporate customers, retail customers, employees, and other stakeholders to use these tools. As we discuss the use of these tools, we explore the reasons why PEG climate initiatives can bypass the fundamental problems that make climate change so hard to address, including uncertainty, mismatched boundaries, the prisoner's dilemma, and polarization.

I. Persuasion

Many PEG initiatives are designed to motivate a company to act by providing information to firm managers about their impact on climate, and how they compare to their peers on managing these issues. The oft-repeated adage that "you can only manage what you measure" underlies PEG initiatives based on information disclosure, which can be thought of as the persuasion tool we discussed in Chapter 3. In addition to creating incentives for better internal management, information disclosure also embodies the words spoken by Supreme Court Justice Louis Brandeis that "sunlight is the best disinfectant." By requiring the publication of information—which can then be reviewed by various constituencies including the public, investors, consumers, NGOs, and others, information can create risks to or enhance a company's public image, reputation, or brand. This in turn can prompt firms to engage in additional forms of PEG to address the underlying risks and challenges. These initiatives can shape the preferences of retail and corporate customers, inform them about how companies' policies and activities square with their preferences, provide information about how to communicate with the company, and motivate customers to act. They also can affect perceptions of the company by employees, local communities, investors, lenders, insurers, and government regulators.

Climate disclosure initiatives typically focus on one of four types of disclosure: corporate, investor and lender, project, or product carbon footprints and risks. We first examine the neutral PEG initiatives that focus on disclosure of corporate, investor, lender, and product carbon footprints and then turn to the normative uses of information. Chapter 9 explores project-based GHG disclosure.

A. Corporate Climate Disclosure

Although naming-and-shaming and other normative uses of information often come to mind when we think about using information as a form of *persuasion*, much more mundane uses of information may be even more important drivers of climate mitigation action. Private organizations and standards have been formed to increase the accuracy and completeness of GHG data, to enable comparisons among sources, and to increase public disclosure. In turn, this disclosure facilitates the many sources of pressure on companies to reduce GHG emissions and facilitates the crafting and adoption of government disclosure requirements by the SEC and other agencies. Understanding the standards for GHG reporting and how to access GHG information is essential knowledge for lawyers, managers and advocates working on private and public climate governance.

1. Emissions Accounting: The GHG Protocol

Many PEG initiatives require information disclosure—often disclosure of GHG emissions. But there can be disagreements about which emissions "count" and how to calculate them. The first of the *persuasion* tools, the GHG Protocol, answers these questions, and serves as the basis for many other PEG information initiatives.

Financial accounting standards increase the accuracy and completeness of financial statements. If widely used, these accounting standards reduce the risk of fraud and enable investors to compare the financial results of companies. More than 100 years ago accountants responded to the need for widely-adopted standards by developing the Generally Accepted Accounting Principles or GAAP. These standards are a form of private governance—they are developed, modified and implemented by private organizations, although they function as a public-private hybrid because their use is required for many types of companies regulated by the states and federal agencies such as the SEC.

In the GHG accounting and reporting area, standards have emerged as the equivalent of GAAP. These GHG accounting and disclosure standards are the product of the GHG Protocol Initiative, a multi-stakeholder partnership of businesses, NGOs, and governments convened by the World Resources Institute (WRI) and

World Business Council on Sustainable Development (WBCSD). The WRI/WBCSD GHG Protocol Initiative is an NGO that functions much like a regulatory agency. It is the secretariat for the GHG reporting standards, so it establishes and amends the standards, generates detailed guidance and tools for applying the standards, and provides technical assistance and interpretations.

The GHG Protocol Initiative has developed seven standards to provide a consistent methodology for calculating and reporting GHG emissions, each designed for different organizations and activities.[1] The most important for corporate reporting is the GHG Protocol Corporate Standard (GHG Protocol). The GHG Protocol Initiative issued the first edition of the GHG Protocol in 2001 and it issued a revised edition in 2004. It also has issued updates to guidance documents and tools that are important resources for preparing or critiquing GHG reports. A steering group guided the standard development process for the GHG Protocol, with members from several environmental groups—including the World Wildlife Fund, the Pew Center on Global Climate Change, and The Energy Research Institute—as well as industry representatives like Norsk Hydro, Tokyo Electric, and Shell. This broad stakeholder involvement likely contributed to the GHG Protocol becoming the dominant global industry standard for emissions reporting: it is now used by over 90 percent of Fortune 500 companies.

The GHG Protocol establishes the requirements for companies that prepare a GHG emissions inventory. The GHG Protocol requires a company that is developing an emissions reporting program to set an *inventory boundary* that includes organizational and operational components. This provides a way to determine which emissions will be included within an organization's boundaries and which will be attributed to other organizations. The company then sets *organizational* boundaries by choosing an approach to consolidate GHG emissions and define its operations for reporting purposes, and it sets *operational* boundaries by "identifying emissions associated with its operations, categorizing them as direct and indirect emissions, and choosing the scope of accounting and reporting for indirect emissions." We focus here on companies, but many universities, NGOs, and governments also use the GHG Protocol for emissions reporting.

As we mentioned earlier in this Chapter, the GHG Protocol identifies three scopes of emissions, *Scope 1* for direct GHG emissions, *Scope 2* for emissions from electricity and steam generated off-site, and *Scope 3* for all other indirect emissions, such as corporate suppliers and employee commuting. The GHG Protocol requires

---

1 GHG PROTOCOL, STANDARDS, available at https://ghgprotocol.org/standards.

corporations to report Scope 1 and 2 emissions, but Scope 3 reporting is optional under the Protocol. Most companies do not report Scope 3 emissions, although Scope 3 reporting is becoming more common. NGOs and governments are increasing pressure on companies to report Scope 3 supply chain emissions, in particular. For instance, the International Sustainability Standards Board (ISSB), an influential private standard-setting organization, in 2022 voted to require supply chain emissions in corporate climate disclosures. Supply chain emissions raise difficult line-drawing questions, though: should only first-tier suppliers be included or lower tier suppliers? How reliable are supply chain data? Should reporting be required if the supply chain is a small part of the company total? The GHG Protocol Initiative has developed the Corporate Value Chain (Scope 3) Standard to provide guidance, and organizations such as the ISSB provide companies with initial flexibility on assessing and reporting supply chain emissions.

A vulnerability of some GHG reporting standards is that they contain reporting thresholds and therefore some emissions may not be reported. For example, the federal GHG reporting program managed by EPA only requires facilities with more than 25,000 tons per year of CO_2e emissions to file public reports. Thresholds are often necessary because they reduce the costs and time involved in assessing emissions, but thresholds also can allow important emissions to escape reporting. A facility that emits 24,000 tons is contributing substantial GHG emissions, but it is not subject to the pressure that arises from public disclosure of its emissions if it is just subject to the EPA reporting requirements.

Unlike many government reporting requirements, the GHG Protocol lacks a uniform reporting threshold. Instead, companies are allowed to determine and disclose a "significance threshold" and to report only the emissions from sources that exceed this threshold. Although this reduces reporting burdens, it creates the risk that some sources may escape reporting if they fall below this self-determined threshold. The GHG Protocol addresses this concern by requiring disclosure of the threshold and by requiring some changes in emissions to trigger a "base year emissions recalculation." In other words, if the emissions excluded by the company make up a disproportionate share of its total emissions, the company is required to revise its approach to include these emissions in its calculations.

2. *Corporate Emissions Reporting: CDP*

The GHG Protocol provides the basic accounting standards for calculating and disclosing GHG emissions, but who creates pressure to disclose and reduce emissions? Who provides platforms to make the results available to the public? Who combines GHG emissions reporting with reporting on climate change risks? Five global NGOs have emerged to improve climate reporting by companies and other organizations, some focusing principally on GHG emissions and others focusing more on climate risks: CDP (formerly the Carbon Disclosure Project), the Climate Disclosure Standards Board, the Global Reporting initiative, the International Integrated Reporting Council, and the Sustainability Accounting Standards Board.

These private reporting organizations are wrestling with two principal problems. The first arises from inconsistent standards, which can increase the costs of preparing reports and undermine the ability of investors and NGOs to compare companies and assess their progress. In addition to these five organizations, government reporting standards exist in the U.S. and other countries, so reporting can be a complex and difficult exercise. The five major private reporting organizations have responded by committing to develop a "comprehensive, globally accepted, corporate reporting system," but this reporting system has not yet emerged. Until that happens, environmental lawyers, managers, and advocates will need to develop familiarity with several of the leading standards.

The second major problem is inconsistency between disclosures in sustainability and ESG reports, and disclosures in periodic financial reports required by governments. Experts disagree on whether sustainability and ESG reports should be integrated into the periodic financial reports that companies prepare in response to legal mandates like securities regulation. Integrating environmental and financial reports could increase the rigor and accountability of the environmental reports, but doing so might induce companies to engage in less reporting out of concern that they lack adequate data on environmental issues. The five major reporting organizations have opted for integrated reporting and have committed to develop a globally accepted standard that includes financial accounting and sustainability disclosure.

CDP is the leading organization that collects and publicly discloses GHG emissions from companies and other organizations. CDP is an NGO that uses the influence of investors with over $100 trillion in assets under management to induce companies to publicly disclose and reduce their GHG emissions using the GHG Protocol for assessing emissions. A 2020 report concluded that roughly 10,000 companies disclosed emissions data to CDP, including many of the largest-emitting companies.

CDP focuses principally on using neutral information disclosure for persuasion, and it does so through aggregating and disclosing company GHG emissions. It does not explicitly engage in naming and shaming, but it provides the information necessary to enable other organizations to pressure companies to reduce emissions and releases issue-specific reports. The Global Reporting Initiative (GRI) also sets standards for GHG reporting, but it has played a more important role in the disclosure of toxic chemical release reporting than GHG reporting, so we discuss it in Chapter 10.

CDP makes emissions data publicly available on its reporting platform. Data and reports on specific types of emissions then enable investors, NGOs, and others to monitor company emissions and commitments. The magnitude of the commitments by companies reporting to CDP is remarkable: A 2018 assessment found that over 2,000 companies pledged at least one climate commitment using the CDP reporting platform. If these companies achieve their goals, annual CO_2 emissions will be reduced by 3.4 gigatons by 2030, more than the emissions of all countries but the U.S. and China.

CDP requires companies to report emissions using the GHG Protocol and requires reporting of Scope 1 and Scope 2 emissions. In recent years, it has escalated pressure on companies to report many types of Scope 3 emissions, not just Scope 1 and 2 emissions. Until a universally accepted global framework for GHG and climate risk reporting emerges, CDP disclosure based on the GHG Protocol will remain the dominant approach.

3. *Corporate Risk Reporting: TCFD and SASB*

Disclosure of GHG emissions provides an indication of a company's contribution to creating climate risks and the financial risks the company faces when government and private decarbonization measures are adopted. But disclosure of GHG emissions alone does not reveal the specific financial risks and opportunities posed by climate change. Standards for climate risk disclosure are emerging from the SEC and other financial regulators in the US and from government agencies in Europe and Asia, but private standard-setting has played a leading role. We focus on the Sustainability Accounting Standards Board (SASB),[2] one of the five leading private reporting organizations, and on a public-private hybrid, the Task Force on Climate-related Financial Disclosure (TCFD).[3]

The TCFD and SASB use *persuasion* by targeting the development of neutral or positive types of information disclosure that focus on financially material climate risks to businesses. Risks arise for investors and the financial system when concentrations of

---

[2] SUSTAINABILITY ACCT. STANDARDS BD., SASB CONCEPTUAL FRAMEWORK 2–3 (2017).

[3] TASK FORCE ON CLIMATE-RELATED FIN. DISCLOSURES, FINAL REPORT: RECOMMENDATIONS OF THE TASK FORCE ON CLIMATE-RELATED FINANCIAL DISCLOSURES 41 (2017).

carbon-related assets in the financial system and the financial system's exposure to climate-related risks are not assessed, disclosed and factored into market prices and decisions by business managers and policymakers. Academics and policymakers have warned of the risks to financial stability of failing to account for climate-related risk.

a. TCFD

The TCFD was established in 2015 by the Financial Stability Board (FSB) after the G20 Finance Ministers and Central Bank Governors asked the FSB to review how the financial sector should account for climate-related issues. The FSB is an international public-private hybrid. It includes members from ministries of finance and central banks from twenty-four countries, the European Union, and international supervisory and regulatory authorities, including the IMF and the World Bank, as well as public and private-sector representatives, such as Unilever, the Singapore Exchange, and the Industrial and Commercial Bank of China.

The TCFD has developed recommendations for climate-related disclosures and has identified two types of climate risks that are also the focus of other public and private organizations: *physical* risks and *transition* risks. *Physical risks* arise from changes to the natural world arising from global warming, such as shifts in precipitation and in extreme weather events. Physical risks include both acute (event-driven) risks and chronic risks (those that arise from longer-term shifts in climate patterns). For instance, acute risks may arise from increased flooding of factories located along rivers when rainfall events are more intense and frequent, whereas chronic risks may arise from the effects of increasing sea levels on port facilities. Companies that are involved with real estate and infrastructure will be most directly affected by physical risks, but companies in many sectors will also be affected by these risks.

In contrast, *transition risks* are risks posed by rapid decarbonisation of the world economy, rather than the underlying changes to the natural environment. *Regulatory risks* are a commonly identified transition risk. An example of a regulatory risk is the effect of a carbon tax on a company whose products are more carbon-intensive than its competitors. This could lead to the stranding of assets like untapped oil and gas reserves if they are no longer economically feasible to exploit.

Technology risks are a type of transition risk that arises when technological improvements or innovations occur as part of the transition to a lower carbon and more energy-efficient economy. In contrast, *market risks* are transition risks that arise from changes in supply and demand driven by climate change. Market risks arise from changing customer behavior, unexpected cost shifts, and re-pricing of assets. Finally, *reputation risks* are risks that arise from changing consumer perceptions, the stigmatization of certain sectors (for instance coal-fired power plants) and stakeholder concerns.

The TCFD framework requires assessment of physical and market risks in four categories: governance, strategy, risk management, and metrics and targets. Under the TCFD's recommendations, "strategy" and "metrics and targets" information should be assessed to determine if the information is material to investors. A materiality assessment is not required for information on "governance" and "risk management." Not surprisingly, according to the TCFD, the impact of climate change on a company's business and strategy has been the most valuable information for experts. Familiarity with TCFD assessment of climate risk is becoming essential for lawyers, managers, and advocates.

All disclosure systems, of course, have limitations. For instance, PEG climate transition risks are implicitly accounted for in market and reputation risks, and the TCFD identifies decreased demand for goods or services and reduction in capital availability as potential financial risks. But the TCFD does not call out the fact that these financial risks are often the result of PEG climate initiatives such as divestment campaigns and supply chain contracting initiatives. Information about the existence and effects of these initiatives may be more important than other types of information for some companies. For example, a supplier to Walmart may take a greater hit to its financial performance if it cannot meet Walmart's Project Gigaton supply chain GHG requirements than if a carbon tax is adopted.

b. SASB

SASB is a private standards board that sets standards for identifying and disclosing climate risks that are financially material. It operates through sector-based committees, with a board composed of university professors, accountants, attorneys, and corporate managers. After identifying sustainability issues that are likely to affect the financial condition of companies, SASB recommends standards based on the materiality of different environmental and climate-related issues to companies in different industries. SASB standards require assessment and disclosure of corporate information that allows data providers and rating agencies to develop tools, analytics, and resources for the capital markets. In turn, these resources improve the ability of investors, NGOs, and others to induce companies to reduce GHG emissions.

SASB publishes sustainability frameworks and sustainability standards. SASB frameworks provide principles-based guidance on how information is structured, how it is prepared, and what broad topics are covered. SASB standards provide specific, detailed, and replicable requirements for what should be reported for each topic. For instance, for the petroleum refining sector, SASB includes broad language identifying areas for disclosure as well specific requirements for disclosure of "risk to reputation due to [an] entity's stance and actions related to the legal and regulatory environment. . . and risk of misalignment with the expectations of customers, investors, and other stakeholders." SASB standards also recommend disclosure of business strategies for emissions reduction. For instance, the SASB oil and gas exploration and production standards require disclosure of "how price and demand for coal and/or climate regulation influence the capital expenditure strategy for exploration, acquisition, and development of assets."

c. Environmental, Social, and Governance (ESG) Disclosures

Many investors and companies disclose climate emissions and commitments as a part of environmental, social, and governance (ESG) reports. The term ESG is used to identify corporate disclosures on these topics and to describe investments that meet ESG criteria. ESG reports often include both persuasion in the form of corporate or investor GHG emissions reporting and other environmental issues and prescriptive requirements in the form of disclosure of information about corporate public commitments to GHG reductions and other environmental actions that will be assessed by a third party under an existing standard. For investors, ESG reports disclose their ESG strategies and the requirements that they will impose on companies.

Many companies and investors produce ESG reports but there are many competing, and sometimes conflicting, private standards for such reporting. These reports include disclosure of GHG emissions and other sustainability data, identify key performance indicators (KPIs), and disclose company commitments. Many companies prepared sustainability reports before ESG reports became common, and the terms sustainability report and ESG report are often used interchangeably. Many ESG reports also address social and corporate governance issues, and the "S" issues—such as diversity, equity and inclusion—are becoming increasingly important aspects of these plans. Some definitions of ESG emphasize the role that values beyond profitability play in the adoption of ESG plans and preparation of ESG reports. But other ESG definitions do not frame ESG as a tradeoff between values and profitability or risk reduction. A review of studies examining the relationship between adoption of ESG strategies by investment firms and financial

ordinal (providing a normative judgment, such as a red, yellow or green stoplight). Simple ordinal labels are most effective for most retail customers when they make point of sale decisions about what to buy. But quantitative information helps corporate managers and NGO advocates make cross-product comparisons and identify sources of emissions. Since labels reduce GHG emissions by affecting both retail consumer and corporate decision-making, experts recommend labels that include both quantitative and ordinal elements.

C. Naming and Shaming Campaigns

The initiatives we have discussed so far principally use information for *persuasion* without signaling moral judgments—they identify what companies and other organizations are doing, not what they should be doing. In contrast, naming and shaming initiatives use climate-related information to create moral or normative pressure for emissions reductions, often by affecting companies' reputation. Reputation is critical to outward-facing companies with recognizable brand names, so they spend large sums creating positive reputations and defending against reputational attacks. They also invest heavily in developing positive brands for their products.

Reputational and brand risks are also important because they arise not only from the operations of the company itself, but also from the company's supply chains, customers, and employees. A company's reputation or brand does not end with the *legal boundary* of a corporation—even though under most circumstances a company cannot be held legally liable for the activities of third-party contractors, a company's customers, employees, investors, and local communities may take a much broader view of the activities that trigger moral judgments. For companies that rely heavily on their reputation, these stakeholder attributions of responsibility are as important as legal line-drawing. In other words, companies also have a *normative boundary*—customers, employees and the general public may hold a company responsible for activities by suppliers and users of their products even if the legal boundaries of the firm and legal liability only extend to the company itself.

Nike learned the hard way about the extent of its normative boundary in the 1990s when the labor practices of its Southeast Asian suppliers led to litigation and to consumer backlash in the U.S. and Europe. Kathy Lee Gifford's popular clothing line also learned this lesson when sales fell dramatically after naming and shaming campaigns revealed the labor practices of suppliers in Central America. The result is that many corporate managers focus attention on developing and maintaining a positive reputation.

The targets of naming and shaming campaigns are often "outward facing" companies with retail customers who focus on climate issues or firms that otherwise may be particularly concerned about brand or reputation issues. These companies may be major consumer-facing retailers such as Walmart or Target, investment firms with retail customers such as BlackRock, banks with a brick-and-mortar presence such as JP MorganChase, or insurers such as Liberty Mutual. In addition, although retail customers are the obvious targets of naming and shaming campaigns, these campaigns also target employee recruitment and retention, as well as community stakeholders and regulators.

As we mentioned in Chapter 1, advocacy groups began targeting the carbon footprint of major banks' loan portfolios in the early 2000s using naming and shaming campaigns directed at retail customers, employees, and corporate executives in the C-suite (the chief executive officer, chief financial officer, etc.). These campaigns are often directed at investors, lenders, corporate buyers, and other actors who can in turn become private regulators of other companies. For instance, numerous banks and financial institutions have adopted policies against lending to Arctic oil development projects, and the number of financial institutions with these policies grew from zero to over fifty between 2017 and 2021.

Naming and shaming campaigns can bypass some of the core problems confronting environmental law and policy that we discussed in Chapter 2. For instance, many companies operate around the world and only succeed if they appeal to broad swaths of their consumer base, so while mismatched political boundaries may enable politicians to avoid majority preferences for climate mitigation, these firms cannot escape that pressure in the same way. The same is true for government gridlock arising from political polarization—if these campaigns make corporate climate actions and emissions (e.g., the carbon footprint of the company or its products) clear to customers, corporate managers and boards may feel economic and social pressure even if politicians are isolated from public pressure by partisan divides and government gridlock.

PEG naming and shaming initiatives raise many important legal and management issues. NGO managers and lawyers need to understand the requirements for gaining access to information, the ability to bring fraud claims, and the limits of public regulations and tort law on intrusions into privacy. They also need to understand when legal risks may arise from counterclaims by the company targeted by a naming and shaming campaign. Rather than taking climate change mitigation actions, the targeted company may sue the NGO for slander, libel, defamation, product disparagement or other legal claims or may bring a legal action known as a strategic lawsuit against public participation (SLAPP). Some states have adopted "Veggie Libel" laws that make disparaging beef a crime, and some states have placed strong limits on entering private property that could affect gathering and publicizing information about slaughterhouses and factories. Similarly, business managers may confront important questions about effects on reputation and brand, and how fiduciary duties and the business judgment rule affect responses to naming and shaming campaigns.

These are just a few of the legal and management issues that are important for the organizers of naming and shaming initiatives and their targets. We will explore how these initiatives drive PEG on many topics in later chapters, but for now the important point is not to overlook the role of naming and shaming campaigns in efforts to drive corporate climate change mitigation.

II. Payments and Penalties

The financial sector, including investors, asset managers, lenders, and insurers, contributes to decarbonization by lowering the cost of capital for companies that are engaging in climate mitigation (payments and penalties) and by imposing requirements on companies for risk and emissions disclosure, emissions reductions, or other actions (prescriptive requirements). Firms in the financial sector often combine these tools, so the payments, penalties and prescriptive requirements tools often reinforce one another.

We examine each type of firm—investors and asset managers, lenders, and insurers—and for each type of firm we examine why they are acting before turning to their climate actions. Their motivations provide insights into the extent and type of pressure that they will exert on companies and the durability of that pressure in the face of political and economic resistance. We then turn to the ways the sector drives decarbonization by using payments and penalties and prescriptive requirements.

A. Investors and Asset Managers

1. *Investment Firm Motivations: Retail Clients, Institutional Clients, and Employees*

Institutional investors and asset managers (collectively, investment firms) have a broad range of motivations to reduce their own GHG emissions, to make investment decisions based on the GHG emissions of the companies they invest in, and to take actions to pressure those companies to reduce emissions. Many PEG climate initiatives focus on motivating investment firms to engage in these decarbonization activities. For instance, the emissions associated with an investment firm's operations (its buildings, electricity use, employee travel, etc.) are often dwarfed by the emissions associated with its investments, so initiatives by climate advocacy groups such as Ceres typically focus principally on disclosure of the carbon footprint of investment firms' portfolios as well as naming and shaming to increase reputational pressure on investment firms from employees, retail investors, pension funds, and other stakeholders.[5] Similarly, 350.org, the advocacy group led by author and activist Bill McKibben, focuses public attention on the need to reduce atmospheric CO_2 levels to 350 ppm to achieve the 2°C goal. The group uses media campaigns to push investment firms' managers and customers to leave fossil fuels in the ground to avoid the financial risks of stranded assets.

The preferences of retail investors—the customers of many investment firms—are important drivers. We focus here on stocks or equities, but many of the same issues arise with bonds or debt. As we have noted, most of the U.S. population supports climate mitigation, and this support is even stronger in Europe and some other regions. The widespread public preferences for climate mitigation affect investment firms by creating market demand for climate-friendly retail investment options. In 2020 retail investors made up roughly 25% of all funds invested in the global ESG market. This retail investor interest has grown over time and has affected the investment priorities of many investment firms.

Public preferences for climate mitigation also contribute to the demands for climate-friendly options by large pension funds, which bring a sophisticated, long-term perspective and substantial market power to bear on investment firms. Some funds have adopted a *divestment* strategy, while others have adopted an *engagement* strategy—an approach that requires the investment firms that manage investments for these pension funds to put pressure on the companies they invest in to decarbonize.

Along the same lines, public preferences for climate mitigation affect investment firms' ability to recruit and retain employees. Many managers and other employees support climate mitigation, and recruiting and retaining the most capable employees is essential to the success of investment firms. Preferences for climate mitigation can be overwhelmed by financial and other rewards, but they are important factors in the decision-making of financial firm managers.

The growth of ESG investing is also consistent with the widespread public support for climate mitigation. Initial decarbonization activities by investment firms had roots in corporate social responsibility (CSR) and socially responsible investing (SRI), but ESG investing is much larger and less reliant on moral or ethical incentives. In fact, an inflection point occurred in roughly 2012, when SRI and CSR investing shifted from a fringe activity to investments

---

[5] CERES, CLIMATE ACTION 100+.

involving a large percentage of all assets and began being framed as ESG investing. Estimates vary, but by 2022 roughly $30 trillion was held in funds with ESG screening criteria. Many managers of investment firms thus face pressure from retail investors, pension funds, and employees to account for climate mitigation in investment decisions. Reports about the investment practices of some of these ESG funds have raised concerns about the integrity of their ESG commitments; this points to a need for enhanced disclosures regarding what precisely ESG investment strategies entail, as well as potential regulatory oversight of ESG claims by investment funds. The EU has adopted such policies in its Sustainable Finance Disclosure Rule, and the U.S. Securities and Exchange Commission is likewise considering such a rule at the time of writing. The key point for our purposes, however, is that investment managers are facing pressure now to engage in climate-friendly investment strategies. Ensuring that these commitments are real will take time and require pressure from a wide range of actors.

2. *Universal or Common Owners: Reducing Portfolio Risks*

The growth of universal or common owners is another important driver of investment firms' actions on climate change, and this development can be viewed as a form of payment or penalty because it affects companies' cost of capital. Even absent pressure from retail investors and others, many investment firms in the last decade have increasingly recognized that they have intrinsic economic motivations to push companies to reduce emissions. This may sound surprising. For generations, the dominant view has been that investors will make more money if they focus on near-term profits to the exclusion of other considerations. CSR and SRI activities by investors and the companies that engaged in them were viewed as altruistic efforts, not ones likely to enhance returns.

Fundamental shifts in financial markets over the last several decades, though, suggest that many investment firms now have economic incentives to structure their portfolios and interactions with the companies they invest in to reduce GHG emissions. Why? Alongside the growth in ESG investing, a shift has occurred in the understanding of investors' incentives. Modern portfolio theory was developed in the 1950s and became the dominant approach to investing. It concluded that investors could not beat the market, so the best investment strategy was to reduce transaction costs by not spending the money to research and select individual companies, but instead to simply assemble a basket of stocks or an index fund to replicate the market or a large share of the market.

The result is that most large institutional investors now function as common or universal owners—they own broadly diversified portfolios, which shifts their focus from firm-specific risks to systematic risks. In 1950, only 6% of U.S. equities were owned by institutional investors. By 2017, the proportion of the stock market owned by these investors reached nearly 80%, and most of the funds managed by these investors were held in large, diversified portfolios. In addition, the 30 largest investment firms hold over half of the shares of all of the Fortune 500 companies. As of 2019 six investment firms that manage large, diversified portfolios controlled 24% of the shares in Exxon Mobil. These same six investment firms controlled similar percentages of the shares of Chevron, PepsiCo, and General Mills. To understand the effect that this shift towards common ownership is having on climate issues, it is important to understand how the interests of a concentrated shareholder—an investor with shares in one company or sector—differ from the interests of common owners or owners of diversified portfolios.

The GHG emissions that drive climate change are classic externalities: if GHG emissions are not regulated or taxed, companies will benefit from not paying for the climate harms they cause, and consumers will over-consume the goods and services produced by these companies because the full costs will not be included in the price charged by the company. An investor that only has shares in these companies can benefit from these externalities because the companies don't bear the cost of GHG emissions while the costs of the climate change the emissions cause are shared with many others.

Investors with diversified portfolios, though, have a different perspective. A common stock or equity represents the right to a company's future cash flows, and the owner of a broad portfolio of equities has the right to future cash flows from the part of the economy represented by the portfolio. Over the long term, the overall performance of the economy measured by gross domestic product or GDP will be directly proportional to the value of a broad, diversified portfolio of equities.[6] In other words, universal owners have an interest in the overall success of the economy over the long term and do not benefit if one firm increases in value by releasing GHG emissions—negative externalities—that cause more harm to the other companies in the portfolio. If Exxon profits by selling oil and gas that contributes to GHG emissions that lead to crop failures that hurt General Mills, PepsiCo and other food companies, the holder of a broad portfolio may not benefit.

The economy-mirroring nature of diversified portfolios can lead investment firms to push for the internalization of inter-firm externalities—in other words, to reduce corporate GHG emissions.

---

[6] PRINCIPLES FOR RESPONSIBLE INVESTING, UNIVERSAL OWNERSHIP: WHY ENVIRONMENTAL EXTERNALITIES MATTER TO INSTITUTIONAL INVESTORS (2011).

Rational investors should support any initiative that will cause an increase in the value of their portfolio from reducing climate harms that is larger than the decrease in value from costs incurred by the implementing firm from reducing emissions.

So, one way to maximize portfolio value is to ensure that externalities are borne by the company that can avoid them at lowest cost. Because diversified investors care about the performance of their portfolio, rather than the performance of any individual company, they have an incentive to support initiatives and vote their shares for corporate boards and proposals that internalize the GHG emissions externalities of the companies in their portfolios. Whether this incentive exists depends on many factors, including the costs imposed by the externality on other firms in their portfolio, the cost of reducing the externality, and the relative amount of shares in each company in the portfolio. Given the physical and transition risks of climate change, though, many common owners will likely find that companies that emit large quantities of GHGs impose costs on the rest of their portfolios that outweigh any savings reaped from the emitting companies. For instance, the Financial Stability Board has concluded that an average temperature rise of 2°C could reduce global financial asset values between 0.7% and 4.2%.

The incentives created by common ownership thus can lead to financial incentives by investors that take the form of the payments or penalties tools. In turn, these tools can provide important economic drivers for GHG emissions reductions, but common ownership has important limitations and risks.

3. *Investor Actions*

Understanding investment firms' motivations to support climate mitigation is the first step; the next is to identify the actions they take. The principal actions fall into three buckets: to reduce their own GHG emissions, to make investment decisions based on the GHG emissions of the companies they invest in, and to take actions to pressure those companies to reduce emissions. These three buckets tend to include PEG measures in the form of penalties, payments, and prescriptive requirements.

a. Divestment and Engagement

Although reducing emissions from investment firms matters, by far the largest effects that investment firms have on GHG emissions arise from divestment and engagement—their decisions regarding which investments to make and the interactions with the companies they invest in arising from their influence as shareholders. Investors' divestment strategies use financial penalties (screening out high-GHG companies or increasing their cost of capital) and payments (a private-governance parallel to subsidies, in which the cost of capital is reduced for portfolio companies with lower climate or environmental risks). Engagement strategies use prescriptive requirements (requiring the companies they invest in to implement decarbonization plans) to motivate companies to engage in mitigation.

Divestment involves using investment screens to identify high-GHG emitting companies and declining to invest in them, in contrast to engagement, which involves using the ownership of shares in high-GHG emitting companies to influence the company's actions. A single investor selling shares may have little impact, but institutional investors and asset management firms can attract negative public attention through divestment, or even affect the share price if the investors own a large percentage of the firm's equity. For instance, many 350.org initiatives have focused on creating pressure for divestment by clients of investment firms such as university and foundation endowments, pension funds, retail investors, and others. Firms that manage ESG funds develop screening criteria to identify companies that do not meet climate and other criteria, which induces investors and asset managers to divest from existing investments in high-GHG companies and to avoid purchasing them when making new investments.

Many investor initiatives focus only on climate mitigation, but they are typically part of the larger effort to incorporate ESG criteria into investment decision-making. In the U.S., the SEC is developing rules "to create a consistent, comparable, and decision-useful regulatory framework for ESG advisory services and investment companies to inform and protect investors while facilitating further innovation in this evolving area of the asset management industry."[7] The SEC has noted that ESG investment funds follow one of three strategies: ESG integration, ESG-focused investing, and ESG impact investing.

In the ESG context, climate divestment efforts are a type of ESG integration or ESG-focused strategy: they account for the climate aspect of ESG concerns in investment decisions. For ESG integration, climate and other ESG factors are not dispositive—integration strategies also account for other factors, including macroeconomic trends or price-to-earnings ratios of companies. A fund with an ESG integration screen could include a high-GHG emitting company if the company had very strong anticipated returns. In contrast, ESG-focused strategies use one or more ESG factors as a significant or

---

[7] See U.S. Securities & Exchange Commission, Enhanced Disclosures by Certain Investment Advisers and Investment Companies: Environmental, Social, and Governance Investment Practices (proposed June 17, 2022); U.S. Securities & Exchange Commission, Investment Company Names (proposed June 17, 2022).

main consideration when making investment decisions or interacting with portfolio companies. An example is a screen that bars investments in high-GHG emitting companies (the use of penalties), combined with an effort to press company managers to engage in decarbonization through direct engagement or proxy voting (the use of prescriptive tools, discussed in more detail below).

The difference between compliance and performance poses a challenge to ESG screens because a company may have a strong record of complying with regulatory requirements; but if GHG regulatory requirements are inadequate, regulatory compliance says little about climate mitigation. For example, companies like Exxon and Xcel Energy have strong compliance records and are included on the S&P 500 ESG Index despite being responsible for the 10th and 7th most emissions in the U.S. in 2019.[8] This is an important vulnerability of ESG screens and ESG funds.

Despite these potential flaws the effect of climate and ESG screening criteria on the allocation of investments is remarkable. According to Reuters, in 2021 global ESG assets were $6.1 trillion, growing over $650 billion that year alone. Similarly, Bloomberg Intelligence, which uses a more expansive definition, estimates that current ESG assets exceed $35 trillion, and it projects that they will reach $50 trillion by 2025. Although divestment or screening decisions can influence company GHG emissions by reducing the stock price or increasing the cost of capital for some companies, in global markets these effects may be limited—studies of divestment initiatives show limited share price effects.

Incorporating climate and ESG criteria into investment decision-making has resulted in the formation of large ESG funds that are held by investors with preferences for ESG actions, as well as smaller funds and investors with a strong ESG or climate focus. The investment firms managing these large ESG funds and smaller climate-focused funds have incentives to reduce company GHG emissions through engagement, which involves using investor influence to press for GHG emissions reductions, rather than simply to use divestment to create pressure by screening out companies with high GHG emissions.

A 2021 announcement by Shell, a major oil and gas producer—suggests one possible effect of investor and asset manager pressure. In a surprising joint press release with Climate Action 100+, Shell announced a goal to reduce the oil major's carbon footprint 20% by 2035, and 50% by 2050. These emissions goals seemed to run counter to Shell's interests. How could an oil company reduce its carbon

---

[8] POLITICAL ECONOMY RESEARCH INSTITUTE, GREENHOUSE 100 POLLUTERS INDEX (2021).

emissions by this magnitude without sacrificing sales—and in turn—profits? The answer lies in the legal, social, and economic options available to ESG impact investors.

As we mentioned in Chapter 5, ownership of equity in a company just gives the institutional and retail owners and asset managers the right to take steps to influence how the firm is managed. Equity holders have the right to elect directors to a corporation's board and the right to offer shareholder resolutions or proposals that would require a firm to address climate issues more aggressively. In the last decade, many corporate shareholder proxy votes have occurred on climate and other environmental, social and governance issues. They can propose shareholder resolutions, alter executive compensation schemes, vote out non-compliant directors, make public declarations in favor or against proposals or directors, or they can use any of these methods as leverage in private discussions with directors and executives.

PEG climate initiatives have increased pressure on investors to exercise their voting power to reduce GHG emissions. According to As You Sow, a nonprofit shareholder advocacy group, in 2022 investors took votes on roughly 300 ESG-related resolutions, with 34 resulting in majorities. Often shareholder proposals are filed but withdrawn after management agrees to take steps requested by the investors or NGOs. Although in some cases a company is not legally required to comply with a resolutions supported by a majority of shareholders, investors can sell (divestment) their shares or vote for new directors (engagement).

For decades, investment firms did not actively engage with most of the companies in their portfolios. Instead, they reduced monitoring and oversight costs by allowing company boards and managers wide discretion to act on behalf of their shareholders. As institutional portfolios have increasingly reflected the entire market, though, the portfolios also have become largely similar to one other. As a result, holders of large portfolios share interests on climate and other ESG issues and can reduce the costs of monitoring and intervening with the companies they invest in by following the leader—by relying on activist investors, NGOs, and other investors when making decisions about how to pressure the companies they invest in to disclose and reduce GHG emissions and climate risks. An NGO called Majority Action plays the role of signaling which directors, climate-focused investors, and asset managers should receive investors' votes. In 2021, it issued company-specific director vote guidance concerning 19 U.S. oil and gas, electric power, and financial services companies that were not on a trajectory to reduce emissions on a pathway that would limit warming to 1.5°C.

Engine No. 1's successful campaign to elect several new climate-concerned members to ExxonMobil's twelve-seat board of directors, which we discussed in Chapter 3, is a good example of an ESG impact investing strategy. The activist hedge fund took the lead with the backing of large institutional investors. Although Engine No. 1 owned only 0.02% of ExxonMobil's shares, the firm was able to convince BlackRock, Vanguard and State Street (who collectively owned twenty percent of ExxonMobil's shares), as well as CalPERS and CalSTERS, the New York State Common Retirement Fund, the Church of England Investment Fund, Institutional Shareholder Services and Glass Lewis, to support new proposed directors with a focus on climate risks. The campaign resulted in electing three new members to the 12-member Exxon board. Also in 2021, investors in Chevron, ConocoPhilips, and Philips66 adopted shareholder resolutions advising these firms to reduce not only their operational emissions, but also emissions in the firms' value chains that arise when its oil and gas products are purchased and used by customers.

b. Climate Action 100+

In addition to collaboration among different types of investors, investor-NGO initiatives and organizations also have emerged to serve the common interests of climate-focused investors and advocacy groups. These investor activist groups enable common owners and other climate-motivated investors to collaborate in ways that reduce monitoring costs, and they use payments, penalties, and prescription along with persuasion to increase the pressure on high-emitting companies. A leading organization is Climate Action 100+, which was instrumental in Shell's 2018 decision to announce emission goals. Climate Action 100+ is an investor initiative led by Ceres, an NGO, which increases the pressure on over 250 of the world's largest companies to reduce GHGs. Climate Action 100+ includes 700 global investors who are responsible for more than $68 trillion in assets under management across 33 markets. Climate Action 100+ includes two categories of asset owners—"participants" who sign the initiative document and take an active role in engaging directly with targeted companies, and "supporters" who sign the initiative document and support the initiative's goals without directly engaging with corporate targets.

Climate Action 100+ initially identified 100 firms responsible for two-thirds of industrial GHG emissions, then assigned financial firms to target each firm on the list. Climate Action 100+ has expanded, and in 2022 it focused on 166 companies in its effort to induce companies to reduce emissions consistent with the 1.5°C Paris Agreement target. These companies account for up to 80% of corporate industrial GHG emissions, so if Climate Action 100+ is successful it will perform a core climate governance function.

To increase pressure on companies to achieve climate commitments, in 2021 Climate Action 100+ developed a Net Zero Company Benchmark, an analytical tool that enables companies, investors, and NGOs to assess companies' performance against GHG emissions reduction, governance, and disclosure goals. The Net Zero Benchmark results are publicly disclosed, increasing pressure on companies by enabling stakeholders to assess progress toward achieving net zero emissions by 2050 or sooner consistent with a 1.5°C pathway. The initial results from the Net-Zero Company Benchmark demonstrated that a sizable gap exists between what is needed to achieve net zero and company actions, prompting Climate Action 100+ to state that "companies are increasingly making ambitious climate commitments, but now need to deliver."

c. Net-Zero Asset Managers' Initiative

NZAMI is another leading investor-led PEG climate initiative. NZAMI describes itself as "an international group of asset managers committed to supporting the goal of net zero GHG emission by 2050 or sooner, in line with global efforts to limit warming to 1.5°C; and to supporting investing aligned with net zero emissions by 2050 or sooner." NZAMI, which is a member of a United Nations-affiliated umbrella organization called Glasgow Financial Alliance for Net Zero (GFANZ), focuses principally on allowing asset managers reduce risks from climate change rather than making major GHG emissions reductions, but it does include GHG emissions mitigation elements. As of 2022, the 273 NZAMI members, who collectively manage $61 trillion, were required to adopt interim decarbonization targets beginning with 2030, ostensibly to set them on pace for an ultimate net-zero target by 2050.

NZAMI and many other PEG climate initiatives have been developed in coordination with government and hybrid initiatives organized by the United Nations and national governments. An example of a hybrid initiative is the Principles for Responsible Investment (PRI), a set of principles developed by investors to guide climate and ESG investing at a global level.[9] Hundreds of major investment firms are signatories, and they commit to six principles. To give you a concrete sense of what such principles look like, we have listed them below.

> Principle 1: We will incorporate ESG issues into investment analysis and decision-making processes.

---

9 PRINCIPLES FOR RESPONSIBLE INVESTMENT, WHAT ARE THE PRINCIPLES FOR RESPONSIBLE INVESTMENT? (2023).

Principle 2: We will be active owners and incorporate ESG issues into our ownership policies and practices.

Principle 3: We will seek appropriate disclosure on ESG issues by the entities in which we invest.

Principle 4: We will promote acceptance and implementation of the Principles within the investment industry.

Principle 5: We will work together to enhance our effectiveness in implementing the Principles.

Principle 6: We will each report on our activities and progress towards implementing the Principles.

ESG and climate investing has provoked legal and policy restrictions on the use of ESG screens for pension fund investments in fossil-fuel heavy states such as Texas and West Virgnia and complaints about "woke capitalism" by some politicians and media commentators. These efforts may affect small investors, but large investors face global market, social, and political pressures that may be far stronger than pressure from specific states.

B. Banks

Banks are playing an increasingly important role in PEG climate initiatives through the screens they use for borrowers, the conditions they impose on borrowers, and the issuance of debt. Banks face many of the same incentives to pursue decarbonization as financial firms, and we will not repeat them here. Banks have the same principal set of options as investors: to reduce their own GHG emissions, to make lending decisions based on the GHG emissions of their borrowers, and to take actions to pressure those borrowers to reduce emissions.

As we mentioned in Chapter 3, banks use the loan underwriting process to manage risk, and many have adopted climate policies that lead them to decline to lend to high-GHG or high climate risk projects. In 2020 all major U.S. banks announced that they would restrict future financing of new coal-fired power plants and coal mining, as well as decline to finance new oil and gas development in the Arctic. Banks not only impose costs or *penalties* on carbon-intensive projects by reducing the number of lenders willing to lend, they also provide *payments* by directing capital flows to clean energy projects or technologies, and engage in *prescriptive requirements* by insisting on specific GHG reduction measures by borrowers. Major banks have mobilized substantial capital—in the hundreds of billions of dollars—to clean-tech and renewable energy investments, green buildings, green bonds, and electric vehicles.

All six major U.S. banks have announced climate commitments regarding their direct operational emissions. Lawyers, managers, and advocates play important roles in the adoption and implementation of those plans. But as with investment firms, the vast majority of the GHG emissions opportunities arise from the loans banks make and how they engage with borrowers.

A first step is to assess the carbon footprint of a loan or loan portfolio. The Partnership for Climate Accounting Financials (PCAF) began as a collection of global banks and financial institutions but has become a multi-stakeholder organization with participation from NGOs like CDP, the UN-convened Net-Zero Asset Owner Alliance, and the Science-Based Targets Initiative (SBTi). PCAF has developed a methodology for financial institutions to account for emissions within their lending portfolios to enable them to align their portfolios with the Paris Agreement goals, and the broad participation in PCAF is designed to ensure that the PCAF metrics both facilitate and are harmonized with other reporting and certification platforms such as CDP and SBTi.

Some NGO efforts target companies that are corporate customers of banks with the goal of having the companies pressure the banks to stop investing in GHG-intensive projects. A study by a group of environmental NGOs examined corporate financial statements and estimated the GHG emissions attributable to the money held by the financial system. According to these calculations, the GHG emissions attributable to the use by banks of the funds of companies like Microsoft, Google, and Meta was more than all emissions attributable to these companies' operations and products. Similarly, the emissions associated with Amazon's $81 billion in cash and financial investments generated more emissions than the emissions from generating all of the energy used by Amazon's facilities.[10]

The effects of these policies are hard to assess, but banks' reluctance to support bids on Alaskan oil and gas leases appears to have undermined a Trump Administration effort to conduct a lease auction in Alaska in 2020–2021. Similarly, large coal companies have identified lender pressure as financial risks. One example from the Peabody Coal 2019 annual report filed with the SEC notes the threat posed by "unfavorable lending policies by lending institutions and divestment efforts affecting the investment community."

Banks also can engage in prescriptive regulation of their borrowers. Historically, banks monitor and regulate their borrowers' financial behavior in order to ensure repayment of the loan. A 2005

---

[10] CLIMATE SAFE LENDING NETWORK ET AL., THE CARBON BANKROLL: THE CLIMATE IMPACT AND UNTAPPED POWER OF CORPORATE CASH (2022).

study of commercial loans found that more than half included environmental disclosure and compliance requirements, although the study did not focus on GHG emissions requirements. To reduce climate risks and comply with climate commitments, banks increasingly include debt covenants with climate-related requirements that must be met by borrowers, such as disclosures of GHG emissions, and covenants regarding future emissions. Banks can also include loan terms decrease the cost of borrowing when the borrower reduces GHG emissions below specified levels and increase the cost when the borrower fails to do so. Banks also have incentives to actively monitor borrowers during the life-cycle of a loan and to insist that borrowers implement climate provisions in loan agreements.

C. Insurers

We noted in Chapter 3 that insurance companies and reinsurance companies are surprisingly important players in PEG climate initiatives. Insurance is both an important actor in the financial sector and one of the tools used in PEG climate initiatives. Insurance works by transferring and pooling risk whereas reinsurance functions as a form of insurance for insurance companies. Insurance companies purchase reinsurance to pool their risk in the event of a disaster that is so costly that the payouts would exceed even an insurance company's ability to pay. Insurers become less profitable if the financial costs from disasters occur in ways that cannot be reflected in insurance premiums. It's not hard to see that climate change-driven natural disasters can reduce the returns on the investments insurance companies make to provide for future payouts. They thus share many of the same climate motivations as investors and banks.

Insurers also have the same principal options: to reduce their own GHG emissions, to make insurance underwriting decisions based on climate risks and the GHG emissions of the companies they insure, and to take actions to pressure those insureds to reduce emissions. Thus, insurance as a tool is a hybrid of penalties (making insurance coverage more costly for high-risk activities), payments (reducing insurance premiums for lower-risk activities), and prescription (dictating terms before insurance can be offered or on an ongoing basis during the life of the policy). Many insurance companies have made GHG disclosures and commitments regarding their operations, but as with insurers and banks we focus on their interactions with GHG-emitting companies.

Insurers exert pressure on their insureds (or potential insureds) through declining to insure GHG-intensive projects and companies. Insurers have joined multi-stakeholder initiatives to create pressure for decarbonization and have adopted internal corporate policies regarding climate change. Roughly two dozen large insurance companies have adopted policies that decline to insure coal-based businesses or projects, including the construction of new coal-fired power plants and coal mines. Many of these insurers decline to underwrite firms that generate more than thirty percent of revenue from coal-mining or energy production from coal.

The securities disclosures of coal firms suggest that these insurer climate policies are having an effect. In 2019, Peabody Coal included insurance risks in its annual report: "the number and quantity of viable financing alternatives available to us may be significantly impacted by unfavorable lending and investment policies by financial institutions and insurance companies associated with concerns about environmental impacts of coal combustion."

The Net-Zero Insurance Alliance (NZIA) is a private organization launched in 2021 at the G20 Climate Summit in Venice. Its eight founding members are all insurance companies: AXA (NZIA Chair), Allianz, Aviva, Generali, Munich Re, SCOR, Swiss Re and Zurich Insurance Group. Over 20 global risk managers, insurers, and investors, representing over 11% of world insurance premium volume, are participants in NZIA, and the total amount of assets under management by the participants is over $7 trillion. NZIA builds on the climate work initiated in 2019 by the Net-Zero Asset Owner Alliance (NZAOA), and, as with many global organizations working on climate mitigation, NZIA is affiliated with a government initiative, in this case the UN Principles for Sustainable Insurance (PSI), an insurance industry-UN collaboration.

The main goal of NZIA is to transition insurance and reinsurance portfolios to net-zero GHG emissions by 2050. To address greenwashing concerns, each insurer must set intermediate 5-year targets and to report on progress annually. NZIA is broadening its reach to other insurance and reinsurance companies and is supporting insurance associations by creating underwriting criteria for the most carbon-intensive projects. NZIA members also are required to support the development of new low-carbon technologies.

Although the NZIA is relatively new, it appears to have made progress in building a global alliance, and it has established six working groups. The Metrics and Targets working group is collaborating with the Partnership for Carbon Accounting Financials (PCAF) to develop an emissions disclosure standard for insurance companies in 2022. The Engagement team has created a document outlining the requirements for "net-zero" in the insurance and reinsurance industries, and it has developed strategies for achieving sustainability in the insurance sector. The Life and Health workstream analyzes methods that life and health insurance businesses can use to make progress toward net-zero emissions. The antitrust workstream engages with legal advisors to ensure compliance with antitrust and competition laws.

As we mentioned in Chapter 3, reinsurers face the greatest risks from climate catastrophes, and they have issued some of the earliest and most unequivocal reports about the financial risks of climate change. The largest reinsurers, Swiss Re, Munich Re and Lloyds of London, were early supporters of government climate mitigation efforts. They also have limited their coverage of coal mining and other GHG-intensive activities.

III. Prescriptive Requirements

Several private initiatives rely on *prescriptive requirements* as their principal tool. Much like a regulatory program that a government might develop, these initiatives identify regulatory goals, pressure companies to meet them, develop accounting methods for calculating GHG emissions, require public disclosure, and provide private sanctions for failing to comply with the requirements.

A. Science-Based Targets Initiative

A leading example of large, corporate-NGO PEG climate initiatives is SBTi, which has over 1,000 participating companies representing over $20 trillion in market capitalization, including roughly 20% of the Global Fortune 500 and including roughly 50 sectors in 60 countries. SBTi is a partnership between CDP, the World Resources Institute, the World Wide Fund for Nature, and the UN Global Compact. SBTi works with companies that are willing to commit to specific GHG reduction targets.[11] SBTi resembles a government regulatory program: it sets a goal of achieving the Paris Agreement 2°C goal or 1.5°C aspiration, it induces regulated companies to reduce emissions at the levels necessary to achieve their share of the global GHG reduction targets established by the IPCC to achieve the 2°C goal or 1.5°C aspiration. Companies and other organizations commit to achieve Paris Agreement-based targets (called "science-based emission reduction targets"), then commit to a GHG emissions trajectory that equals the companies' share of reductions necessary to achieve the Paris Agreement goals, including 50% GHG emissions reductions by 2030 and net-zero emissions by 2050.

SBTi experts conduct a detailed review of a company's GHG reduction commitments against their scientific criteria to validate the legitimacy of corporate reduction commitments. To maintain the

---

[11] WHO WE ARE, SCIENCE BASED TARGETS INITIATIVE (SBTI).

SBTi validation companies must show meaningful progress toward the target and publicly report progress annually. To reduce concerns that companies are excluding important emissions from their supply chains or making claims that push action into the future or rely on paying others to make reductions, in 2021 SBTi published a sustainability standard that establishes criteria that companies will need to meet to reach validated science-based "net-zero" GHG reductions across the entire supply chain.

SBTi provides a forum for companies to make public commitments to achieve science-based targets, specifies disclosure standards, provides technical support, and assesses how likely the companies are to meet the targets. SBTi also revises its criteria on a regular basis to assure consistency with the latest climate science. Once a company has made an SBTi commitment, compliance is not legally compelled but it is not entirely voluntary. Although SBTi lacks the ability to bring a civil or criminal legal action against companies that fail to comply, the reputational harms of failing to comply can be significant, and companies may be under pressure from investors, lenders, and corporate buyers to participate in SBTi.

SBTi's program includes many of the attributes and operational functions that are needed for a private climate change governance approach to be an effective and legitimate measure and complement to government requirements, including science-based ambition, public reporting, steps to foster implementation and innovation among the regulated community, and accountability for participants.

In a private governance system, the consequences for a company that misses its targets can be substantial. A company is open to criticism by its stakeholders, reduced ESG rating scores, loss of supply chain customers, potential claims from false disclosures, and breach of contract actions, and may suffer reputational damage. Absent fraud, there is no corresponding threat of civil and criminal enforcement by government agencies if targets are not met.

As with other PEG initiatives, it is difficult to assess the specific emissions reductions attributable to SBTi, but an SBTi study of 338 participating companies concluded that they collectively reduced their annual GHG emissions by 25% between 2015 and 2019, a reduction of 302 million tons of $C0_{2}e$, the equivalent of all the emissions of a medium-sized country or the annual emissions from 78 coal-fired power plants.

B. Investment Firm Commitments

The first action is a form of *prescriptive governance*: Most major financial firms have climate or ESG plans that include climate commitments, often "net zero" commitments. These are self-imposed requirements, so they are voluntary in the sense that firms typically are not legally obligated to adopt them and could change them without the approval of a third party. These commitments may be prescriptive if they are verified by a third-party that has set standards the firm commits to meeting. Firms face many types of pressure, though, to adopt and implement these plans: the firms that make them often publicize them with customers and employees in ways that make them vulnerable to naming and shaming if they fail to follow through and may subject them to legal liability if the commitments and plans are used in regulatory filings or mislead customers.

C. Supply Chain Contracting Requirements

Climate-focused supply chain contracting requirements are growing rapidly and are an example of *prescriptive requirements* in PEG climate initiatives that may be enforced not only via economic and social pressures, but also via legal contract actions. A recent study demonstrated that more than 80% of the largest firms in seven global sectors included environmental requirements in their supply chain contracting in 2020, up from roughly 50% in 2004. Large companies are the targets of many *persuasion* campaigns and have the resources to participate in PEG initiatives, but 80% or more of the GHG emissions in many sectors arise from the value chain—the suppliers to these companies. These suppliers are often small companies that are not as often subject to NGO naming and shaming campaigns. Supply chain contracting initiatives are extending decarbonization pressure to these smaller companies and are an increasingly important component of the work of lawyers, managers, and advocates.

As explained above, the GHG Protocol divides emissions into three categories (Scope 1 from owned or operated facilities, Scope 2 from off-site electricity and heat, and Scope 3 from all other sources). Supply chain emissions are included Scope 3, and many disclosure organizations such as CDP are increasing pressure on companies to report supply chain and other Scope 3 emissions after initially focusing largely on Scope 1 and 2 emissions.

If companies commit to reduce GHG emissions but exclude supply chain emissions, these commitments can contribute to greenwashing—they can create the appearance that the company is taking important climate mitigation steps while it is actually ignoring a large share of emissions. Or the company can announce supply chain contracting policies that are weak or unenforced. But supply chains also represent a major opportunity for GHG reductions—they can create a global network of private requirements for emissions reductions that bypass limits on government action.

The leading example is Walmart's Project Gigaton. Walmart worked with several leading NGOs to commit to a gigaton (a billion tons) of GHG emissions from its suppliers worldwide. Walmart's business model and environmental and employee record have been heavily criticized, but regardless of your overall view about Walmart, Project Gigaton is an important PEG climate initiative: the NGO involvement suggests that the commitment is more than greenwashing, the emissions reductions are large—equal to Germany or Japan going carbon neutral for a year—and the decarbonization pressure will extend to many companies, facilities, and countries that have thus far escaped mitigation pressure. This type of supply chain contracting also can bypass polarization problems. Research shows that when moderates and conservatives learn about Walmart's Project Gigaton they become more concerned about climate change and more supportive of public and private climate mitigation.

Global networks of supply chain decarbonization pressure are particularly important because they provide a partial solution to the mismatched geographic and political boundaries problem we identified in Chapter 2. GHG emissions occur locally but have global effects. They also often arise from sources outside of a country's boundaries, and a country that has committed to GHG reductions cannot regulate the sources in other countries. In the absence of effective international requirements—which do not exist for GHG emissions—government regulation is not an option, but supply chain requirements can provide private emissions limits and a mechanism for companies to transfer expertise and resources to suppliers.

The ability of supply chain contracting pressure to transcend geographic and political boundaries provides opportunities to address the mismatched boundaries problem and reduce incentives for another problem we discussed in Chapter 2—the race-to-the-bottom. One NGO has noted that this mismatch enables "jurisdictional arbitrage"—playing one government off another to reduce regulatory costs. But supply chain requirements can reduce opportunities for this type of arbitrage and the resulting race-to-the-bottom. Countries may compete for businesses and jobs by lowering climate requirements, but if those businesses are subject to private supply chain requirements, there is less competitive advantage to locating in a country with less stringent standards and less likelihood that businesses—and countries—will act in ways that are individually rational but collectively deficient.

The ability of supply chain contracting requirements to transfer pressure from companies in countries with stakeholders who are insisting on GHG reductions to companies located in countries with customers who are creating less pressure to decarbonize is a core benefit of PEG supply chain contracting initiatives. However, supply chain contracting requirements also raises equity concerns. Should companies be able to create procurement-based pressure on companies in countries that do not support climate mitigation? Should the companies and workers who will suffer the effects of that emissions reduction pressure suffer the consequences of failing to do so if their governments have rejected doing so on a national basis? If supply chain contracts also are ways that corporate buyers provide information and expertise (persuasion) and financial incentives (penalties and subsidies) to corporate sellers that enable them to be more competitive in decarbonizing global markets, are supply chain contracting initiatives a net benefit to smaller firms? If catastrophic climate change cannot be avoided without this pressure, is procurement pressure an acceptable option even if it imposes costs on smaller producers? We defer these issues to our climate change justice discussion at the end of this Chapter.

Supply chain requirements can lead not only to direct emissions reductions by suppliers, they can also lead to innovations across sectors. Author and activist Bill McKibben has noted that Google worked with its suppliers to reduce the substantial emissions associated with the aluminum casings on its new Pixel 5 phones, and "when Google did the work on its aluminum casings, the company noted that its suppliers had agreed to make the recycled aluminum 'available to the consumer electronics industry as a whole,' because 'it's a core Google principle to try to lift all boats.'"[12] Whether or not Google is attempting to lift all boats, diffusion of innovation and the transfer of expert knowledge is an important aspect of PEG supply chain initiatives.

Many recent PEG climate initiatives have focused on increasing supply chain contracting commitments by creating incentives for firms to disclose and reduce the GHG emissions from suppliers. For instance, CDP (formerly the Carbon Disclosure Project) has developed the CDP Supply Chain Initiative and the Environmental Defense Fund (EDF) has developed the EDF Supply Chain Solutions Center. Both efforts are designed to provide expertise and increase pressure on companies to disclose and reduce supply chain emissions. CDP has produced annual reports discussing companies' supply chain emissions and praising companies that have disclosed supply chain emissions and taken steps to reduce them. By inducing firms to calculate, disclose, and reduce the GHG emissions of their entire value chain, including suppliers, these NGO initiatives create incentives for the firm to serve as a private regulator of other firms.

---

[12] Bill McKibben, *Could Google's Carbon Emissions Have Effectively Doubled Overnight?*, THE NEW YORKER (May 20, 2022).

The motivations for and elements of supply chain initiatives are apparent from recent commitments by Maersk, a shipping firm that accounts for a quarter of all goods shipped by sea. Under pressure from half of its 200 largest customers, including retailers like Unilever, Maersk has committed to a net zero GHG trajectory and to shipping all goods from its climate-committed customers using low-GHG ships. Corporate SEC disclosures such as this Intel 2019 annual report statement, also reveal the motivations for companies to reduce supply chain emissions:

> Actively managing our supply chain creates business value for Intel and our customers by helping to reduce risk, improve product quality, achieve environmental and social goals, and raise the overall performance of our suppliers. Over the past five years, we completed more than 600 supplier audits using the Responsible Business Alliance Code of Conduct standard. We actively collaborate with other companies and lead industry initiatives on key issues such as advancing responsible minerals sourcing, improving transparency around climate and water impacts in the global electronics supply chain, and addressing risks of forced and bonded labor.

The growing focus on supply chain contracting has not only led to supply chain-focused disclosure programs by CDP, but also efforts to develop broad standards for the minimum elements in procurement requirements, such as the Responsible Business Alliance Code of Conduct mentioned by Intel. Sector-specific procurement initiatives also have emerged, such as the Electric Utility Industry Sustainable Supply Chain Alliance, an industry effort targeting climate procurement practices for electric utilities.

The use of procurement requirements and climate provisions in supply chain contracts has increased the importance of supply chain contracting expertise for environmental lawyers. In the U.S. and United Kingdom, PEG climate initiatives are underway by the Environmental Law Institute and the Chancery Lane Project to develop model supply chain contracting provisions. The Chancery Lane Project is an NGO that has served as a forum for hundreds of lawyers to develop over 100 model supply chain contract provisions. The model climate provisions developed by the Chancery Lane Project reduce companies' transaction costs, enabling smaller businesses to deploy supply chain contracting requirements even if they do not have a large legal staff. When model provisions are developed in an open, inclusive process with broad stakeholder input, they also can reduce NGO concerns about greenwashing and provide companies with comfort that using the provisions will leave them less vulnerable to NGO naming and shaming campaigns.

D. Sector-Specific Initiatives

In addition to the broad efforts to reduce GHG emissions across multiple sectors through SBTi, net zero, and supply chain contracting efforts, numerous sector-specific PEG climate initiatives have emerged that use prescriptive requirements, persuasion and other tools. Private sector organizations and public-private hybrids have emerged. An example of a hybrid is a global effort to reduce carbon emissions from shipping, which includes Maersk and other large shipping firms. Another example is the Fashion Industry Charter for Climate Action, which is a United Nations-sponsored industry-NGO collaboration focusing on reducing the carbon footprint of the fashion industry. Dozens of widely-recognized companies such as Adidas, Chanel, Nike, and Ralph Lauren are signatories, and the goal is to reach net zero by 2050 consistent with the 1.5°C aspiration of the Paris Agreement. Fashion brands are particularly vulnerable to naming and shaming and supply chain contracting pressure from retailers, but they are also under enormous pressure to respond to consumer interests for cheap, new designs and investor pressure for profits.

IV. Property Rights

Two types of PEG climate initiatives use *property rights* as a principal tool for GHG emissions reductions: carbon offsets and internal carbon trading systems.

A. Offsets

Offsets are arguably a hybrid of several tools, including private creation of *property rights*, *prescriptive requirements*, and *payments and penalties*. A GHG emissions source can reduce emissions or pay others to do so. Carbon offsets are created when emissions reductions by one party are used to reduce the emissions attributed to another party. In other words, it may be cheaper to pay another party to reduce its emissions than to reduce at source. Since GHGs are global pollutants, it does not matter where the reductions take place. Examples of activities that generate offsets include capturing methane from landfills and planting trees or reducing deforestation. PEG climate initiatives have created entitlements in carbon emissions through private carbon offset programs, and the market for private carbon offsets is massive—it accounted for $523 million and 101 million tons of GHG emissions in 2012. The market growth is estimated to reach billions of dollars by 2030 for the simple reason that many of the companies making net zero commitments will need to rely on offsets to meet their goals.

An example of a PEG climate initiative that relies heavily on offsets is Climate Neutral, a private labeling and certification system for retail brands. Climate Neutral requires companies to use the GHG Protocol to assess and disclose their carbon emissions, including supply chain and other Scope 3 emissions, to commit to an emissions reduction trajectory, and to achieve near-term carbon neutrality by purchasing offsets for any emissions not reduced directly. To reduce the risk of false climate neutrality claims, Climate Neutral requires brands to purchase offsets that meet the requirements of one of four private offset standard-setting organizations: the Gold Standard, Verified Carbon Standard, Climate Action Reserve, and American Carbon Registry.

Offsets can reduce the cost and accelerate the pace of decarbonization so long as the offsets are additional—if they reduce emissions that would not otherwise have been reduced absent the offset—and if they do not create moral hazard by limiting the firm's incentives to reduce its own emissions. If one NGO or company can reduce emissions at much lower cost than another, having the second pay the first to make reductions it would not otherwise make can be an efficient way to achieve decarbonization.

Offsets have provoked criticism, though, because the lack of clear, rigorous standards for many offsets has enabled some companies to claim they are meeting climate goals by relying on offsets that do not represent additional GHG reductions. Reliance on carbon offsets also may enable companies to delay fundamental changes necessary for long-term decarbonization. Equity concerns may arise if wealthy emitters pay economically disadvantaged emitters to make reductions rather than making them directly. Offsets are further discussed in Chapter 11's section on forestry.

B. Internal Carbon Trading and Pricing Systems

Some companies and other organizations have created internal systems for trading or pricing carbon emissions. To the extent these systems involve caps and trading within the organization, they are a type of internal *property right* tool, and to the extent they use an internal tax on emissions, they are a form of *penalty* or *payment*.

Many business firms, notably Microsoft and Disney, have adopted internal carbon pricing; and Yale University was among the first universities to adopt internal carbon-pricing in the private non-profit world. The core concept is for the organization to calculate GHG emissions, to place a shadow price on the emissions, and to charge units within the organization based on the quantity of emissions. The revenue collected from the internal carbon price can be used for carbon mitigation or the price can simply send signals about the GHG emissions associated with various activities. Pricing carbon should lead to more efficient allocations of GHG emissions within the organization and reduce the cost of achieving emissions reduction goals.

Problem Exercise: Corporate Climate Strategy

As you review the opportunities—and limits—of PEG climate initiatives, think through what you would do as a corporate sustainability officer or outside environmental advocate organizing a PEG climate initiative to encourage MaxCo or MinCo to reduce GHG emissions or were helping them respond to a PEG initiative:

> *MaxCo* is a large publicly traded corporation with 10% of its stock owned by InvestCo, a large institutional investor, as part of diversified portfolios managed for pension funds. MaxCo has borrowed $100 million from U.S. Bank, a large international bank headquartered in New York, to fund its ongoing operations. MaxCo has comprehensive general liability insurance from Acme, a member of the Net-Zero Insurance Alliance. MaxCo's headquarters building and manufacturing facilities are located in San Francisco, California. MaxCo makes widgets, which it sells to Walmart and Target in the U.S. and Unilever in Europe. MaxCo uses Maersk as its preferred firm for shipping widgets to customers around the world. The production of MaxCo's sophisticated widgets requires a great deal of expertise, so many of MaxCo's employees are recruited from universities with strong computer science and data analytics programs. The processes MaxCo uses to make widgets result in very large GHG emissions. MaxCo is studying whether to secure project finance funding to open a new widget manufacturing facility in Indonesia.
>
> *MinCo* is also a corporation, but it is not as large as MaxCo and most of its stock is held by the family of the company's founders and a fund that just invests in the widget sector. MinCo has borrowed the same amount as MaxCo, but its bank is a low-profile lender headquartered in Birmingham, Alabama. MinCo's insurer is Beta, a regional insurance company that is not part of the Net-Zero Insurance Alliance. MinCo's headquarters building and manufacturing facilities are located in Atlanta, GA. MinCo also makes widgets, but it sells them to corporate buyers in China. MinCo uses several small shipping firms depending on which offers the lowest costs. MinCo's widgets require less technical expertise and it relies less on recruiting employees with that expertise. As with MaxCo,

the processes MinCo uses to make widgets result in very large GHG emissions. Minco is also studying whether to use its own capital to finance construction of a new widget manufacturing facility in Indonesia.

To review your understanding of the PEG tools and climate initiatives we have discussed in Chapters 7 and 8, consider these questions using the MaxCo and MinCo hypothetical:

- Which actors and tools will be most valuable in reducing MaxCo's GHG emissions?
- Will those same actors and tools be valuable in reducing MinCo's emissions?
- Are the universal owners who invest in MaxCo more likely to push for decarbonization measures than the concentrated investors in MinCo.?
- Is MaxCo's international lender more likely to press for decarbonization than MaxCo's bank?
- Is MaxCo more likely to face pressure from its NZIA-member insurer than MinCo is from its insurer?
- Will MaxCo be subject to greater decarbonization pressure from its major US and European retailers than MinCo?
- Which is most likely to be subject to supply chain contracting pressure?

QUESTIONS AND DISCUSSION

1. Assume that you are a lawyer or manager who has been asked to provide advice on whether an investment firm should join Climate Action 100+ or the Net Asset Managers Climate Initiative. What legal, social or economic risks and benefits should you mention? Would your advice change if the investor is a universal owner?

2. Why might an investor with a large, diversified portfolio of stocks have an incentive to pressure an oil and gas company to sell less oil and gas? What prisoner's dilemma problem do many companies face that is not faced by universal or common owners?

3. Universal owner theory raises difficult questions about the fiduciary duties of the investment firms' managers and the managers of the companies they invest in. An investment firm manager with only diversified portfolios may have fairly clear obligations to reduce systemic risks like climate change. But what about an investment firm manager with diversified portfolios, sector-specific portfolios, and portfolios that are not diversified? Similarly, at the company level, managers have a fiduciary duty to protect the interests of their shareholders. But a company's shareholders may include some with diversified portfolios and others with concentrated investments in their company or sector. These shareholders' interests may diverge, raising questions as to how managers should balance those different interests. To what extent are managers are likely to be able to balance these competing interests under the protection of the business judgment rule, which we discussed in Chapter 5. To what extent is common ownership likely to induce investment fund managers and corporate managers to engage in PEG initiatives?

4. Assume you are a lawyer or manager asked to provide advice on whether a company should join the Science Based Targets initiative. What advice would you provide? Would your advice differ if you represented MaxCo or MinCo?

5. Assume that you are advising an NGO that is concerned about the quality of corporate net zero commitments. What are the ways in which net zero commitments may contribute less to GHG emissions reductions than they may promise? What commitments would you want to receive from a company about a net zero pledge to ensure that it will yield major GHG reductions?

6. Assume you are advising an institutional investment company that manages both a large fund with a diversified basket of stocks that replicate the economy as a whole, a diversified fund made up of stocks that meet ESG criteria, and a sector-specific fund with stocks in the oil and gas industry. A group of NGOs and shareholders have pushed the investment company to vote it shares against boards of directors who do not support reducing corporate emissions consistent with a 1.5C pathway. What advice would you provide to the investment company on whether it has conflicting fiduciary duties to the clients in the large diversified fund and clients in the sector-specific oil and gas fund? Does it have a fiduciary duty to shareholders in the diversified fund to account for climate change and in the ESG fund? Does it have a fiduciary duty not to account for climate change in the oil and gas fund?

7. Many of the largest companies in the world have made "net zero" commitments, including Apple with a market capitalization at No. 2, Microsoft at No. 3, Alphabet (Google) at No. 4, Amazon at No. 5, Tesla at No. 6, and Meta at No. 8. These are self-imposed prescriptive requirements enforced through the range of PEG pressures that induce companies to engage in climate mitigation. The "net" component of "net zero" means that the company does not commit to eliminate all GHG emissions, but it commits to purchase offsets equal to any emissions that it does not eliminate and to reach a net zero accounting for both, often by 2050. In addition, the timing of the emissions reductions matters for climate change—reductions that begin in the near term will reduce global warming far more than reductions that continue in the near term and decline sharply by 2050. The timing of emissions reductions and the balance between emissions reductions and offset purchases have become a source of contention among companies and NGOs. Many companies have announced ambitious goals but have yet to take major steps to implement them. For instance, a 2022 survey of 25 large

global companies[13] concluded that corporate carbon neutrality claims are often misleading. At the same time, company managers have responded that few organizations, whether companies or governments, understand the options sufficiently and have the technologies or other aspects of decarbonization in place to include in climate plans. What incentives does a company have to comply with net zero commitments? What PEG initiatives could create these incentives and monitor compliance?

8. By Executive Order and regulations, the U.S. federal government requires major suppliers of goods and services to government agencies to disclose Scope 1 and Scope 2 emissions, and Scope 3 emissions if they make up a large share of the carbon footprint of the suppliers' products. Is this likely to reduce U.S. GHG emissions? What effects is this likely to have on PEG supply chain contracting initiatives?

9. In what ways might PEG climate initiatives increase the likelihood of major government climate measures like the procurement requirements discussed in question 8? Might PEG climate initiatives decrease the likelihood of government action in some cases? How?

10. Assume you are representing an NGO that is pressing for near-term carbon emissions reductions from small and medium-sized businesses. What type of commitment should you suggest? What timelines should be included? Should offsets be an option?

11. A major concern raised by critics of PEG is that common ownership leaves substantial power in the hands of institutional investors. Common owners can use the powers outlined above in less social-regarding ways than combating climate change, such as setting monopoly prices and monopsony wages. Additionally, all relevant actors in common ownership are unelected officials. Should we allow these investors to make decisions about PEG that affect climate mitigation strategy? Or would doing so offend our democratic ideals? What if common owners better represent public preferences on climate change than policymakers?

12. A gap between commitments and action exists for the companies in Climate Action 100+, NZAMI, and other PEG initiatives. For instance, a November 2021 analysis found the NZAMI targets to be "both unambitious and gameable," and it concluded that the NZAMI targets would only achieve 40% of the emissions reductions necessary by 2030 to keep the world on track to achieve Paris Agreement 2°C goal. We mentioned in Chapter 4 that the relevant question for PEG climate initiatives is often not whether they will *solve* the climate problem, but whether they are *contributing* to the solution. Is a 40% reduction a positive development or, because some of these initiatives seem to promise "net zero" or other more complete solutions, is this a troubling form of greenwashing?

13. Referring back to our policy toolkit, what types of tools do each of these PEG climate initiatives rely on?

---

[13] New Climate Institute, *Corporate Climate Responsibility Monitor 2022*, available at https://newclimate.org/wp-content/uploads/2022/02/CorporateClimateResponsibilityMonitor2022.pdf.

a. A bank policy not to lend to fossil fuel-heavy projects.

b. Investment firm vote for climate-concerned board members against the wishes of a company's management team.

c. A bank's low interest loan to a renewable power project.

d. Asset manager requirement for companies in its portfolio to join the Science-Based Targets initiative.

e. A company purchases offsets to achieve its net zero goal.

Chapter 9

THE ENERGY TRANSITION, CLIMATE ADAPTATION AND CLIMATE JUSTICE

Chapter 7 described why companies care about addressing climate change. Chapter 8 explored the full toolkit of PEG instruments in the climate space. Chapter 9 turns to PEG initiatives in three specific settings. Because emissions from fossil fuels play a central role in driving climate change, the energy system is undergoing a major transition to decarbonized energy sources. We begin Chapter 9 by examining the many PEG initiatives that are designed to accelerate the energy transition, blurring the boundary between climate initiatives and energy initiatives. Even if climate mitigation and energy transition efforts succeed in achieving the goals of the Paris Agreement, though, a substantial amount of adaptation to climate change will still be necessary, and our second section examines PEG adaptation initiatives. Third, we wrap up the chapter by exploring the significant environmental justice concerns raised by PEG energy transition and climate adaptation initiatives.

I. The Energy Transition

Roughly 80% of GHGs are the product of fossil fuel use, so PEG initiatives often focus on transitioning the energy system to low-carbon or zero-carbon fuels. We focus below on three aspects of the role of private governance in the energy transition: renewable power initiatives, the Equator Principles, and energy transactions.

A. Renewable Power Initiatives

Many private organizations help companies reduce the collective action problems we discussed in Chapter 2 by serving as a forum for companies to reduce the transaction costs of coordinating, to gain the benefits of credible public commitments, and to gain expertise. Roughly half of the world's end-of-use of electricity occurs by companies in the commercial and industrial sector, and two leading initiatives led by non-governmental organizations (NGOs) have emerged to push for and coordinate corporate renewable power commitments: the RE100 initiative and the Renewable Energy Buyers Alliance (REBA)/Clean Energy Buyers Alliance (CEBA).

1. RE100

RE100 is a global initiative that includes close to 400 companies that have committed to powering their operations with 100% renewable electricity (hence the name "RE"). RE100 is managed by

CDP and the Climate Group, an international non-profit specializing in working with businesses on climate and energy initiatives.

RE100 focuses on companies with very large electricity demand, typically over 100 GWh annually. The participating companies span a wide range of sectors, from technology, pharmaceuticals, and manufacturing to fashion. They currently include well-known companies such as IKEA, Google, Apple, and General Motors. The large energy demand and size of RE100's membership send signals to markets and governments about private sector demand for renewable power. RE100 provides a platform for companies to make public commitments to using 100% renewable power, to follow widely-adopted standards for assessing how much renewable power they should purchase and what types of power qualify, to create incentives for other companies to make similar commitments and to push for governments to improve the regulatory environment for renewable power. To participate in RE100, companies are required to match 100% of the electricity they use across their global operations with electricity produced from a range of renewable sources (such as contracts with electricity suppliers or renewable energy credits). By focusing on private commitments for renewable power around the globe, RE100 not only reduces the transaction costs of collective action, but also bypasses the geographic and political boundaries that are barriers to government action on energy and climate change.

As with any public or private regulatory system, lawyers and managers advising clients on whether and how to participate in RE100 focus on the risks and benefits of joining, the commitments required, and the process of joining and leaving the organization. For RE100, companies must commit to 100% renewable power by 2050, with interim steps of at least 60% by 2030 and 90% by 2040. The permissible renewable sources include electricity from the market or produced by the company and can include wind, solar, geothermal, biomass (including biogas), or hydropower. Participating companies can procure renewable electricity directly by purchasing from generators and suppliers in the market through power purchase agreements (commonly called "PPAs") and can make retail renewable power purchases and buy stand-alone "unbundled" renewable energy instruments. RE100 also requires participating companies to join the campaign at the group level (not to just have a subsidiary or unit join) and commit to a set of core criteria. To give a concrete sense of these criteria, they are set out below:

- *Commitment.* A 100% renewable electricity public commitment that includes all of the company's operations, including Scope 1 emissions from electricity generation, Scope 2 emissions from company activities, and emissions from the operations of business units operating under the brand or company group.

- *Verification.* Third party verification of renewable energy consumption and if necessary of generation and sales.
- *In-Grid Sourcing.* Sourcing of renewable electricity from within the boundary of the market in which the company is consuming the electricity, excluding small loads (small offices, retail outlets) of up to 100 MWh/year, per market, in markets where renewable energy sourcing is not technically feasible.
- *Reporting.* Annual public reports on progress annually via the RE 100 Reporting Spreadsheet or the CDP climate change questionnaire.
- *Policy Advocacy.* A commitment not to engage in political lobbying in support of fossil fuels over renewable energy production, increasing holdings in fossil fuel assets, or other activities that would undermine the RE100 mission.

RE100 members must be able to show that they have a claim to meet all of their reported renewable electricity usage through use of unique renewable electricity production. The requirements for a credible renewable energy usage claim typically include factors such as credible generation data, exclusive ownership of attributes (double counting is not permitted), geographic market limitations of claims, and vintage (year of production) limitations. These requirements are often met by purchasing Energy Attribute Certificates (similar to Renewable Energy Credits) but contracts can also be used. The membership approval process follows 8 steps, including an analysis of the technical requirements for RE100 membership by the company, a corporate expression of intent, an RE100 analysis of whether the company meets the criteria for joining, an application, a decision from the RE 100 management, and a new member announcement.

2. Renewable Energy Buyers Alliance (REBA)/Clean Energy Buyers Alliance (CEBA)

REBA was formed in 2018 as an alliance of over 300 large energy buyers, energy providers, and four NGOs. REBA was one of the first NGOs to focus on renewable energy purchases, and it facilitated commitments by many companies to procure 100 percent renewable power.[1] Many large scale company renewable power purchases have been made by REBA members. One example is Google (via Alphabet), which disclosed in 2019 that it had purchased 1,600 megawatts of renewable energy. The disclosure indicated that Google did so through participation in over eighteen new energy deals and noted that it anticipated construction of $2 billion in new energy infrastructure.[2]

The initial REBA goal was to catalyze 60 gigawatts of renewable energy by 2025, and the combined efforts of REBA and RE100 make that goal feasible. By facilitating corporate renewable power commitments and actions, REBA and other corporate-NGO collaborations also increase pressure on utilities to provide renewable power even in states that are either on the sidelines or actively hostile to government climate regulatory efforts.

Despite its success facilitating private renewable power commitments, REBA is also an example of the limits of PEG climate initiatives. Its members faced resistance to adding renewable power to local grids from some government agencies and state public utility commissions, and REBA ultimately transformed into CEBA (Clean Energy Buyers Alliance). CEBA is structured as a lobbying organization that advocates for government legislative and regulatory changes to promote renewable power. With a membership list that includes Google, General Motors, McDonald's, Target and other leading companies, CEBA has the support to play a strong lobbying role. CEBA has a goal of achieving a 90% carbon-free U.S. electricity system by 2030, and it now combines REBA's initial focus on facilitating private renewable power commitments with its new focus on changing government energy policy to make it easier for members to achieve those commitments. In 2021, CEBA released a list of top clean energy purchases that included more than 100 projects totaling 11.06 GW of contracted capacity, an amount equal to roughly 20 major power plants.

The transition from REBA to CEBA also reflects an important difference between "renewable" and "clean" energy. Renewables typically include wind, solar, geothermal and hydro, but clean energy typically includes a broader set of sources, including often biogas and nuclear. The acceptance of clean rather than just renewable energy by CEBA reflects the challenge of supporting large increases in power demand, including in storage, software, and data systems.

---

1 OUR VISION, RENEWABLE ENERGY BUYERS ALLIANCE.

2 Alphabet, Inc., 2019 10K, at 8.

B. Equator Principles

Carbon disclosure occurs at the company, investor, product, and project or facility levels. We discussed company, investor, and product disclosure in Chapter 8, and in Chapter 3 we introduced the Equator Principles, which are private standards for disclosing the environmental impacts of new projects or facilities funded by project finance lenders. Project finance lending occurs when a project, whether a bridge with tolls or a power plant that sells electricity, uses the funding generated by the project to repay the loan.

In the 1990s, growing concern about the environmental impacts of project finance-funded pipelines, dams, and power plants in developing countries culminated in efforts by numerous advocacy groups and banks, with support from the World Bank and International Monetary Fund (IMF) and International Finance Corporation (IFC), to form the Equator Principles. Project finance lending has historically been opaque to the general public, but advocacy groups targeted major banks with retail businesses using naming and shaming campaigns based on the environmental effects of the banks' project finance lending. A leader was the Rainforest Action Network (RAN), which led protests against Citibank's lending to multiple projects with large ecological footprints. Citibank then played a leadership role in the effort to establish the Equator Principles, which were patterned after World Bank and IMF/IFC lending guidelines.

The Equator Principles initiative consists of three elements: the Equator Principles, a private standard that requires participants to disclose the environmental harms of projects funded through project finance loans; the Equator Principles Association (EP Association), an NGO formed to administer the standard; and the Equator Principles Financial Institutions (EPFI), the lenders that have committed to abide by the Equator Principles. More than 75 leading banks are committed to the Equator Principles, representing well over 70% of all global project finance lending at a global level.

According to the EP Association, the purpose of the Equator Principles is "to serve as a common baseline and risk management framework for financial institutions to identify, assess, and manage environmental and social risks when financing Projects." As with many environmental initiatives, the effects of the Equator Principles' project-level disclosure on carbon emissions are difficult to assess, but the types of projects subject to Equator Principles disclosure (e.g., pipelines and other major infrastructure projects), suggest the potential for large effects, and anecdotal examples of success have emerged. For instance, the Equator Principles provided the foundation for a 2016 RAN naming and shaming campaign regarding the Dakota Access pipeline. In an effort to induce Citigroup to stop funding the pipeline and to persuade the developers of the pipeline to halt construction, RAN argued that Citigroup's leadership role in financing the pipeline contradicted its Equator Principles commitments on climate and other issues. RAN used the fact that Citigroup is a signatory to the Equator Principles to argue that Citigroup was being hypocritical. Citigroup later announced that it had adopted a comprehensive environmental policy with standards related to climate change, endangered ecosystems, ecologically sustainable development, and other issues.

The EP Association uses a process to generate and amend the Equator Principles that resembles the informal rulemakings that federal agencies conduct under the Administrative Procedure Act: the EP Association proposes a standard, receives comments on the proposed standard, amends the proposed standard, and then publishes it in final form with explanations about how the final version addressed stakeholder comments. As of 2022, the current version of the Equator Principles is the fourth version, known as EP4.

The Equator Principles are organized much like government regulations, with main text, annexes, and exhibits. Under EP4, the Equator Principles assessments only apply to projects over $10 million. General requirements vary based on the size of the proposed project (identified as A, B & C Proposed Projects), but all must include an assessment of the environmental and social impacts of the project. For projects in non-OECD countries (non-industrialized countries, which may not have strong assessment requirements in place or the resources to enforce them), EP4 requires an assessment based on IFC standards & guidelines. For projects in OECD countries, EP4 requires an assessment of compliance with the laws of the host country.

In several ways, the EP4 requirements exceed the requirements of its federal analogue, the National Environmental Policy Act (NEPA). In parallel with NEPA, the Equator Principles require participating lenders to conduct environmental and social impact assessments before financing projects. EP4 requires not only an assessment of the environmental impacts of a project, which NEPA requires, but also a review of the project's environmental management and social systems, and environmental and social management plans, which NEPA does not.

Do the Equator Principles require reductions in environmental impacts or just assessment? NEPA only requires assessment, not mitigation of environmental impacts, but EP4 requires an action plan to reduce impacts. This requirement to include mitigation—not just analysis and disclosure—of negative environmental and social impacts has the potential to drive GHG emissions reductions if it is implemented.

What about enforcement? Since government agencies are not involved, it is easy to assume that the Equator Principles are simply "voluntary," but that perspective misses the ways that information and contract requirements affect corporate behavior. The EP4 requires use of an independent environmental and social consultant, disclosure of the environmental impacts identified in the report, and covenants in loan documents requiring compliance with the EP4 terms. There is no guarantee that a lender will enforce these provisions, but the risk that the lender will do so or even declare that the loan is in default increases the incentives of the project developer to comply with the EP4 requirements. The Chancery Lane Project, a PEG climate initiative headquartered in London that involves hundreds of corporate and NGO lawyers, has developed model covenants to increase the enforcement of climate-related IFC and Equator Principles provisions in project finance and other transactions.

Are the Equator Principles likely to play a role in climate mitigation? In addition to general requirements for environmental assessments, EP4 includes specific requirements for climate change assessment and disclosure in the EP4 standard and in Annex A. GHG assessments are required for projects with the potential to release 100,000 tons or more of CO_2e. Assessment and reporting are required to comply with the private carbon accounting and reporting standards of the GHG Protocol and CDP standards discussed in Chapter 8. Scope 1 and Scope 2 reporting is required, but Scope 3 is not, and the reporting must include not only project-specific emissions, but also aggregate emissions.

As with many other PEG energy and climate initiatives at the global level, the Equator Principles are largely driven by the private sector, but they have public-private hybrid features. The formation of the Equator Principles occurred with support from several quasi-public institutions such as the World Bank, and for projects in non-OECD countries, the standards incorporate compliance with IFC lending standards. The Equator Principles also buttress the activities of the United Nations' Principles for Responsible Banking and with the United Nations Environment Program's Finance Initiative, which has focused on assessment and disclosure of the Scope 3 emissions from lending and investment portfolios.

C. Energy Transactions

Achieving the 1.5°C or 2°C Paris Agreement targets will require rapid and widespread decarbonization of the energy system. Fossil fuels account for roughly 80% of global GHG emissions, so meeting these targets will require this energy transition to occur at a global level. Research shows that viable options exist to achieve the energy transition. For instance, decarbonizing electric generation, electrifying transportation, and electrifying buildings can achieve roughly 70% emissions reductions in the U.S., and comparable reductions can be achieved in many other countries.

At the same time, fossil fuels provide energy for the economic activity that supports the global population, a massive physical infrastructure exists to extract, transport, and use fossil fuels, and fossil fuel interests are powerful economic, social, and political actors around the globe. Many of the most disadvantaged populations around the world have limited access to electricity and other forms of energy, leading to a desire for a just transition.

These conflicting features of the energy system result in a complex energy market and regulatory framework and have created demand for private governance responses. In particular, the combination of increasing energy demand and pressure for decarbonization is driving a high volume of energy transactions. In some cases, these agreements involve the financing and construction of wind farms or solar facilities and the power purchase agreements companies use to purchase power from them. In other cases, they involve the building of gas-fired power plants, pipelines and other infrastructure, which can contribute to a reduction in carbon emissions if the power plants displace coal-fired power or if they include carbon capture and storage, but which ultimately must be replaced by non-carbon sources to achieve a 2050 net zero goal. No new coal-fired power plants are planned for the U.S. and many other developed countries, but deals involving the building of coal-fired plants, coal mines, and related infrastructure are continuing around the world.

Energy transactions involve all of the tools of public and private governance, including not only the financing and transfer of assets (payments, penalties, and property); but also investigations, disclosures, and representations and warranties (persuasion); covenants (prescriptive requirements); and indemnities (insurance). Energy transactions are too varied and the state of the art shifts too quickly to capture all of the nuances here, but this brief overview of the common features of energy transactions and how they contribute to the energy transition is a starting point for lawyers, managers, and advocates. To focus the analysis, assume that a company has joined RE 100 and plans to enter into a power purchase agreement to purchase the electricity generated by a solar farm. An equity investor and a bank are providing financing for a developer to construct and operate the solar farm. As we review the most important steps in the in the transaction, think about how the transaction may affect the company's carbon emissions.

1. Financing

As we have seen, investors and asset managers, banks, and other financial sector firms are heavily engaged in the energy transition. As NGOs have pointed out, the finance sector is simultaneously funding renewable and other decarbonization projects and fossil fuel-based projects. The PEG pressure to shift away from high-GHG projects in the finance sector arises from the investor initiatives we have discussed, including ESG screens and engagement through Climate Action 100+ and other investor-NGO initiatives; bank pressure through lending screens and climate engagement policies; project finance lending disclosure and pressure through the Equator Principles; and many other PEG financial sector climate initiatives.

Financial sector pressure is expressed through decisions about whether to finance particular energy projects, the effects of those decisions on the costs of capital, the disclosures required, and the conditions imposed on the companies and projects receiving the financing. Specific provisions in the agreements between firms in the finance sector and the companies they fund are too numerous to describe here, but the Chancery Lane Project provides examples of climate-friendly provisions for many finance-related agreements.

2. Investigations, Disclosures, Representations, and Warranties

Participants in an energy transaction have an interest in gathering relevant information, and the gathering and disclosure of this information can drive substantial GHG emissions reductions. Investigations are often called "due diligence" because they are conducted to ensure that the buyer or other party has met a basic standard of care regarding gathering the information necessary to know what it will be buying or leasing, whether that is land, goods, or services. Often lawyers or business managers retain environmental engineers, accountants, and other experts to conduct the diligence, and although they are not government inspectors, the participants in due diligence investigations have many of the same incentives to uncover liabilities, operating costs, or violations of laws and standards as a government inspector.

The scope of due diligence is massive. As Michael Gerrard of Columbia Law School has noted, roughly $500 million is spent on private environmental investigations every year in the U.S., an amount larger than the entire EPA enforcement budget. Site investigations that do not involve sampling are often called Phase I assessments, and if sampling is involved they are called Phase II assessments. Importantly, Phase I and II assessments are often designed to meet the requirements for reducing liability for hazardous substance releases under the federal Superfund statute, but many are not designed to assess compliance costs or market risks associated with GHG emissions or other environmental matters.

In addition to private environmental investigations, energy transactions often involve disclosures, representations, and warranties. Typically the selling party or landlord will disclose information requested by the prospective buyer or tenant. In our hypothetical the disclosure might include information about the prior uses of the land on which the solar farm will be built and information about the ability of the developer to build and operate the solar farm. The parties then often make explicit representations and warranties regarding the most important disclosures. The representations identify the extent and limits of the disclosures and the warranties provide the basis for legal remedies in the event of a breach of the representations.

Parties sometimes benefit by making their goals clear through disclosures called "recitals" at the beginning of a transactional document. For instance, recitals frame climate change issues as important considerations and make the parties' intentions unambiguous in the event of future contract disputes. They also can be valuable in the event of climate-related oversight by advocacy groups or others. An example from the Chancery Lane Project is a recital that identifies the parties' goal of ensuring that a transaction is part of an effort to limit the global temperature increase to 1.5°C above pre-industrial levels and achieve net zero or net negative emissions by 2050 or sooner.

3. *Covenants*

Covenants are promises made between the parties to the agreement. Because they are enforceable through breach of contract actions or other enforcement provisions in the agreement, they are prescriptive requirements that function much like regulatory requirements, except that the enforcing actor is a party to the contract, not a government regulator. An example is the Chancery Lane Project's model covenant regarding compliance with the climate-related IFC and Equator Principles provisions in project finance and other transactions.

4. *Indemnities*

In many cases a buyer or seller will agree to indemnify the other party for climate or other damages that may arise in the future. An example might be that a buyer of an older industrial company might insist on an indemnification in the event lawsuits are filed based on the company's historical GHG emissions. As another example, a firm constructing a new solar array might insist on an indemnification from project developer in the event that it is subject to a naming and shaming campaign because the construction of the solar facility destroyed historical artifacts or culturally valuable property.

After the indemnification is agreed to, the indemnifying party has an interest in policing the activities of the indemnified party to reduce the risk of having to make an indemnity payment. This places the indemnifying party in the role of an inspector and enforcer regarding the actions of the indemnified party. In some cases one of the parties will agree to purchase insurance rather than provide a direct indemnity, and in that case the insurer has essentially the same incentives as the indemnifying party. The Chancery Lane Project has developed model disclosures and other provisions between insurers and insureds regarding climate change risks.

Other Commercial Transactions. Although this overview has focused on energy transactions, many other types of commercial transactions occur that have important PEG implications. For instance, a sample of the agreements filed with the SEC indicated that publicly traded firms, which include many of the largest and highest GHG-emitting firms, filed more than 1,000 merger and acquisition agreements in 2001, and that total is likely to be much higher now. The study concluded that more than 70% of these agreements included environmental provisions.[3]

The total value of all mergers and acquisitions in the United States in a recent year exceeded $795 billion, so the investigations, contract provisions, and enforcement may have a large effect on climate and other environmental issues. Similarly, although the total value of commercial real estate transactions in the United States ranges widely from year to year, it was $875 billion in 2021. More than 80% of all commercial leases include environmental provisions, and comparable percentages arise from commercial land sales.

The incentives to identify, disclose, and reduce risks induce buyers, sellers, landlords, tenants, lenders, and others involved in these transactions to engage in many of the same investigating, standard-setting, and enforcing functions as government environmental agencies. As the physical and transition risks of climate become clear, environmental lawyers, managers, and advocates increasingly are focusing on GHG emissions and climate risks through the use of these types of commercial transactions.

---

[3] See Michael P. Vandenbergh, *The Private Life of Public Law*, 105 COLUMBIA L. REV. 2029 (2005).

II. Climate Adaptation

Temperature increases since preindustrial times are already approaching 1.5°C, and damage is occurring from anthropogenic climate change. If mitigation efforts fail, the climate effects will be more severe, but even if mitigation efforts achieve the 1.5°C or 2°C targets, adaptation will be necessary to respond to sea level rise, increased heat waves, more intense wet weather events, and other changes arising from climate change. Of course, achieving the 1.5°C or 2°C targets will be very difficult, and the more global average temperatures exceed the targets, the more adaptation will be essential.

Governments are increasingly focusing on the need for climate change adaptation, but just as uncertainty, public goods, collective action, and polarization problems are barriers to government climate mitigation efforts, they are also barriers to government adaptation efforts. In fact, the use of the term "resilience," rather than climate adaptation, has become a common way to try to bypass the polarizing effects of mentioning climate change. Not surprisingly, adaptation is also becoming an increasing focus of the private sector. Lawyers, managers, and advocates have been engaged in PEG adaptation initiatives for more than a decade, but these initiatives have proliferated in recent years.

The difference between mitigation and adaptation is important. Climate change mitigation involves reducing the causes of climate change through decreasing the release of GHG *emissions* into the atmosphere or increasing GHG *sinks*. In contrast, the IPCC has defined climate adaptation as "the process of *adjustment* to the actual or expected climate and its effects" and has noted that adaptation actions seek to moderate harm or exploit beneficial opportunities, as opposed to reducing the amount of climate change.[4] Adaptation includes both imminent actions such as responses to impending climate disasters and non-imminent actions such as accounting for increased sea level when renovating or constructing buildings, roads, and bridges. Adaptation also includes anticipatory measures (actions taken in advance to minimize the expected negative impact of climate change), as well as reactive measures (actions taken after negative impacts occur).

The principal challenge for defining PEG adaptation is to identify when private sector adaptation initiatives constitute a form of governance. We view adaption as being a form of PEG when private actors take actions that provide the types of societal benefits typically provided by government laws, policies and programs, such

---

[4] INTERGOVERNMENTAL PANEL ON CLIMATE CHANGE (2014).

as when a company, under pressure from NGOs, employees, and neighbors, includes a town within its new sea wall. In this case, it is providing a public good to the town and engaging in PEG adaptation. If the sea wall simply protects the company's factory and exclusively benefits the business rather than the broader community, we would label this private adaptation but we would not call it private governance.

Why do companies and other private organizations undertake PEG adaptation activities? For many firms, investing in adaptation creates new business opportunities. Additional drivers of PEG adaptation are likely to parallel the drivers of PEG climate mitigation, including reputational concerns, retail and corporate customer pressure, investor, lender and insurer pressure, employee pressure, and responding to manager norms.

The United Nations Framework Convention on Climate Change maintains a database of private sector adaptation initiatives, and the United Nations Environment Program and other organizations have identified private sector adaptation efforts. Examples of these efforts include the following:

A. Retail

Coca Cola has collaborated with the World Wildlife Fund and other organizations to establish watershed restoration and community natural resource management projects in Vietnam and Thailand. Coca-Cola set the goal to return water to communities in an amount equivalent to what it uses in the production of all its products, in part through replenishing water via local restoration projects. These local adaptation initiatives have public and private benefits. They increase long term production stability by protecting and replenishing water supplies, which in turn protects the surrounding communities (who often make up the workforce) and the resources needed to make products. Coca-Cola initially selected specific watersheds based on their biodiversity and potential for conservation gains. The effort also supports local communities through water quality testing, wastewater treatment, and financing.

Mars has engaged in PEG adaptation efforts with Basmati rice farmers in Pakistan. Recognizing that climate change threatens the supply of Basmati rice, Mars worked with Rice Partners Ltd. to develop a program to decrease water usage and improve rice farming practices. The program aimed to educate roughly 500 farmers about alternative practices that use less water and require fewer inputs, and then encouraged the farmers to share lessons learned with others to drive wider adoption of efficient practices. To determine which practices to promote, Mars conducted assessments of current farming practices and invested in research on less water-intensive alternatives. Mars has set goals for engagement rates and water reduction, and it projects that the alternative practices could increase net income for farmers by 30%.

B. Insurance

The insurance industry is well positioned and motivated to engage in climate change adaptation. For example, reinsurance companies Swiss Re and Munch Re have supported adaptation in developing countries via innovative insurance-related risk management tools. As we mentioned in Chapter 3, insurance firms can reduce premiums for actions that promote protection of properties against climate-related risks, such as proactive landscaping to reduce fire risk, moving electrical panels or equipment to higher levels of buildings in flood-prone areas, or constructing or retrofitting properties to be more resilient to high winds. We also noted that healthy coral reefs can act like natural sea walls and reduce storm surges, and we noted that some insurers have begun to take steps to protect coral reefs and other ecosystems that promote climate adaptation. Insurance firms have begun to insure against damage to coral reefs, with the insurance policy guaranteeing immediate funds to repair damage to the reef caused by high winds above specific speed thresholds.

Swiss Re, in collaboration with the advocacy group Oxfam, the Ethiopian government, and other partners, developed the Horn of Africa Risk Transfer for Adaptation (HARITA) project to assist farmers. The project combines financing of community climate resilience projects with weather risk insurance and microcredit. The program allows cash-poor farmers to work for their insurance premiums through community-identified projects that improve irrigation and soil management, thus reducing risk and building climate resilience. The project measures its success by the growing number of people it serves and the increasing number of farmers who can "graduate" from working on projects to paying in cash.

In the United States, the insurance industry is engaging in PEG adaptation in response to the increasing risks of sea level rise and flooding. Private insurers are increasingly wary of insuring properties that are subject to flooding and are increasing rates or denying coverage in these areas. These private actors are thus pushing their insureds to adapt to climate change even though governments are often undermining market incentives, such as by subsidizing flood insurance.

C. Banking

Many banks are also becoming involved in PEG adaptation efforts. For instance, mortgage lenders often account for risks over a thirty-year period, and they are beginning to account for sea level rise, increasing storm damage, and other climate risks. These mortgage lenders are thus engaging in adaptation by making mortgages more difficult to obtain in climate-affected areas, even as the federal government continues to both directly and indirectly encourage development in coastal areas subject to sea level rise.

Banks also engage in some activities that more clearly qualify as PEG adaptation. For example, Banco do Brasil conducted assessments across various watersheds in Brazil to assess climate change vulnerabilities. It determined that conventional agriculture processes (such as inadequate soil management), coupled with a lack of local knowledge regarding sustainable alternatives, put many watersheds at particular risk. In response, Banco do Brasil developed the Aqua Brasil program, which it funded and developed in partnership with Brazil's National Water Agency, and WWF-Brasil. The program coordinates and funds actions that encourage sustainable rural production practices to improve water levels and the quality of target watersheds, and farmers can receive financial incentives (funded by the bank) to adopt sustainable technologies. The program has helped produce a 60 percent reduction in erosion in some watersheds.

D. Finance

The private sector is helping fill the need for financing climate adaptation, and the United Nations Development Program has prioritized increasing private sector funding of adaptation efforts. For instance, the market for corporate green bonds (bonds whose proceeds are committed specifically to finance climate-friendly projects) has grown substantially since the early 2010s. In 2018, the corporate sector, including large companies like Toyota, Apple, and Unilever, issued green bonds worth $95.7 billion. Although green bonds focus principally on mitigation, many address climate adaptation. Unilever, for example, has set climate adaptation requirements for its green bonds. Because the green bond market is not publicly regulated, private voluntary certification systems, such as Climate Bond Standards and the Climate Resilience Principles have been developed to increase transparency and address greenwashing concerns.

E. Energy

PEG adaptation is also occurring in the energy sector. For instance, the Energy Development Corporation (EDC) Philippines has responded to recent typhoons by increasing the resilience of existing energy infrastructure with the support of a green bond issued by the IFC. The EDC is also boosting community resilience through disaster response training for schools, residents and local government officials, and it has established a network of first responders at project sites across the country.

Across multiple sectors, PEG climate adaptation initiatives are likely to become more common as the damages from climate change increase. A growing number of activities qualify as PEG adaptation, and lawyers, managers, and advocates are likely to deploy many of the same tools for climate adaptation as they do for climate mitigation, including payments, prescription, and persuasion.

III. Climate and Energy Justice

As we noted in Chapter 2, climate change justice poses difficult issues for public and private governance. Justice or equity is often thought of as a concern of public governance, but it also is important for understanding PEG climate mitigation, adaptation, and energy initiatives. Examples at the local and global levels provide a sense of how justice issues are affecting the PEG initiatives of companies and advocacy groups.

A. Linking Justice and Renewable Power

ClearLoop is a new company that operates in several communities in the United States. Its motto is "turning everyday purchases into clean energy." Initially an independent company, it is now owned by Silicon Ranch, a large solar developer, which in turn recently was acquired by Shell. ClearLoop enables investors and companies to direct funds toward the development of new solar power facilities and collects the information necessary to ensure the accuracy of emissions reductions claims.

Substituting solar power for coal or natural gas-fired power plants reduces carbon emissions, and by reducing the long term climate threats caused by the carbon emissions it has *intergenerational* environmental justice implications. But what makes ClearLoop fascinating is the way it is addressing *intragenerational* environmental justice issues: ClearLoop's clients receive carbon credits, but the company also uses a screening methodology to develop solar projects in locations that yield the highest environmental, social, and economic impact.

ClearLoop's screening methodology uses data collected and analyzed by Economic Innovations Group (EIG.org) to enable siting of facilities based on a distressed community index, which accounts for poverty, education, and other social factors. ClearLoop focuses on communities that fall in the at-risk-to-distressed ends of the spectrum, and this allows ClearLoop to locate projects in the most economically disadvantaged communities, not just the most carbon-intensive electric grids. The solar development then includes programs that support workforce training and career awareness around renewable energy, focusing on workers in construction, design, and other fields. This social justice aspect of Clearloop's business has attracted business from a private equity firm, a call center, a retailer and others.

B. Intra- and Intergenerational Justice

Difficult climate justice issues arise not only at the local level, but at the global level. Many companies in the Global North have made climate commitments that will promote intergenerational justice by reducing the risk of climate change, but the commitments can only be fulfilled if the companies achieve emissions reductions from their supply chains, which make up 80% or more of the emissions from many companies. These suppliers often have limited financial resources and are often operating in Global South countries with large disadvantaged populations. Companies confront difficult justice questions in these situations, and some supply chain initiatives have been criticized as simply a new form of colonialism.

But in some cases win-win solutions have emerged. Corporate responses to pressure to reduce the toxic chemicals and carbon emission from global supply chains provide one example. Many companies are finding that they cannot simply demand less toxics releases or lower carbon emissions from suppliers in Global South countries—they need to provide the information and financial resources necessary to build capacity and enable their suppliers to meet the corporate buyers' requirements. In other words, the PEG responses by these companies are providing private sector-based payments or subsidies as well as technical expertise to their suppliers. These transfers of money and information are not a solution to the climate and justice problems, but they can play a role in protecting accelerating decarbonization while providing jobs and other economic benefits.

For instance, some global companies are using procurement requirements that combine phased-in toxic chemical use restrictions with several types of subsidies, including capacity building for suppliers in the form of training and guidance materials for disclosing releases of toxics to air, water, and land. A working group hosted by the Environmental Law Institute has developed a model supply chain contract that facilitates this type of transfer of support to Global South factories in the pharmaceutical sector. Similarly, in the mining sector the Responsible Minerals Initiative manages an audit fund through which corporate members voluntarily seek to offset the initial costs of obtaining an audit for upstream smelters and refiners. The fund provides for audits, not toxic emissions reductions, but these audits can increase the pressure for reductions.

Perhaps the best example of payments that address intragenerational justice involves GHG emissions rather than toxic chemicals. Apple has made carbon emissions reduction requirements that extend to its supply chains, but many of its suppliers are in China, which relies heavily on coal-fired electric power. This leads suppliers to produce goods with large carbon footprints and makes it difficult for corporate buyers like Apple to meet their climate goals. In response, rather than just shifting to different suppliers when its low carbon requirements could not be met, Apple provided a private subsidy to give suppliers access to low carbon power. It did so by forming the China Clean Energy Fund, which has enabled Apple to invest in clean energy projects totaling more than one gigawatt of renewable energy in China—an amount equal to the production of roughly two major power plants.

These local and global responses to environmental justice concerns are certainly not panaceas. They do not address a wide range of institutional and other inequities. But they provide examples of how environmental lawyers, managers, and advocates can account for environmental justice not only in government laws and policies, but in PEG climate and energy initiatives as well.

QUESTIONS AND DISCUSSION

1. Assume you work for an advocacy group that opposes the construction of a coal-fired power plant in a country with no GHG regulations and no public law equivalent to the National Environmental Policy Act, which requires disclosure of the environmental effects of major federal government actions. Would you want to know whether the plant is being financed by a project finance lender that has committed to the Equator Principles? What options are available if the lender has committed to the Equator Principles but the project developer is not planning to conduct an Equator Principles environmental assessment? What options are available if the assessment will be conducted but will ignore GHG emissions? If the assessment does not include a plan to reduce GHG emissions?

2. Do corporate commitments to procure 100% renewable power play a different role in California than in Georgia or Mississippi? What leverage do these corporate commitments provide to climate mitigation advocates in these states?

3. Assume you are a lawyer or manager for an investment bank that has committed to achieve net zero GHG emissions by 2050 in its investment portfolio. A potential client is looking for financing for a new natural gas-fired electric plant. The deal would generate large profits for the investment bank, but natural gas is a potent GHG, and large quantities of CO_2 are emitted from burning natural gas. What requirements would you want to be included in the terms of the deal or the transaction documents?

4. Assume you represent a climate justice advocacy group. A new company proposes to build a large wind farm that will generate renewable electricity and accelerate the closure of a nearby coal-fired electric plant. The wind farm is located in an area near a large economically disadvantaged population. What is the equitable or just strategy? How should you account for the interests of the current generation that will be affected by the wind farm and future generations that will be affected by climate change?

5. Archimedes Industries plans to build a major new coal-fired electric plant near Bangkok, Thailand. Assume no Thai law requires an environmental assessment and the U.S. National Environmental Policy Act does not apply. The bank providing the project finance funding is a U.S. bank that has committed to comply with the June 2013 version of the Equator Principles (EP).

- Is the bank required under the EP to reject the loan or to report on its environmental effects?
- Must Archimedes, the project developer, commit to reduce greenhouse gas (GHG) emissions?
- What recourse does the project developer have if it believes the bank is asking for something that the EP does not require?
- What recourse does an environmental non-governmental organization (NGO) have if it objects to the project?
- What recourse does the bank have if it believes Archimedes is not complying with the EP?
- Is a procedure available to change the EP?
- Why might a bank or other for-profit organization be motivated to adopt and enforce the EP even absent government requirements?
- Are the EP an example of private or public environmental governance?
- When might PEG initiatives reduce or increase the likelihood of more effective government measures?

Part III

PEG IN ACTION: TOXICS, WASTE, WATER, AND NATURAL RESOURCES

Chapter 10

TOXICS AND WASTE MANAGEMENT

In Chapter 10 we discuss how PEG initiatives respond to the environmental and human health risks arising from toxic substances and hazardous wastes. The toxic substances in the household products you use, the steps environmental lawyers, managers, and advocates take to reduce the risks of toxics, and the tools available to protect fenceline communities from hazardous wastes are driven as much by PEG initiatives as government regulations, and in some cases even more so. The PEG initiatives that target toxic substances deploy many of the same types of tools—including informational regulation, prescriptive requirements, and payments and penalties—as the PEG climate initiatives we reviewed in the last several chapters.

Along the way, we detail the specific difficulties of addressing toxic substances and hazardous wastes, how PEG toxics initiatives interact with public environmental governance, and how these initiatives reflect environmental justice concerns. PEG initiatives that address toxics and hazardous waste management problems were among the first private governance initiatives to emerge—often long before the PEG climate change mitigation initiatives that we discussed in the last several chapters. PEG tools that address toxics are woven into the daily work of many environmental lawyers, managers, and advocates, so we have a lot of ground to cover, but a full understanding of these issues is well worth the investment.

I. The Toxics Problem

The governance challenge for toxics and hazardous wastes begins with the massive volumes and wide variation of chemicals produced every year. It is difficult to know how many types of chemicals are in circulation, but the best estimate is that the total exceeds 100,000, with new substances being produced at a rate of nearly 700 per year. The chemical manufacturing industry is massive, employing over 800,000 people and contributing over 20% of the gross domestic product (GDP) in the United States. Major producers include the agricultural, industrial manufacturing, and household product sectors. Toxic substances are used for a wide range of purposes, from familiar substances found in many households—shampoo, food preservatives, and finishings for furniture—to industrial substances—agricultural pesticides, gasoline additives, and substances used in manufacturing processes.

Toxic chemical releases have been slowing in recent years. Since 2011, according to the U.S. Bureau of Economic Analysis, toxic chemical releases in the U.S. have decreased by 27%, led by a 34% reduction in air releases. This reduction has occurred while economic activity (as measured by GDP) increased by over 40%. According to the EPA, the reduction has been driven by new technologies that limit the need for toxic substances, and the development of improved toxic chemical management methods such as recycling, energy recovery, and treatment. Despite these promising trends, chemical production and consumption remain high; toxic substances are integrated into many of our everyday products; new risks are being identified, such as from PFAS; and many of us live in a "toxic cloud" of emissions arising from the products we use in our daily activities.

When toxic substances are disposed of they are often considered to be hazardous wastes under federal and state environmental laws. Hazardous waste generation has declined in parallel with the declines in toxic chemical releases: according to the EPA, hazardous waste generation has declined by roughly 30% since 1980. The enactment of the federal Resource Conservation and Recovery Act (RCRA) in 1976 and the Comprehensive Environmental Response, Compensation and Liability Act (CERCLA) in 1980 created incentives to reduce hazardous waste generation and resulted in the cleanup of many major disposal sites (called "Superfund sites") over the last several decades. Many smaller disposal sites are still being discovered and cleaned up, though, including lightly contaminated industrial properties often called "brownfields." Disposal sites and brownfields are often located near low income communities and communities of color, and studies show that these communities also bear a disproportionate share of the exposures to hazardous wastes. The extent of human exposure to toxic substances arising from disposal sites has been the subject of extensive and sometimes conflicting research, but a recent meta-analysis found a strong positive correlation.[1]

The substantial amounts of toxic substances produced each year highlight an important difference between toxics and conventional pollutants: toxic substances are sometimes produced because they are valuable products, not just unintended byproducts. As a result, public and private regulators face difficult decisions not only about how to reduce emissions, but also over the tradeoffs that arise from restricting the production, use, and release of toxic substances. The core governance challenges include assessing the risks, determining what levels of risk are tolerable, and selecting the best regulatory

[1] Kathleen Gruschow, "Effect of Residential Proximity and Exposure to Municipal, Industrial, and Hazardous Waste Sites on Cancer Risk: A Literature Review," Master Essay, University of Pittsburgh (2023).

tools. The challenge is to assess both the risks and benefits of toxic substances in order to develop regulatory systems that strike the best balance between reducing risks while also providing the social and economic benefits of these compounds.

A. Human Health and Ecological Effects

In 1972, the EPA banned the pesticide widely known as "DDT." Nearly a decade of research followed the 1962 release of Rachel Carson's best-selling book, *Silent Spring*, which raised widespread public concerns about the toxicity of DDT to humans and the environment. Over the following ten years, the government enforced a gradual transition away from DDT before a final ban became effective in 1972. Although DDT has been removed from the market in the United States, thousands of other toxic and potentially toxic substances are still produced, included in consumer products, and released into the environment. One category that has garnered a great deal of attention in recent years includes per- and polyfluororalkul substances (PFAS), also known as "forever chemicals," because they persist in the environment and the human body, and do not easily break down. As a class, these substances have been used in stain- and water-resistant fabrics, as well as fire-fighting foam, Teflon (non-stick) cookware, and even in dental floss. They were invented and entered into widespread use because of their effectiveness in consumer and industrial products; however, in recent years more has become known about their negative environmental and health effects. Some serve their purpose without any significant human health or environmental harm but for many of them, such as DDT or PFAS, substances that many people and animals are exposed to have harmful health or ecological effects. These are the substances that public and private governance are designed to regulate.

1. Risk Assessment

A core challenge regarding toxic substances is that assessing the risks they pose is often difficult, expensive, and time-consuming. Risk assessment challenges include assessing the probability and severity of harm, the extent to which the risks are voluntarily assumed (driving a car) or imposed externally (living next to a factory that produces cars), how the risks are distributed in the population, whether adequate information exists to assess the risk—(which becomes uncertainty when the information is inadequate)—and who gets to decide whether to regulate.

At the outset, perhaps the greatest challenge is that the risks of toxic substances are often just that: risks of harm, not guaranteed harms. Unlike many types of workplace injuries and diseases such as typhoid or cholera arising from microbes in drinking water, which unequivocally cause a direct harm, toxic substance releases may increase the probability that a harm will occur. The probability that the harm will occur and whether responsibility can be assigned to a specific toxic substance depends on complex assessments of its fate in the environment, how humans or other organisms are exposed to it, and how they respond when exposed. Returning to our DDT example, unlike the sickness that immediately arises from water contaminated by typhoid or cholera bacteria, toxics like DDT often increase the chronic, long-term risk of cancer or other diseases. Thus, regulation of toxics often rests on assessments of the probability that harms will occur. This creates difficult challenges for regulators—whether public or private—because determining the precise probability that a given exposure will cause a given harm is difficult.

Risk assessment also is complicated by the need to calculate not only the probability of harm but also its magnitude. If a toxic substance increases the likelihood of someone developing a minor rash, we will be less concerned about addressing it than if it increases the likelihood of a stroke or cancer. The extent to which an exposure is voluntary or involuntary is another important consideration. We may be less concerned with addressing the carcinogenic substances in first-hand cigarette smoke if we view smoking as voluntary—informed adults can decide for themselves if smoking is worth the risk—than if exposure occurs involuntarily via second-hand smoke. Similarly, risks arising from exposure to air pollutants when released into the air by a factory smokestack may trigger greater concern than exposure to the same pollutants from a fireplace in the home.

The distribution of risks across geography, populations, and time also affects our appetite for risk and decisions about the appropriate level of regulation. If 100 people die in one city because of the release of a certain chemical, we may react more strongly toward that chemical than if 100 people die across the entire country. Similarly, the distribution of the harm within the population matters. Environmental justice concerns arise if the exposure occurs disproportionately in disadvantaged or minority populations, a topic we address in more detail later in this Chapter.

Time matters, too, and whether a harm occurs today, five years from now, or five generations from now affects the assessment of risks and regulatory decision-making. Immediate risks tend to provoke more support for regulation than long-term risks, but scientific research in the last several decades has identified concerns that increase the focus on long-term risks. For instance, since the early days of DDT research, scientists have understood that some toxic substances accumulate in tissue and can be passed to organisms that are higher on the food chain in a process known as "bioaccumulation" that can take many years to reach humans.

Scientists also have long understood that some toxic substances can cause genetic mutations and other genetic changes that can affect future generations. As science progresses, these types of developments will further complicate toxic substance risk assessment and governance.

2. *Uncertainty*

The distinction between risk and uncertainty adds another layer of complexity. Risk assessment is difficult when adequate information is available, but uncertainty exists if insufficient information exists to fully assess or quantify the probability and likelihood of harm. And this is often the case. Uncertainty may arise from a lack of information, raising important questions about what tests should be conducted and who is responsible for testing. Uncertainty also may arise from the difficulty of assessing cancer and other risks. A chemical may only be toxic at extremely high levels or it may be toxic at very small exposure levels. Some toxics even cause harms with U-shaped dose-response curves, causing harm at very low and very high doses rather than intermediate ones. If a 10% chance of developing a serious health condition exists at very low exposures, a ban or heavy restrictions may be warranted. But if a 10% chance exists of developing a certain condition at a high exposure level but only a one in one billion chance at a lower exposure level, strict regulation may not be necessary. It is thus critical to understand how much risk is associated with different exposure levels, but for many toxic substances that may not be possible with certainty. Given the inadequate information regarding some toxic substances, the cost of testing, and the pace at which new toxic substances are being produced, it is no wonder that uncertainty remains a substantial problem for many substances.

B. The Advantages and Disadvantages of PEG-Based Toxics Regulation

As the complexity of risk analysis suggests, government responses to toxics can take many years after initial research identifies problems. Depending upon how much evidence is required before restricting toxic substances in the flow of commerce, regulators may be suffering from "paralysis by analysis," where action is long delayed while examining ever more data. This delay reduces the risk of over-regulating, but it also can undermine the ability of government agencies to prevent harms before they occur and undercut confidence in public governance.

One response to uncertainty and other risk assessment challenges is to adopt the "precautionary principle," which places the burden to prove that a chemical is nontoxic on the producer rather than requiring the regulator to prove toxicity. European regulations of toxic chemicals tend to follow this precautionary approach, but most toxics-related statutes in the United States, including the Toxic Substances Control Act, do not follow the precautionary principle, so regulators must conduct tests or review industry tests of a new chemical's risks before regulating.

PEG initiatives do not suffer from the same institutional constraints—private actors can assess the toxicology or epidemiology literature and perform their own assessments much more quickly than can a government agency, and these private actors may be less vulnerable to delays arising from the administrative law requirements and judicial challenges. This can enable them to act in a thoroughly precautionary way, imposing private restrictions on substances with potentially toxic properties without going through laborious government regulatory process and restricting chemical sales until more comprehensive research has been done. PEG initiatives thus may be able to respond more quickly to new information about environmental risks than government regulatory initiatives. PEG initiatives also often rely on the government-funded research necessary to detect and evaluate toxic chemical risks, though, and acting based on incomplete information creates governance risks. For instance, PEG initiatives may be more likely to over- or under-control toxics releases if later studies fail to confirm initial concerns, the process fails to include important public input, or private regulators overreact to public pressure.

PEG to address toxics is not a panacea, however. Some private actors may have incentives to sell popular products (such as nonstick cookware or fire retardant fabric), even in the face of environmental and health concerns, and consumer or other pressure to avoid these chemicals. Two additional complicating factors of PEG toxics initiatives are their inability to apply to all sources within any one nation on the one hand and their global reach across national boundaries on the other. Toxic substances are sold in national and global markets, and are found in many different environments around the world. National governments have numerous regulatory tools that they can apply to all of the companies within their boundaries, and governments can use civil and criminal enforcement tools to motivate compliance. This ability to impose regulatory requirements on all companies within a nation's boundaries is not matched by PEG initiatives, which lack the broad reach and coercive tools of government agencies. This PEG limitation—which applies to many types of PEG, not just PEG initiatives directed at toxics—means that some companies will be able to avoid private pressure regarding the production and use of toxic substances within any one nation.

At the same time, PEG initiatives can transcend national boundaries in ways that national and subnational government regulations cannot. A nation typically cannot enforce its toxics requirements beyond its boundaries; in contrast, PEG initiatives such as supply chain and investor requirements have a global reach—they can use global contracting, finance, and information networks to extend private requirements to toxics manufacturers and users in countries with weak toxics laws or weak enforcement. For instance, even if country A hasn't adopted strong toxics regulations or does not enforce its regulations, supply chain pressure from a corporate buyer in country B may provide a level of private regulation for a company using toxic substances in country A. The effects of PEG initiatives on the development of government requirements for toxics are complex, and we discuss those effects later in this Chapter after we introduce the types of PEG initiatives.

II. Private Environmental Governance Toxics Initiatives

The PEG toxic chemical initiatives that have emerged in the last several decades deploy many of the tools we've discussed in earlier chapters, but most fall into two categories: persuasion and prescription. This section discusses the leading PEG initiatives that use persuasive and prescriptive tools to reduce the risks of toxic substances.

A. Persuasion

Persuasion regarding toxics often includes the disclosure of factual information—such as through toxic chemical emissions reporting for products. The use of factual information involves collecting and disclosing information without an explicit moral characterization or judgment to create incentives for better management of toxic chemical handling. In other cases persuasion involves more normative or value-laden uses of information—such as through the naming-and-shaming that occurs when companies are included in an advocacy group's "dirty dozen" campaign. In either case, the goal of these persuasion initiatives is to drive change through collecting and disclosing information about toxic chemical releases and risks.

Government and PEG initiatives have used persuasion through public disclosure of toxic chemical information to reduce the releases and risks of toxic substances. The leading public law examples are the Toxics Release Inventory (TRI) reporting requirements of the Emergency Planning and Community Right to Know Act (EPCRA), and California Proposition 65, which requires labels on products containing carcinogenic substances. These disclosure laws often have multiple, overlapping targets, including retail consumers, the media, corporate directors, corporate managers and other employees, investors, lenders, and regulators. PEG initiatives use similar tools.

1. *Information Disclosure: Global Reporting Initiative*

The Global Reporting Initiative (GRI) is a private organization headquartered in Amsterdam, the Netherlands, that describes its mission as helping "businesses and other organizations take responsibility for their impacts, by providing them with the global common language to communicate those impacts." GRI uses the collection and disclosure of information to reduce toxic chemical releases and improve corporate environmental performance. GRI generates reporting standards for many facets of business operations, including labor rights, corruption, energy use, and waste management. It is the most widely used reporting standard in the world with over 10,000 corporations and other organizations from over 100 countries using its standards. GRI divides its reporting requirements into universal standards, sector specific standards, and topic standards (i.e., waste or emissions).

The sector-specific focus of the standards allows disclosure of toxics to be tailored more specifically to individual companies or sectors. For example, there may be no need to track the toxic releases of an employment services firm while an agricultural firm may be required to engage in substantial toxic release reporting. For those sectors that release substantial quantities of toxics, though, the GRI disclosures can be important gap-fillers when no government standard is applicable. GRI toxics disclosures also supplement the government-required disclosures such as the TRI disclosure program administered by the federal Environmental Protection Agency (EPA). EPA only requires TRI reporting of chemical releases for facilities with more than 10 employees and above certain use thresholds for different types of releases, and the reporting requirements only apply to facilities in the United States. Thus, GRI reporting is particularly important for companies with small facilities or facilities operating outside the United States.

Although the GRI requirements do not include a dedicated "toxics" standard, toxic chemical reporting is incorporated into many of the GRI standards, including standards on waste management, water effluent, and others. For instance, for the agricultural sector, GRI standard 306–1 on "waste generation and significant waste-related impacts" requires an organization to disclose its "significant actual and potential waste-related impacts," including "the inputs, activities, and outputs that lead or could lead to these impacts; [and] whether these impacts relate to waste generated in the organization's own activities or to waste generated upstream or downstream in its value chain."

Like CDP—as discussed in Chapter 7—GRI does not use the information it receives through reporting to engage in naming-and-shaming or to take direct actions regarding the toxic chemical handling by participating companies. Instead, GRI sets information collection and disclosure standards that organizations can use in annual reports on their environmental performance to ensure that the reporting is accurate and can be compared across different organizations in the same sector. By creating rigorous, uniform standards for the types of data that should be made available to the public, GRI encourages firms to report on the most important sustainability metrics. In turn, this allows managers to identify vulnerabilities and allows advocacy groups, investors, and others to apply more effective pressure on firms to reduce toxic releases. In this way, GRI's information-based standards serve as a foundation for other PEG initiatives, including calling out companies as a part of the "dirty dozen" largest polluters, as we explore below.

2. Naming and Shaming

The information disclosed through GRI and other private and public standards enables other PEG actors to engage in naming and shaming, pressuring companies based on what they should or should not be doing. Naming-and-shaming campaigns attack the reputation of a firm or the brand of its products. This can damage its position with consumers, investors, corporate suppliers and purchasers, other stakeholders, and regulators. This subsection will detail two naming and shaming campaigns relevant to toxics chemicals.

Since 2004, the Environmental Working Group (EWG), a non-profit environmental advocacy organization, has released an annual Shopper's Guide to Pesticides in Produce. EWG uses thousands of samples taken by the FDA and USDA on pesticide content in 46 different types of produce to develop their "Dirty Dozen" and "Clean Fifteen" lists. For the dirty dozen, EWG recommends that consumers buy organic because of the relatively high probability of substantial pesticide contamination. They note, however, that their reliance upon FDA and USDA research limits the comprehensiveness of the Dirty Dozen since certain pesticides are not tested. For example, because the USDA does not test for glyphosate—one of the most commonly used pesticides—on oats and grains, it is possible that high levels of glyphosate would not be reflected in the Dirty Dozen. In spite of this, the Dirty Dozen continues to achieve widespread media coverage and appears to be an effective naming and shaming campaign.

Unlike many naming and shaming campaigns, the ESG Dirty Dozen effort does not target any specific brands or companies. Instead, it provides general information about trends in crop cultivation, focusing on industry-wide norms rather than any individual actor. By doing this, the EWG's naming and shaming campaign induces consumers to shift their preferences to produce that relies on less heavy pesticide usage and creates incentives for producers to use less pesticides in order to avoid EWG including their crops on the Dirty Dozen. Even if companies that sell produce such as strawberries—which often top the Dirty Dozen—choose not to take the major step of following requirements to be organic, they have incentives to reduce pesticide use.

Although it is not possible to know whether naming and shaming campaigns were the cause of increased consumer demand for organic products, consumer pressure has contributed to large increases in the amount of organic food available to consumers. In California, by far the largest crop producing state in the United States, agricultural land devoted to organic production increased 265% between 2009 and 2016. And this shift toward organic production has occurred among many of the products commonly included in the Dirty Dozen list. For instance, despite an overall reduction in the volume of strawberries shipped to consumers between 2010–2020, the volume of organic strawberries tripled during this period.[2]

Naming and shaming campaigns often work in tandem with more neutral forms of information disclosure. Although persuasion is often effective—especially when it is directed at consumer-focused (business to consumer or "B-to-C") businesses—it typically does not create legally enforceable obligations and is only effective if consumers, investors, employees, managers, other stakeholders or regulators are induced to act. This brings us to our next type of PEG tool.

B. Prescription

The prescriptive tools used in PEG toxics initiatives involve more explicitly coercive actions than the persuasion tools. Coercion often occurs through business practices such as supply chain contracting requirements, the investigations and contract terms that are now common in commercial real estate, merger, lending, and project finance transactions, and the adoption of environmental management systems. The PEG prescriptive tools also rely on many of the same types of standards as are common in government toxic

[2] Rural Migration News, *Strawberries: Growth and Labor* (UC Davis 2021).

substance statutes: health-based, feasibility, risk-benefit, and risk-risk standards.

- *Health-based standards* are designed to prevent significant health risks and only consider the adverse health effects, not the costs of regulating or the risks of substitutes. A prominent example is the Delaney Clause in the Food, Drug and Cosmetic Act (FDCA), which for many years prohibited *any* carcinogens in food additives regardless of the costs of the ban or health effects of substitutes. The Food Quality Protection Act of 1996 shifted the Delaney Clause language from an absolute ban on all carcinogens to a "reasonable certainty of no harm" standard, but the approach remains one that focuses on the health effects of the substance, not on costs or the effects of substitutes. The PEG parallel arises from bans by Walmart, Target, and other retailers on the use of certain toxics by suppliers.
- *Feasibility standards* are set the level of required risk reduction based on what is technologically or economically feasible. Examples in public law include requirements for preventing drinking water contaminants in the Safe Drinking Water Act and many worker safety standards in the Occupational Safety and Health Act. The PEG parallel is that many commercial agreements include language requiring a seller or borrower to take feasible steps to remedy prior releases of toxics or reduce toxic emissions.
- *Risk-benefit balancing* standards require the regulator to account for the benefits of the toxic substance when determining whether to allow the substance to be sold and the restrictions on its use. Examples in public law include the Federal Insecticide, Fungicide, and Rodenticide Act (FIFRA), which regulates pesticides produced or used in the United States, and TSCA, which regulates new chemical substances. FIFRA requires regulators to balance risks and benefits by considering the economic and human health benefits provided by pesticides. Many agricultural substances are toxic to humans and ecosystems if exposed, but those same substances may make food production more productive, reduce hunger, provide healthier diets, and increase agricultural sector profits. PEG initiatives typically do not explicitly require risk-benefit balancing, but the profit incentives of many companies

likely induce managers to consider some benefits when assessing whether the risks are acceptable.

- *Risk-risk standards* resemble risk-benefit standards, but they require regulators to determine not only the risk posed by a chemical, but also the risk of likely alternatives. If chemical A has a 1/100,000 chance of causing cancer, but chemical B, a substitute for A, has a 1/100 chance of causing the same cancer, an agency can regulate A less heavily to prevent wider adoption of the relatively riskier chemical B. In the *Corrosion Proof Fittings* case, a federal court concluded that TSCA requires EPA to compare the risks of a chemical to the risks of the substitutes that would be used if the chemical were banned, and to pursue the least burdensome regulatory alternative. Although a rational approach in theory, this can produce paralysis by analysis since there are many possible substitutes, each posing its own risk assessment challenges. As with risk-benefit standards, PEG initiatives typically do not explicitly follow risk-risk approaches, but it is likely that many private actors give implicit consideration to the risks of alternatives.

Many types of private actors, including corporations, religious organizations, medical centers, colleges and universities, and civic and cultural organizations, can apply prescriptive pressure to other organizations and individuals, and this section detail several of the most common prescriptive tools, beginning with supply chain contracting.

1. *Supply Chain Contracting*

Many businesses today are not vertically integrated. In other words, rather than making all of the products they sell, they contract with suppliers for components that they assemble into final products or offer to consumers in retail stores. This means that much of what retail consumers, companies, governments, and other organizations purchase has gone through the doors of multiple other companies on its way to the shelves. For example, Apple has several hundred first-tier suppliers in its supply chain, and these suppliers account for 98% of their spending on materials, manufacturing, and assembly. In turn, these suppliers have thousands of suppliers, which are known as second-tier suppliers, and they in turn have third-tier suppliers, and so on. Thus, even though you are buying an iPhone or Mac from Apple, it is the result of a long and complex global network of supply chain contracts.

These global supply chain networks can enable corporate buyers to evade government toxic chemical regulations by enabling companies to buy products produced in countries with less stringent toxics requirements or less capacity to enforce those requirements. Outsourcing also can limit legal liability by enabling corporate buyers to rely on third party contractors to conduct the most toxics-intensive aspects of their production. But many consumers and others hold companies responsible for the environmental harms associated with their products without regard to the legal limits imposed by national boundaries or the way the law treats third party contractors. In other words, the normative boundary of the company is much larger than the legal boundary. This creates pressure on companies to reduce the toxic emissions from their supply chains even if governments do not require them to do so and even if the company is not vulnerable to litigation for the actions of its suppliers.

Companies have responded by acting in ways that turn supply chain networks into prescriptive PEG tools that regulate toxic substances even when government regulations or other legal requirements are ineffective. These requirements are increasingly widespread and are becoming a core tool of environmental lawyers, managers, and advocates. A recent study concluded that 80% of the largest firms in seven global sectors include environmental requirements in their supply chain contracting, up from 50% a little over a decade ago. For instance, Apple has substantial ability to influence the toxic chemical use and releases of its supply chain. Apple is a major buyer for many of these suppliers and is therefore able to make demands of them which, even when increasing the costs of production, will often be in the economic interest of these suppliers given the advantages of selling to Apple.

In some cases, procurement or supply chain pressure will arise from screening mechanisms—requirements that determine who can qualify as a supplier and exclude companies that are unwilling or unable to commit not to use or release certain toxic substances. A good example of this approach is Whole Foods' Responsibly Grown pledge. The current version of this pledge, which went into effect in 2017, lists 90 pesticides that are prohibited for food and flowers sold by Whole Foods.[3] These prohibited toxics follow a precautionary approach—they go beyond current EPA regulations and intentionally target pesticides that have been identified as "high risk" but are nonetheless approved for use in agricultural production in many countries. As a major grocery chain, Whole Foods has the ability to create strong economic incentives for producers to meet its requirements, so despite not actually growing any food or flowers,

---

[3] WHOLE FOODS MARKET, WHOLE FOODS MARKET RESPONSIBLY GROWN PROHIBITED AND RESTRICTED PESTICIDES POLICY FOR PRODUCE AND FLOWERS.

Whole Foods exerts substantial influence over the toxic substances released during their production.

Supplier screening regarding toxic substances extends across multiple sectors. For instance, the jewelry company Amalena has adopted screening or exclusive contracting requirements for the suppliers that mine the gems and metals used in its jewelry. In the process of mining, polishing, and concentrating gold, the use of toxic substances is common—especially mercury and bleach. In fact, small-scale gold mining represents the largest source of mercury pollution in the world. In response to consumer and other pressure focused on these toxic emissions, Amalena has adopted a policy of contracting exclusively with gold producers that do not use mercury or bleach at any point in their production process.[4] Compliance with these requirements can be a problem, but in many countries few alternatives exist to buyers exerting this type of supply chain pressure.

In other cases, a corporate buyer such as Whole Foods, Apple or Hewlett-Packard may not just screen out buyers based on toxic substances criteria, but also may include requirements regarding the use of toxic substances in the terms of its contracts. Contract terms often include representations and warranties regarding chemical handling and releases (in other words, disclosure requirements with the right of the buyer to receive damages or walk away from the contract if the seller's representations are inaccurate). The contract terms also often provide the buyer with the right to conduct investigations of toxics issues during the term of the contract, and impose requirements on the seller regarding which toxic substances can be used during product manufacturing or can be present in the products. Some contracts also include requirements regarding the handling and release of substances from the manufacturing and shipment of the products, as well as provisions that enable the corporate buyer to terminate the contract and collect damages if the toxics provisions are violated. The corporate buyer may face difficulties recovering damages from a breach of these provisions in a contract unless the buyer can demonstrate a monetary loss, but the contract sends a clear message about the expectations of the buyer and puts the buyer in an advantageous position to exert informal contract pressure or to prevail in the event of breach of contact litigation.

[4] AMALENA, ECO-GOLD (2018).

Case Study: Model Supply Chain Contracts

As environmental supply chain contracting requirements have expanded in recent years, teams of nonprofit lawyers working with the Environmental Law Institute (ELI) in Washington and the Chancery Lane Project (CLP) in London and New York have developed model contract provisions, many of which address toxic substances.[5]

The ELI model toxics contract is designed to combine persuasion and prescription: it includes requirements for disclosure and reduction of toxic substance releases by facilities making products for the pharmaceutical sector in countries without strong government toxics disclosure requirements. The preamble recommends that a company disclose the number of suppliers having "significant actual and potential negative environmental impacts." It implements that goal by requiring that the "[s]upplier shall review the annual quantity of chemicals used and generated at the Supplier site(s) and compare to the chemical thresholds established in [USEPA Toxics Release Inventory Chemical List] [EU Pollutant Release and Transfer Registry] [other chemical use threshold list]. Supplier shall document this review and make available for review by Buyer if requested." As to reduction of toxic substance releases, the section on "Supplier Chemical Release Reduction Plans" provides that the "Supplier shall be responsible for developing and implementing any needed Chemical Release Reduction Plan and for paying all costs thereof" and that the "Buyer, upon request from Supplier, shall review and provide input to Supplier's Chemical Release Reduction Plan."

The CLP has generated numerous contract provisions that are designed to be used at the global level, and CLP is increasing its focus on provisions that are specifically designed for companies in the United States. Examples in the toxics context include the following:

The *Conservation Covenant for Soil Preservation and Enhancement* provision, which is designed to apply to private, non-agricultural land, prohibits the use of chemical pesticides and fertilizers. It also requires that soil health, which is affected by toxic metals, must improve each year.

The *Supply Chain Sustainable Land Use Clause and Questionnaire* includes prescriptive requirements as well as questions that corporate suppliers are required to answer. Two of the questions are related to toxics use and ask about the use of agro-chemicals as well as pesticides specifically.

The *Promotion of Carbon Sinks and Ecological Restoration in Lettings of Rural Land* clause requires that the signatories, including rural or agricultural land holders, create and follow a pest management plan that "limits the use of pesticide and other interventions to levels that are economically and ecologically justified and minimises risks to human health and the environment."

2. *Project Finance*

We introduced the Equator Principles in Chapter 3 and discussed their role in climate mitigation in Chapter 8, but they are also important for governing toxic substances. The large capital investments needed for major infrastructure projects such as toll roads, power plants, and major factories often makes these projects impractical or impossible to undertake without large sources of outside financing. The field of project finance has emerged to fund these projects. The essential feature of project finance is that an entity is formed to build and operate the project (the project developer), and that entity serves as the borrower. Lenders loan funds to the project developer that are necessary to build the project, with the expectation that the developer will repay the loan from the revenue generated by the project. If the developer defaults, the lender's recourse is to repossess the developer's assets (which consist largely of project infrastructure).

These kinds of projects are difficult to build without large amounts of capital, and they are critically important to the project developers that will operate them, so lenders have substantial coercive power over the developers. Thus, lenders that adopt PEG policies are able to enforce environmental compliance by their clients. Financial institutions have their own incentives to impose toxics and other environmental conditions on project developers. Companies that fail to meet government environmental regulations may be subject to fines or civil suits. And even if no laws are violated, naming-and-shaming campaigns and community opposition can halt projects and interfere with developers' ability to pay back project finance loans. These factors create financial incentives for project finance lenders to conduct environmental investigations before lending and impose disclosure and management requirements on project developers regarding toxic substances and other environmental issues.

In response to toxics and other environmental risks, nearly 140 financial institutions representing the vast majority of all project

[5] All quotations in this Case Study come from The Chancery Lane Project.

financing have signed onto the Equator Principles, a set of private standards that govern lending for large infrastructure projects. Signatories are required to meet each of the ten Principles before agreeing to a contract for a major infrastructure project that is covered by the Principles. In general, these Principles apply to lending for projects over $10 million. The Equator Principles also have industry-specific requirements, and certain sectors have unique compliance benchmarks.

Under the Equator Principles, lending institutions are required to ensure that extensive environmental assessments are conducted before lending to evaluate and disclose the environmental impacts of the construction and expected use of the infrastructure. For example, if Bank A is considering whether to lend $30 million to Company B to construct a new chemical processing plant, Bank A will want to review both the direct emissions of toxics from the construction as well as the likely emissions of the plant once operating. To be clear, the Equator Principles do not prohibit lending to projects with high potential for environmental (or social) risks. Rather, they impose stricter requirements for the assessment, management, and disclosure of these risks, and many lawyers, managers, and advocates have become heavily engaged in this process.

3. Environmental Management Systems

Environmental management systems (EMSs) are systems adopted within companies and other organizations to improve their management of environmental concerns such as toxic substances. Public and private organizations have developed standards for EMSs, and there are some indications from empirical studies that these standards improve firm environmental compliance with environmental laws and overall environmental performance. Corporations have incentives to adopt EMSs to reduce reputational risks, comply with supply chain provisions, and respond to investor pressure. A 2005 study concluded that supply chain contacting and other commercial transactions often require adoption of EMSs. In addition, in the event of a violation of a government environmental regulation, the existence of an EMS may enable a corporation to reduce its penalties from EPA or state government environmental agencies and may induce the federal Department of Justice to treat a violation as a civil matter rather than pursue criminal charges.

The best-known standard for EMSs is the International Organization for Standardization (ISO) 14001 standard. ISO is a hybrid public-private organization headquartered in Switzerland that sets standards for everything from the size of screw threads to environmental management. Businesses and other organizations use private third-party auditors to certify ISO 14001 compliance.

Although few nations require firms to have EMSs in place, more than 250,000 firms around the world have certified compliance with ISO 14001. EMSs can affect toxic substance management by requiring measurement and disclosure of toxic releases, management standards, whistleblower programs, and periodic assessment and updating of management systems.

4. Commercial Transactions

Toxic substance management also occurs through many types of commercial transactions other than supply chain contracts and project finance deals. Key elements of such transactions include environmental due diligence investigations, disclosures, terms in agreements, and the formal and informal enforcement of those terms. Transactions that are important for toxics also include commercial real estate leases and sales, commercial lending, merger and acquisition (M&A) transactions, and securities offerings. This section provides examples of how toxic substances may be addressed in these transactions and identifies key concepts.

Commercial transactions are a core aspect of PEG, and they are important to many environmental lawyers, managers, and advocates. One study concluded that almost all of the largest law firms in the United States work for clients on the environmental aspects of commercial transactions. Another concluded that more money is spent each year on the private environmental investigations conducted in connection with commercial transactions than the entire EPA enforcement budget. We focus here on three aspects of commercial transactions: due diligence investigations, contract terms, and contract enforcement.

a. Environmental Due Diligence

Companies have been conducting investigations to understand the subject matter of the transaction—whether the boundaries of the land that is being leased or purchased, the ability of a borrower to repay a loan, or the value of a factory that is being purchased—since long before environmental issues became an important consideration. A company buying another company needs to know if the property has risks of all types that should affect the purchase prices, and a bank needs to know the risks associated with collateral for loans and the ability of the borrower to repay the loan.

The adoption of federal and state environmental statutes in the 1970s increased environmental compliance costs. The adoption of the Comprehensive Environmental Response, Compensation and Liability Act (CERCLA or Superfund) in 1980 upped the ante by creating strict, joint and several, and retroactive liability for owners, operators, transporters and generators of hazardous substances that result in cleanup costs. This threat of liability even for historical contamination not caused by the current owner or operator created additional incentives for the parties to commercial real estate transactions, loans, M&A deals and other transactions to conduct more extensive investigations. Over time, a private standard emerged for conducting environmental investigations (issued by the American Society for Testing and Materials or ASTM). Following a series of court decisions, EPA policies, and statutory amendments, the ASTM standard was incorporated into an EPA rule. Parties attempt to meet these requirements not only to learn about the environmental risks arising from transactions, but also to qualify for the "innocent landowner" and "bona fide prospective purchaser" defenses that are available under CERCLA and some state laws. These defenses insulate new landowners and operators from liability if they conducted certain forms of due diligence.

Environmental due diligence often involves teams of lawyers, business managers and environmental experts who assess the legal, economic, and physical risks arising from a transaction and summarize the risks for a client. These investigations have private purposes—to identify and reduce risks—but they uncover many of the same issues as government enforcement inspections and often trigger reporting requirements and contractual cleanup requirements. These investigations also generate information that may assist advocacy groups and investors who push for environmental improvements, and litigants in toxic tort cases who seek to establish facts about the handling and disposal of toxic substances. In addition, in anticipation of these private investigations, companies that contemplate selling, leasing, or encumbering a facility or company may increase compliance with environmental laws or conduct remedial work to get their house in order before the investigations begin.

b. Contract Terms

Transactions differ substantially in the types of contract terms that affect toxic substances management and other environmental issues, but several types of provisions are common across many types of transactions and are important for toxic substances management. Representations and warranties are common in most commercial transactions. They provide an opportunity for the parties to state information that they want to convey to the other party (the representations), such as the compliance status with toxics requirements and whether the release of hazardous substances has occurred on a property. These formal contract terms then provide the other party the ability to sue if the representation is false (the warranty). Covenants typically form the core of an agreement, and they identify the specific commitments made by the parties, such as a loan document in which the borrower agrees not to handle any of a list of toxic substances.

Indemnities are included in some agreements. They require one party to pay another for or conduct environmental remediation activities, such as to pay for cleanup work from historical hazardous substance releases. In some situations, third-party insurance contracts are used to cover toxic chemical and other environmental cleanup costs and other risks. Indemnity clauses are often included in real estate purchases and corporate acquisitions.

Imagine that Company A owns and operates a chemical production plant that it is selling to Company B. Company B recognizes that it will take Company A at least six months to complete a cleanup of on-site contamination at the plant, but Company B wants to complete the transaction with the next several months. Company B may agree to buy the plant and conduct the cleanup but insist on an indemnity requiring Company A pay for—indemnify—Company B for the cleanup costs that arise after the sale. So, even though Company A and Company B both may be liable after the sale under federal and state law, the indemnity may enable Company B to buy the plant quickly, recover its cleanup costs from Company A, and sue Company A if A does not comply with the terms of the indemnity. Environmental indemnities are common features of acquisition agreements, and a search of public company filings with the Securities and Exchange Commission found that these types of indemnities were present in 500 of 516 acquisition agreements filed in 2022.

A copy of a 2012 acquisition agreement between Dole and Itochu is available in a Securities and Exchange Commission public database and provides an example of the kinds of environmental terms that are common in commercial transactions. The agreement for the sale of two Dole subsidiaries includes clauses that create requirements for shipping pesticides and other toxic substances.[6] Even though Dole sold the rights to and likely transferred the liability for these subsidiaries, it maintained an interest in its operations because Dole provided some indemnities for environmental compliance. Dole's indemnity agreements thus created economic incentives for it to become a PEG regulator of Itochu's pesticide handling after the transaction.

---

[6] See *Acquisition Agreement By and Between Dole Food Co. and Itochu Corporation* (2012), available at https://www.sec.gov/Archives/edgar/data/18169/000119312512399881/d413707dex21.htm.

c. Contract Enforcement

Contract enforcement can occur informally through contacts between corporate managers or through formal legal breach of contract actions. For instance, if a company commits to a bank in a commercial loan agreement not to use toxic substances in factory or in the production of its products, a bank loan officer may learn about a violation of the loan agreement but may conclude that it is not sufficiently serious to warrant formal litigation with the company. The loan officer may conclude, though, that the company is creating liabilities that will undermine its ability to repay the loan or that the actions suggest broader management problems. The loan officer may contact the chief financial officer of the company and threaten to treat the use of toxic substances as an act of default if the company does not address the problem. The chief financial officer may be concerned about defaulting one loan and having to obtain a new loan at a higher interest rate. If the bank and company managers ultimately cannot resolve the conflict, they may litigate over whether the toxic chemical use occurred, whether its use constituted an act of default, and the available legal remedies. Similarly, when an environmental indemnity or insurance policy is in place, the party providing the indemnity or insurance often has an incentive to reduce the risk that it will incur costs for environmental harms, so it will monitor and enforce the environmental activities of the company that is subject to the policy.

Commercial transactions also can facilitate environmental enforcement in more subtle ways. For example, environmental issues that might otherwise be overlooked may draw attention during major purchases or loans. As we mentioned earlier, companies also may clean house in anticipation of entering into commercial transactions.

Of course, financial agreements such as for commercial lending can lead to perverse incentives. For instance, a company may sell a subsidiary that has created large historical toxic substance releases in the hopes of avoiding liability. Or a bank may pressure a borrower to save funds for loan repayment by reducing spending on environmental compliance or by increasing use of toxics. An example in the agricultural industry arises from the fact that increased pesticide use often leads to higher yields and more revenue, so to ensure their loans are repaid commercial lenders may have incentivizes to encourage pesticide use above the socially optimal levels.

5. *NGO-Corporate Agreements*

In addition to commercial transactions between for-profit corporations, in some cases non-profit and for-profit organizations enter into agreements to collaborate to reduce hazardous and other wastes. Perhaps the best known and the first agreement of this kind was a partnership between McDonald's and the Environmental Defense Fund to reduce McDonalds' solid waste. Together, they took steps to investigate where waste was coming from, sought ways to reduce that waste, and to implement strategies to ensure waste reduction was a permanent development. As a result of this partnership, McDonald's eliminated 300 million pounds of packaging, reduced restaurant waste by 30%, and saved $6 million per year.[7] Though this example is slightly different from the commercial transactions described earlier, its logic and implementation are similar: a private firm facing public backlash for its pollution enters negotiations with an activist organization to reduce its environmental impact in a way consistent with the desires of the firm's stakeholders.

III. Interactions Between Public and Private Governance

How do PEG initiatives and government initiatives interact? Do they complement or compete with one another? We examined public-private interactions regarding climate change mitigation in Chapter 8, and many of the same types of interactions occur regarding toxics. If PEG initiatives create an impression in the public that a specific toxics threat has been addressed or that markets and the private sector can always be relied upon to address toxics problems, support for government regulation may decrease. This is a problem if the PEG initiative does not actually address the threat and government could have done so. It is also a problem if focusing on private actions undermines support for government actions more generally. In addition, many agreements require that any disputes be handled in arbitration, rather than through litigation. If disputes are handled through arbitration, this can limit public access to environmental information. It is also possible for companies to use asset sales and other transactions to circumvent regulatory requirements.

PEG efforts also can stimulate government action, though, and a recent example is the development by Walmart, Target, and other retailers of stringent toxic chemical procurement policies for their major suppliers. Advocates from the Environmental Defense Fund, a leading environmental group, and the American Chemistry Council, a chemical industry trade association, both pointed to the growth of these retailer-based PEG initiatives as a reason why Congress adopted the 2016 Lautenberg Amendments to TSCA, the principal federal toxics statute. Why were environmentalists and industry

---

[7] See Environmental Defense Fund, *McDonald's Saves Billions Cutting Waste*, available at https://www.edf.org/partnerships/mcdonalds.

both motivated by PEG initiatives to support the new legislation after many years of opposition to amending TSCA? Environmentalists could take some chances on legislative reform because a private backstop was in place for many toxics. And industry was pushed to the bargaining table because it feared that PEG initiatives would impose increasingly stringent private requirements on toxics even if the chemical industry succeeded in convincing EPA and Congress not to strengthen the public toxics regulatory system. In fact, the EPA has noted the critical role of private actions, especially in toxics management given the lengthiness of testing and extreme backlog of EPA testing.

IV. Private Environmental Governance Toxics Initiatives and Environmental Justice

Toxics have disproportionately affected communities of color and economically disadvantaged communities. An area often referred to as "Cancer Alley," an 85-mile stretch between Baton Rouge and New Orleans, Louisiana, is among the clearest examples of this environmental in-justice. Decades of research shows that production of toxic chemicals tends to take place in poorer communities, with race playing an additional role and exacerbating the other drivers.[8] A challenge for PEG initiatives is to address these harms and prevent further disproportionate harm against marginalized communities. Several PEG-driven, environmental justice initiatives have emerged the last decade. This section discusses two examples, exploring both domestic and international frameworks.

A. Domestic: Good Neighbor Agreements

Plans to construct a new chemical production facility may face significant local backlash. People tend not to want a polluting plant in their back yard; especially communities that have historically had many similar facilities in their direct vicinity. Several PEG responses have developed in the last two decades. One of the most important is the Good Neighbor Agreement (GNA), in which a business reaches an agreement with local community groups to ameliorate the risks of a new or expanded facility. GNAs can include provisions regarding emission tracking and reporting, limits on emissions more stringent than the level required by government, or public funding for parks and healthcare provided by the private firm. By signing a private agreement, companies can avoid substantial local resistance and government oversight. Fenceline communities can benefit from legally binding contractual commitments that require environmental protections exceeding federal, state, and local requirements.

---

[8] See ROBERT BULLARD, RACE AND ENVIRONMENTAL JUSTICE IN THE UNITED STATES (1983).

An example of a GNA can be found in Manchester, Texas, where community organizers demanded an agreement after a Rhône Poulenc plant in the town released sulfur dioxide, hospitalizing 27 people. Even in an area known for petrochemical plants, the residents of Manchester were able to negotiate an agreement requiring an independent environmental audit performed by an expert chosen by the residents themselves, public disclosure of company documents, and a guarantee for residents of the right to accompany auditors and conduct their own investigations. Similar agreements have been reached regarding a refinery in the San Francisco Bay area and elsewhere throughout the country. Although they remain relatively rare, GNAs provide one way for companies to address environmental injustice through PEG. By engaging directly with community organizations, these agreements can be tailored to the specific needs of a neighboring community. They may also serve as effective preventative measures, providing for environmental commitments prior to the start of production.

B. International: Supply Chain Contracting Requirements

Supply chain contracts, discussed in depth in this Chapter as a PEG toxics management technique, can also serve the international goal of environmental justice. In many cases, supply chains start in the Global South in countries with environmental regulations or enforcement that are less stringent than those in the United States. So, companies in the Global North can contract with suppliers in these countries to reduce production costs by externalizing their releases of toxics. This outsourcing may lead to more releases than would be legally acceptable if their production occurred domestically. This result has attracted attention to the fashion and textile industries and generated images of rivers in China and Bangladesh dyed the same color as clothes made from the textiles produced in those countries. The fashion industry is a major polluter in many countries, but it represents just one of dozens of industries that generate striking amounts of pollution in the Global South. Other examples abound related to the discovery of lead in children's toys or jewelry produced in China, or toxic chemicals in other household products.

In response, some private firms have begun to impose additional toxics requirements on their suppliers, and some have provided compliance assistance. Walmart, a company that imports more merchandise from China than almost any country, has been very public with its strict supplier requirements. Hewlett-Packard, a large electronics manufacturer, and Target, the seventh largest retailer in the United States, also have announced toxics requirements that apply to overseas suppliers.

Interestingly, climate supply chain and procurement requirements can achieve co-benefits with respect to toxic emissions reductions. After half of its 200 largest clients adopted climate pledges, the Danish shipping giant Maersk announced that it would allocate an additional $1.4 billion to making the first ever carbon-neutral vessel.[9] Because the dominant fuel in large ships like Maersk's has been heavy in sulfur and other hazardous air pollutants, by moving away from fossil fuel combustion these vessels are likely to reduce toxic emissions of co-pollutants as well. Despite being the largest shipping company in the world with massive bargaining power, Maersk was forced to respond to pressure from its customers to induce a major reduction in greenhouse gas and toxic emissions.

These domestic and global initiatives are only small pieces of the environmental justice puzzle, and corporations have many adverse effects on environmental justice. For instance, Walmart has come under fire for some disposal practices, and the State of California has sued the company for illegally dumping toxic electronic waste in a landfill.[10] Similarly, supply chain contracting requirements of all types at the global and domestic levels are no guarantee of superior performance. The Rana Plaza building collapse in Pakistan, which killed hundreds of workers and occurred despite local companies' supply chain contracting requirements with major clothing retailers, is a visible recent example.

QUESTIONS AND DISCUSSION

1. Assume you work for an advocacy group that is seeking to force a chemical plant owned by Company A to reduce its release of toxic substances. How would learning that Company A supplies chemicals to a company that has an environmental procurement policy affect your strategy? How would learning about a recent bank loan to Company A, or a potential acquisition of Company A by another company affect your strategy?

2. What incentives might a corporate buyer have to enforce the environmental provisions of a supply chain contract? When are those incentives likely to be greater than the any cost savings from not investing in better toxic substance management? When are they likely to be less than the costs of better toxics management?

3. The list below includes several types of companies. What types of businesses are most vulnerable to naming-and-shaming campaigns? Which

---

[9] Maersk, *Maersk Will Operate the World's First Carbon Neutral Liner Vessel by 2023—Seven Years Ahead of Schedule, MAERSK* (Feb. 17, 2021).

[10] Oladele A. Ogunseitan, *The Environmental Justice Agenda for E-Waste Management,* 65 ENVIRONMENT: SCIENCE AND POLICY FOR SUSTAINABLE DEVELOPMENT 15 (2023).

are least vulnerable? Which types of campaigns are most likely to be effective against each?

- A technology company that sells to retail consumers.
- An iron ore mining company that sells iron ore to steel manufacturers, who in turn sell steel to automobile manufacturers.
- A large bank with retail and commercial operations.
- A small business in San Francisco, California.
- A small business in Birmingham, Alabama.
- A retail store that sells household cleaning products.
- A chemical manufacturing firm that sells to wholesale and retail product manufacturers.

4. How can good neighbor agreements reduce toxic substance exposures in disadvantaged and minority communities? Are they likely to increase or decrease the likelihood of federal, state, or local government toxics regulations?

Chapter 11

FISHERIES, FORESTS, AGRICULTURE, AND HABITAT

The environmental harms and resource management issues arising from fisheries, forests, agriculture, and habitat or land use are among the most difficult problems confronted by environmental lawyers, managers, and advocates. These problems reflect many of the barriers to public governance that we outlined in Chapter 2—they often involve multiple, small, hard-to-regulate sources of pollution, as well as sources such as farmers that have been surprisingly successful at resisting government regulation. They also often create water and air pollution problems that cross national and state government boundaries. Many of these problems arise in commons situations, such as open oceans that create motivations to over-exploit resources that are outside the regulatory boundaries of any one government. Moreover, concentrated resource interests such as the agriculture and timber lobbies can have strong influence on legislatures and agencies. This chapter examines how PEG initiatives have emerged in response to these barriers for regulation of fisheries, forests, agriculture, and land use. The chapter also explores how PEG initiatives on these topics often use a combination of the instruments in the PEG toolkit, including persuasion, payments, and prescription.

I. Fisheries

A. The Marine Stewardship Council

We explained the origins of the Marine Stewardship Council (MSC) in Chapter 1 and discussed how it has filled gaps in the international regulation of major fisheries. Now that we have explained the motivations for PEG and the tools commonly developed by lawyers, managers, and advocates, it's time to examine where MSC fits into the governance of fisheries and how it functions. As we mentioned in Chapter 1, MSC is a leading example of a certification, standards, and labeling system that emerged as a result of a gap in government action. The World Wildlife Fund and Unilever formed the MSC in response to concerns by European consumers and environmental groups about the sustainability of the fish sold in Europe. The MSC is now a global organization.

The MSC uses prescription (via standards and certification requirements for fisheries) and persuasion (via labels for seafood from certified fisheries). It develops and administers standards for sustainable fisheries, updates the standards periodically with input from a stakeholder advisory group, evaluates fisheries, allows those fisheries that meet its sustainability criteria to label their fish as MSC certified, and includes a dispute resolution process at several steps in the process.[1] Private auditors assess a fishery's compliance with the MSC standards and report the status of the fishery to the MSC. Like public governance mechanisms, the MSC also modifies its standards and implementation in response to shifting stakeholder wishes and new scientific developments.

Importantly, the administrative process followed by the MSC and other resource certification and standards systems closely tracks the administrative law processes that public agencies must follow. As described in Chapter 1, the MSC uses a notice-and-comment process to develop and modify its fisheries standards, and this process parallels the approach required for informal rulemaking by the U.S. Administrative Procedure Act and many state analogues. The MSC process is more flexible than the process followed by government agencies, though. For instance, any stakeholder at any time may propose new or revised standards. Proposals are submitted to the Board of Trustees, which makes the decision to accept or deny the proposal after consultation with the Standards Advisory Board (SAB) on technical issues and the Stakeholder Advisory Council (STAC) on stakeholder engagement issues. An accepted proposal is then distributed for a period of public consultation (one sixty-day period for revision, two for new standards) during which time all stakeholders can submit suggestions for modifying the proposal. Following the public consultation period(s), the MSC staff submits the final draft of the standard again to the SAB and STAC, which make final comments before the Board formally adopts the standard.

Once adopted, fisheries have up to three years to come into compliance with a new standard. Should they fail to do so—or should they fall out of compliance with an existing standard—MSC will revoke their certification. Upon revocation, the MSC instructs the fishery to stop selling fish with an MSC label until it is re-certified. Fisheries then have two avenues to pursue re-certification: correction or adjudication. Fisheries may submit a correction plan and corresponding documentation proving that the correction plan has been fully implemented and has addressed the issue that resulted in suspension. Alternatively, if the fishery believes its certification has been improperly suspended, it may challenge the decision and enter adjudication. If the fishery and MSC are unable to reach an agreement, the complaint is submitted to an independent adjudicator who, after hearing arguments from the MSC and the affected fishery,

---

1 See ABOUT US, MARINE STEWARDSHIP COUNCIL.

makes a final decision on suspension. If a fishery fails to correct issues that warrant suspension, the MSC will withdraw the fishery's certification.

In addition to enforcing its private standards, the MSC explicitly builds on and adds a private enforcement mechanism to applicable government fisheries standards. For instance, although the MSC was formed by private organizations and does not operate under government control or with government funding, one of its requirements for achieving certification as a sustainable fishery is compliance with the nonbinding Code of Conduct developed by the United Nations Food and Agriculture Organization. The result is that the private auditors that assess fisheries for MSC often add a private enforcement team to the limited number of government enforcement staff for national and international fisheries standards.

Today the MSC certifies nearly 20%[2] of the wild caught seafood for human consumption in the world, and this percentage is higher in many countries. For instance, roughly 60% of the seafood caught for human consumption from U.S. fisheries is certified or is from fisheries that are under assessment for certification. Firms such as Walmart, which through Sam's Club is one of the largest sellers of fish in the U.S., sell only wild-caught fish from MSC-certified fisheries, and in 2013, McDonald's announced that it would sell MSC-certified fish at all of its U.S. locations. In 2020, the supermarket chain Kroger pledged to source 100% of its wild-caught seafood from MSC-certified fisheries. The adoption of the MSC standards by large retailers also has spawned a mini-industry in the fisheries area, with for-profit and not-for-profit firms providing technical assistance to fisheries attempting to make improvements to satisfy the demands of large buyers for certified fish.

B. Aquaculture

Private standards, certification, and labeling systems also have emerged for aquaculture in recent years with procedures, standards, and implementation systems that roughly track those of the MSC. More decentralized and with greater public oversight than the PEG systems for wild-caught fish overseen by the MSC, aquaculture PEG is driven by organizations including the Monterey Bay Aquarium's Seafood Watch, the Aquaculture Stewardship Council, and Best Aquaculture Practices. The standards for aquaculture focus more on effluent release, animal health, and water quality than do the MSC's standards, but the processes for standards review, certification, and adjudication remain much the same.

---

[2] OUR COLLECTIVE IMPACT, MARINE STEWARDSHIP COUNCIL (2023).

The growth in PEG initiatives that target aquaculture is particularly important because aquaculture accounts for much of the increased seafood consumption that is accompanying global population growth. In 2020, total inland and marine aquaculture production was 97 million tons, and aquaculture accounted for 49% of all global fisheries products.[3] A significant portion of the wild catch is used for fishmeal, however, so aquaculture provides 56% of the global catch intended for direct human consumption. At the global level, approximately 8% of aquaculture production (~7.5 million tons) is certified through third-party inspection each year.

II. Forests

A. The Forest Stewardship Council

The Forest Stewardship Council (FSC) was one of the first certification and standards systems developed to address national and global sustainability concerns. It focuses on forests and remains the leading global forest certification program. In 1984, a coalition of environmental activists planted the seed that would later become the FSC. Troubled by rising fears of deforestation, the activists pressured Burger King to end tropical beef imports by staging a global boycott. By the end of the "Whopper Stop Month" in May 1986, Burger King's sales decreased by 11%, forcing the company's board to cancel a $35 million contract and to pledge only to use domestically produced beef. The success of this campaign encouraged environmental activists to press for further actions by tropical lumber producers and other industries that affect forest health. After a disappointing failure to establish international forest regulations at the 1992 UN Earth Summit at Rio de Janeiro, Brazil (also known as the Rio Convention), in the following year environmentalists and human rights groups joined with several leading wood products companies and traders to establish the FSC.[4]

The basic design of the FSC closely resembles the MSC. The FSC's governing body consists of a wide range of private for-profit and not-for-profit stakeholders, sets standards for well managed forests, and provides a certification based on private third-party verification. Forest products harvested from certified forests are permitted to display the FSC label. The processes followed by the FSC also closely resemble the MSC notice-and-comment approach to standard development. In addition to concerns about whether the FSC standards and enforcement are adequate, a limitation of the FSC is that the bulk of the FSC-certified forests are in temperate

---

[3] *See* TOTAL FISHERIES AND AQUACULTURE PRODUCTION, FOOD & AGRIC. ORG. OF THE UNITED NATIONS, THE STATE OF WORLD FISHERIES AND AQUACULTURE (2022).

[4] *See* OUR HISTORY, FOREST STEWARDSHIP COUNCIL (n.d.).

zones even though the need for systems to ensure sustainable practices is greatest for tropical forests.

B. Other PEG Forest Initiatives

In response to objections about the more stringent requirements of the FSC system, the Sustainable Forestry Initiative (SFI), a competing group with a stronger corporate focus, emerged after the formation of the FSC.[5] In addition, the Programme for the Endorsement of Forest Certification (PEFC) was formed in 1999 to provide a forest certification program for small forest owners.[6] Academic research has warned that when labeling systems have variable stringency and consumers have inadequate information, one may undercut another by loosening the requirements for certification and enabling industry to adopt the least stringent approach. Other research, however, suggests that in some cases labels complement rather than undercut one another.

Forest sustainability systems have been widely adopted around the world. Today, more than 30% of global productive forest area (roughly 363 million hectares) is certified to FSC and PEFC standards. Forestry certifications have also spread rapidly through supply chains. More than 20,000 companies have achieved PEFC Chain of Custody certification. Whether these systems have resulted in more sustainable forest practices and forests is less clear, and critics have pointed to examples of environmental harms and effects on local communities that have occurred in forests that participate in the FSC, SFI, and PEFC programs.

C. Forest Offsets

In recent years, ambitious commitments to reduce greenhouse gases have become the new normal. Thirty-three nations have announced net zero commitments (including the European Union, Canada, and the UK) as well as more than 5,200 companies globally. Some of these reductions may come from direct reductions in emissions, but a substantial fraction will come from "carbon offsets," a market predicted to exceed $200 billion per year by 2050.

Carbon offsets are greenhouse gas emissions reduced or avoided offsite that are then claimed by a party seeking to reduce its own emission levels. For example, a company that has made a net zero promise may continue to emit carbon dioxide in its own operations but claim to meet its target by paying others to plant trees or reduce levels of deforestation. Offsets can also take the form of paying a third

---

[5] See SUSTAINABLE FORESTRY INITIATIVE.

[6] PROGRAMME FOR ENDORSMENT FOREST CERTIFICATION

party to upgrade machinery or switch to more fuel-efficient technologies. Our focus here is on forest offsets.

In principle, offsets make good sense. The costs of reduction opportunities are heterogeneous, and greenhouse gases are global pollutants. It can be more efficient to pay for low-cost reductions offsite than more expensive reductions onsite. Thus in a corporate net zero promise or other voluntary program, offsets allow the business to continue to emit in its own operations while meeting, or claiming to meet, its net zero promise. Given how challenging it is to reduce emissions in many sectors (such as steel, cement manufacturing, or air transport), corporate net zero promises currently rely to a large extent on offsets. Indeed, a large fraction of the Intergovernmental Panel on Climate Change's projections for reducing global greenhouse gas emissions are premised on offsets and other "negative emissions" mechanisms.

Globally, the world is losing forests the size of Switzerland every year. Some see offsets as a powerful tool to battle this rapid deforestation, particularly in the tropics. Offsets provide a way to funnel funds to forest communities, making trees worth more standing than cut down.

Offsets, however, have become a popular target of criticism. Critics denounce them as bogus, greenwashing, and scams. In 2023, a major lawsuit was filed against Delta airlines, alleging that its claims of progress toward net zero were fraudulent because of sham offsets. Even the comedian John Oliver dedicated part of his popular show to attacking offsets. And when John Oliver is going after you, you know things are bad.

The critiques focus on several separate concerns. The most serious is the issue of "additionality." Additionality refers to the requirement that reductions in emissions be *additional* to those that would have otherwise occurred in the absence of the offset regime. For example, if the trees that a company pays to have planted were going to be planted anyway, or the forest an organization promises to conserve was never going to be logged, there are no additional emissions reductions to offset the company's emissions onsite. Issuing offset credits or paying for actions that otherwise would have happened wastes money for no additional benefit. A number of high-profile media stories have exposed offsets that clearly were not additional (such as payments for a pledge by an environmental group not to log in what was revealed to be a bird reserve, probably the last place logging would occur).

A second concern with offsets is "permanence." Carbon stored in forests may be released if the forest burns or is logged. Once that happens, there is no longer any offsetting reduction in emissions or removal. Offsets also face a third concern over "leakage." Leakage arises if the emissions reduced by an offset simply shift to another location. For example, preventing deforestation on one plot of land does no good if the plot next door is deforested instead. As with permanence, counting offsets without adjusting for leakage can provide more reduction credits than are warranted.

A final criticism, unrelated to the quality of the offset, is strategic—that offsets allow polluters to continue to pollute when they should instead be focused on reducing their own emissions. Although the concern takes a variety of forms, the underlying worry is that stopping climate change requires shifting away from fossil fuel use, and allowing polluters to use offsets delays that shift, possibly locking in fossil fuel infrastructure that will continue to pollute in the future.

To address these concerns and bolster credibility, a number of private certification organizations have emerged that provide standards for carbon offsets. The largest is Verra's Verified Carbon Standard, with over 60% of all registered offsets. Under the Verra system, offset providers must pay third-party certifiers who verify whether the standard has been met. To ensure additionality, for example, the standards seek to establish whether the offset project would have otherwise been required or have been financially feasible without the offset payment. Some large companies have created their own standards for offsets. Amazon, Nestle, Unilever, and other major corporations joined together to create the Lowering Emissions by Accelerating Forest finance (LEAF) Coalition. The group has pledged to mobilize $1 billion to reduce 100 million tons of greenhouse gas emissions through forest conservation.

In 2021, in light of the multiple standards to address carbon offsets, the Voluntary Carbon Market Integrity Initiative (VCMI) was launched to address many of these concerns in a more systematic way. In 2023, as of the time of writing, the VCMI issued a rulebook with guidelines that require firms to be transparent about how they are reducing emissions, to disclose an annual greenhouse gas emission inventory, to set emissions reduction targets, and to disclose how much money they are spending on offsets. The system further divides offsets into "silver," "gold," and "platinum," with specific requirements if a firm wants to make a claim in one of these categories. All claims must be verified by a third party.

D. United States Green Building Council

Forests can be protected not only by standards such as FSC that are designed to reduce the *supply* of unsustainable forest products by targeting forest products companies, but also standards that increase the *demand* for sustainably harvested forest products by targeting builders and other users of forest products. An example of a PEG initiative that follows the demand-side approach is the complex set of private standards established by the U.S. Green Building Council's (USGBC), known as the Leadership in Energy and Environmental Design (LEED) standards. The LEED standards influence the design and construction of many buildings in the United States by allowing builders to certify compliance with efficiency and environmental requirements at several levels of stringency (Platinum, Gold, Silver, and Bronze).[7]

The USGBC is an NGO that establishes, modifies, and administers the LEED standards with input from stakeholder groups. The LEED process also involves private verification that is financed in part by certification charges. The USGBC developed and follows private procedural standards much like the MSC standards. Not surprisingly, advising clients on the LEED standards is now an important aspect of the practice of law for many environmental and land use lawyers, and industry groups now lobby the USGBC regarding the content of the LEED standards in ways that might have been directed at Congress or the Environmental Protection Agency several decades ago.

LEED was founded in 1998, and it has experienced rapid growth in recent years. From 2017 to 2021, the number of LEED certified residential buildings grew over 2.5 fold, and the number of certified non-residential buildings nearly doubled. In October 2022, LEED certified its 100,000th project, with the total number of projects collectively accounting for over 11 billion square feet. As we note in Chapter 8, widespread use of green certifications will not always result in better environmental results. Green certifications can create misimpressions and lead to greenwashing, and critics have noted that it is possible to receive LEED recognition for a building that does not use less energy than relevant benchmark buildings so long as other environmental requirements are satisfied.[8]

III. Insurance and Private Finance for Natural Resources

When you think about insurance, the first thing that comes to mind is probably not coral reefs. Insurance is a tool that allows you to spread and pool risk. By paying a small amount of money upfront monthly or annually as a premium, you can protect yourself against catastrophic losses. Insurance is an important tool for risk management, but it also promotes beneficial economic activities that

---

[7] See LEED, U.S. GREEN BUILDING COUNCIL.

[8] See Pamela-Jean N. Driza and Nam-Kyu Park, Actual *Energy and Water Performance in LEED-Certified Educational Buildings*, 6(4) SUSTAINABILITY 227–232 (2013).

might not take place in the absence of insurance. It is also a tool to address disasters and promote resilience. In the case of catastrophic events like hurricanes, floods and tornadoes, insurance can provide resources to individuals and businesses that allow them to rebuild.

As we noted in Chapter 3, in discussions about environmental resources, scholars and policymakers often think about insurance as a tool that can create incentives for better behavior—for policyholders to take better care in exchange for a lower premium. For example, an insurance company could lower the premium for a firm located near the coast and at risk of flooding from storm surges if that firm moves its electrical equipment out of the basement and onto a higher floor. Or, for a homeowner located in an area subject to hurricanes, the insurance company could lower the homeowner's premium for installing bracing around the home to withstand higher winds. At the most extreme end of the spectrum, an insurance company could simply decline to issue a policy if the risk is too high, which might lead people to move away from a risk-prone area. In 2023, several insurance companies stated publicly that they would not write new homeowners' insurance policies in California and Florida because the wildfire and hurricane risks and other extreme weather conditions are too high. In some cases, governments (either at the state or federal level) may choose to step in either to mandate insurance or to subsidize insurance markets if the failure of private markets to provide insurance conflicts with an important policy goal. In other cases, governments may choose not to intervene, if government intervention might induce individuals and businesses to rebuild in areas that will be subject to repeated wildfires or flooding in a warming world.

The most common types of policies for both homeowners and business are *indemnity*-based insurance. In the event of a loss, the policyholder makes a claim, and the insurance company sends out an insurance adjuster to evaluate the amount of the loss. The policyholder receives payment equal to the amount of the loss sustained. This process can be subject to delays and some uncertainty over the repayment amount. These kinds of policies can promote resilience when natural resources are either under threat or are themselves posing the threat to policyholders.

But there is a second kind of insurance policy that is important to understand in the natural resources context—*parametric* insurance. Unlike *indemnity*-based insurance, a parametric policy is triggered by an objective, predetermined event, such as the wind speed as measured on a specific wind gauge, or the level of a river as measured on a specific flood gauge. Once that threshold has been triggered, the policy pays out to the insured immediately in a set amount. There is some *basis risk* involved in parametric insurance, meaning that the payout will not cover the actual losses. However, in contrast to *indemnity*-based insurance, the payout is a set amount, and the payment is triggered by an objective event, so there is no waiting for the loss adjuster to evaluate damages.

Why discuss the ins and outs of parametric insurance in the context of a chapter focusing on natural resources? In an innovative context, a parametric insurance policy was recently underwritten to protect a coral reef off of the coast of Mexico. Why? Because after a busy hurricane season in Mexico in which hotels, residences, and other businesses suffered approximately $8 billion in losses, scientists observed that the hotels and beaches near Puerto Morelos, Mexico suffered less harm and damage than nearby areas. There is a significant coral reef system adjacent to the beaches in Puerto Morelos, and scientists concluded that the reef provided an important ecosystem service: it acted as a natural "sea wall," protecting the upland properties against storm surges from the hurricanes. The coral reef ecosystem also provides habitat for fish and other aquatic life, and therefore aesthetic and recreational services to tourists, generating revenue for the hotels in the area.

The irony, unfortunately, is that while the coral reef protects the beaches and upland properties from storms, the reef itself is subject to damage from those very same storms. Chunks of coral can break off, not only damaging the reef's natural ecosystem, but damaging the reef's ability to protect the coastline from future storms. Having identified this catch-22, The Nature Conservancy began working with the Quintana Roo State Government in Mexico, as well as the Cancun and Puerto Morelos Hotel Owners Association, and the major reinsurer Swiss Re to create a Coastal Zone Management Trust. The purpose of the Trust, which was officially created in 2018, was to build resilience in this area by financing maintenance of the coral reefs and beaches and to purchase an insurance policy to ensure quick restoration of the coral reef in the event of extreme weather events. The Trust ultimately purchased a parametric insurance policy in 2019 that would be triggered by certain wind speed thresholds. If the wind speed thresholds are met, the policy pays out a set amount of money which can then be used to immediately repair the reef. If the wind speed thresholds are not met but the reef still suffers damage, the Trust can act as a self-insurance mechanism to repair the damage. The Nature Conservancy is working actively to build on this model in other parts of the world.

IV. Agriculture

A. Supply Chain Contracting Initiatives That Target Agricultural Products

1. *Retail Food Stores*

Environmental advocacy groups have increased the pressure on retail food stores to reduce the environmental harms of agricultural commodity production, often relying on retail customer interest in more sustainable foods. In turn, retailers often transfer pressure to suppliers to upgrade the sustainability of their supply chains. An example is an initiative by Whole Foods Markets, Inc. to increase the pressure on its agricultural product suppliers:

"We encourage our suppliers to implement systems that are designed to minimize the impact on the environment through their supply chain, the production process, and the products themselves . . . . Where implemented, such systems must track and document the environmental impact, including the use of energy, air emissions, waste, water, pollution, hazardous materials, and recycling. We encourage suppliers to use insights from these systems to pursue initiatives that minimize energy, water waste, and greenhouse gas emissions, and seek ways to use renewable sources of energy. . . . Whole Foods Market expects that suppliers adopt a management system to drive continuous improvement and ensure compliance with applicable laws and this Supplier Code."

These food retailer-driven supply chain initiatives have extended far beyond the organic or health food markets. Procurement requirements by retail food giant Albertsons Cos., Inc. provide an example of the pressure large general retailers are placing on suppliers' agricultural products. In articulating its standards for dairy and meat producers, Albertsons states that "[s]uppliers are expected to. . . Take steps to reduce or eliminate air emissions, water contamination, soil contamination and waste." Also as to meat suppliers, Albertsons indicates that "[s]uppliers are expected to. . .[e]xplore options such as converting methane to fuel, waste to fertilizer and other practices that reduce waste and/or convert waste products into fuel or energy." As to dry goods and oils, the expectation is for suppliers to "[s]trive to reduce or eliminate natural resource destruction, air emissions, water contamination, soil contamination and waste."

It is difficult to assess whether these requirements are enforced or create pressure on producers to reduce water and air emissions. Notice that Whole Foods uses language like "encourage" rather than "require" and "when implemented" rather than "in all cases." Similarly, Albertsons' language is ambiguous as to exactly what the suppliers must do to comply with Albertsons' standards and retain its business. Suppliers are "expected" rather than "required" to act, and what they must do is "take steps" to reduce pollution rather than achieve particular standards.

Nevertheless, retailers like Whole Foods and Albertsons are using these procurement policies to send messages about their expectations to agricultural product suppliers, and in competitive markets suppliers may worry that not meeting these expectations will reduce their chances of contracting with the retailers. In addition, in many cases these retailers' policies are pushing for more than just compliance with government requirements. For instance, Whole Foods' direction to suppliers to "minimize the impact on the environment" of their activities is a requirement not found in environmental laws that apply to agriculture in the United States. Whole Foods' requirement that its suppliers adopt environmental management systems is also well beyond what any federal environmental laws require in the United States, and research suggests that companies with environmental management systems are better environmental performers than those without them.

More research will be needed before it is clear whether and how these private standards are enforced and how their impact compares with government requirements. But it is important to remember that the environmental harms from agriculture have been among the most difficult for federal, state, and local governments to address and that government requirements are often either blocked by lobbying or are not aggressively enforced. So, as always, an important question when evaluating the effectiveness of these systems is: As compared to what viable alternative?

2. *Food Product Companies*

In recent years many environmental NGOs have worked with food producers and retailers to bypass the barriers to government regulation of agricultural companies and farmers. A leading example is the Environmental Defense Fund's (EDF) effort over the last decade to work with Smithfield Foods, the largest pork producer in the United States. The focus of this joint initiative has been on using supply chains to reach farmers who sell commodity crops to Smithfield. These types of PEG agricultural initiatives often combine the prescription, persuasion, and payments tools: the NGO helps the corporate buyer develop requirements for reducing water and air pollution from farms and livestock operations, and the corporate buyer provides farmers with information on best management practices and financial incentives to try them.

These NGO-agricultural company-supply chain initiatives often focus on agricultural nutrient management (fertilizer use) and water pollution (fertilizer and pesticide runoff). For instance, a 2013 Smithfield initiative focused on reducing fertilizer loss and protecting soils on the farms that supply the corn for the animals that farmers sell to the company. With an initial goal of engaging 75% of the farmland used by Smithfield's suppliers, the initiative created financial incentives for farmers that included access to cheaper wheat seed, more efficient non-genetically modified (non-GMO) crops, and long-term biogas contracts to farmers who invest in manure-to-energy infrastructure.[9] These initiatives enabled Smithfield to surpass its 75% goal by 2018, affecting more than 560,000 acres of farmland and incentivizing manure-to-energy projects that aim to capture 86,000 metric tons of methane. By improving manure handling, the project will contribute to meeting climate change goals and reducing the risk of nutrient runoff to waterbodies. The point is not that pork production has small environmental impacts—it does not—but that this PEG initiative bypassed barriers to government action to reduce some of those impacts.

In a similar category, Walmart partnered with EDF on implementing Project Gigaton, which we discussed in Chapter 7. When EDF learned that much of Walmart's scope 3 greenhouse gas emissions are attributable to commodity crops in the firm's supply chain, EDF worked with other nonprofit groups and Walmart to create financial incentives for farmers to reduce fertilizer use and take other steps that would reduce greenhouse gas emissions and non-point water pollution.

In addition to company-NGO partnerships, larger multi-party initiatives have developed to reduce non-point water pollution from agricultural crops. For instance, the Midwest Row Crop Collaborative is an important player in the private governance of nutrient (fertilizer) management. The Collaborative's approach prioritizes the payments and persuasion tools—financial incentives and knowledge sharing—rather than prescriptive mandates in supply chain contracts. Focusing on farmers, the Collaborative increases the economic incentives to farmers to try sustainability solutions that, even if desired by producers, might otherwise be viewed by farmers as risky. Similarly, Field to Market connects producers with economic resources and a national database of sustainable agriculture initiatives to facilitate innovation and sharing of information. With participation from more than 170 member organizations—including major retail firms like PepsiCo, Unilever,

---

[9] *See* DATU RESEARCH, SHARED VALUE: HOW SMITHFIELD FOODS CREATES ENVIRONMENTAL AND BUSINESS BENEFITS THROUGH SUPPLY CHAIN PARTNERSHIPS, ENV. DEF. FUND (2018).

and Walmart—Field to Market has extended its platform to 126 sustainability projects across the US and Canada.[10]

A number of the nutrient management projects developed by commodity trader and food processing companies are motivated by GHG reduction goals (especially the reduction of nitrous oxide emissions resulting from fertilizer overuse); but as we've seen with Walmart's Project Gigaton, these projects often address water quality as well. These initiatives rely largely on payments and persuasion—financial incentives and information to help farmers improve sustainability—and rarely rely on prescriptive or regulatory pressure. When fertilizer optimization and improved nutrient management practices prove profitable and gain farmer support, buyers may expect farmers to continue the nutrient management practices on their own. At that point companies and company-advocacy group initiatives may shift to a more prescriptive approach in the form of supply chain contracting requirements, and this shift may already be underway.

Pesticide companies that are feeling government and private pressure to reduce the water pollution from their products have also entered the private governance space by providing farmers with financial incentives and information to reduce pesticide and nutrient runoff. These efforts are a good example of how corporate sellers of chemicals, not just corporate buyers, sometimes have incentives to push for less harmful use of their products. Critics have noted that the involvement of pesticide companies in these initiatives can create environmental risks. For instance, if these initiatives increase farmers' use of cover crops, this increase could bolster the use of pesticides for "terminating" cover crops before the planting season. In turn, terminating cover crops planted to manage soil erosion and to improve soil fertility with pesticides can be counterproductive if these pesticides disrupt the natural soil microbiomes, adversely affecting the soil's fertility and its ability to sequester carbon.

B. Certification Systems for Agricultural Products

Certification systems for food are among the oldest forms of private governance. For instance, Tim Lytton has demonstrated how kosher and halal standards established centuries ago provided early forms of food safety and environmental governance systems for agricultural products. Today, surprisingly large shares of agricultural products sold in international commerce are subject to modern private certification and standards systems. These systems typically follow the basic organizational and procedural structures of the MSC and FSC. In 2010, approximately 20% of all bananas were

[10] *See* Continuous Improvement Accelerator Project Directory, Field to Market.

sold under a certification scheme, while 8% of global coffee sales were sold as certified and 17% of global coffee was produced as compliant with these standards (in other words, the coffee was not certified, but it met the certification standards). Also in 2010, 7.7% of global tea was sold as certified, and between 2005 and 2010, global tea certification grew by 2000%. Since then, the growth rate of compliant production of these crops has continued to outpace the growth rate of conventionally produced foods. Conventional coffee supply increased, on average, 1.5% per year between 2008 and 2019 while environmentally compliant production has grown, on average, 13–19% each year during the same period. Similar trends have emerged in the banana (0.75% annual growth rate for conventional, 32–35% for compliant) and tea (0.71% annual growth rate for conventional, 35% for compliant) markets.

C. Commodities Roundtables

Many foods and other agricultural products are sold in commodity markets (e.g., corn, wheat, and other grains), and their supply chains are difficult to identify. In other words, a food producer that buys a ton of wheat in a commodity market may have little knowledge of what farm produced the wheat or what farming practices were used to produce it. And the retailers and consumers buying the finished product may know even less. Unlike the pressure that led to the development of the FSC and MSC certification systems, direct retailer or retail customer pressure may have little effect since the food producers, retailers and customers know little about the provenance of the commodities used in the products. To overcome the barriers to development of private governance systems for these types of commodities, environmental groups, retailers, producers, and others have formed commodity roundtables for palm oil, cotton, and other commodities in the last decade. As with many international private governance initiatives, the private activities in this area include governmental involvement in some cases and in others exist alongside similar government initiatives.[11]

Palm oil is a commodity that has been targeted by several PEG initiatives. The development of palm oil plantations has led to the destruction of tropical forests, losses in biodiversity, displacement of local communities, and many other adverse effects. Palm oil is an ingredient in nearly half of all supermarket products, and these products often have blends of many different types of palm oil. In response to these challenges, several NGOs and private sector firms formed the Roundtable on Sustainable Palm Oil (RSPO), which seeks to create an adequate chain of custody and to certify suppliers of palm

[11] For example, the Sustainable Commodity Initiative promotes development of voluntary sustainability initiatives focused on commodity production.

oil. The RSPO uses these information-driven efforts to enable food producers to identify sustainable palm oil and to make claims about their use of sustainable oil in their product labeling. These efforts have reduced recent deforestation, although a 2020 study found that 75% of RSPO-certified land had been recently deforested (deforested since 1990) and that the deforested land served as critical habitat for many endangered animals (orangutans, tigers, and rhinos). In addition, allegations of human rights abuses on RSPO-certified palm oil plantations led the RSPO to form a Human Rights Working Group in 2021. It is too early to tell whether this working group will have positive effects on labor practices at certified palm oil plantations.

Palm oil presents a challenge because different sources are frequently mixed in the finished product. Thus, certifying only a subset of palm oil producers will not necessarily result in large quantities of palm oil supply that are totally from certified sources. Switching the entire supply chain to sustainable palm oil is likewise difficult given the large volumes used around the globe. In response, the World Wildlife Fund started GreenPalm, an initiative that combined environmental certification with a trading system for palm oil. The GreenPalm plan allowed a business to obtain a certificate for every ton of palm oil it can certify as sustainable. Businesses could then trade these certificates to offset unsustainable production. Although this approach resulted in products that have some noncertified palm oil being labeled as certified, it led to the production of one million tons of certified palm oil in the first two years. This resulted in a payment of nine million dollars to producers to stimulate the development of sustainable palm oil production. GreenPalm has since been replaced by a new tradeable credit and certification program, Palm Trace, which was launched in January 2017. An RSPO Palm Trace credit certifies that one ton of sustainable palm oil has been produced, and buyers are then able to purchase the credit and use the RSPO trademark on their products.

Problem Exercise: Palm Oil Certification in Indonesia

Because demand for agricultural commodities is a leading cause of tropical deforestation, the rise of commodity roundtables in the early 2000's created a great deal of excitement and optimism. As described above, roughly 20% of global palm oil production is certified. This requires, among other things, that the land used to produce certified palm oil not be the result of clearing primary or high conservation-value land. Twenty percent seemed an encouraging number, but was the certification meaningful?

In a 2020 peer-reviewed study, researchers sought to answer this question by focusing on palm oil certification in Indonesia from 2009 to 2016. Their findings were disturbing. Certification was having a statistically insignificant impact on deforestation. Certification sounded good for the company's public relations, but it was not making a difference on the ground.

There were two main reasons for this failure. Growers were certifying lands that had already been cleared with little remaining forest. While these lands were protected from further forest loss, there was significant "spillover"—deforestation to make fields for new palm oil planting was taking place on lands that were not certified. Deforestation was simply displaced outside the certified areas.

More recent studies, however, show that deforestation rates in Indonesia have dropped significantly, due in part to changes in the certification process following the revelations that certification was not slowing deforestation.

What changes do you think were made to the palm oil certification process following the finding of no impact that led to such a change in effectiveness?

Cotton is another commodity crop that is produced using large amounts of pesticides and water. Cotton producers, processors, and distributors have responded by developing industry-wide initiatives to overcome the decentralized production of cotton. One example is the Textile Exchange (TE), a non-profit founded to promote organic cotton in the international textile trade. In 2010 TE developed universal standards for fiber manufacturing, sustainable fiber certifications, and textile roundtables. TE also has used persuasion by increasing communication among participants in the supply chain, which has allowed many types of stakeholders to participate in setting and enforcing sustainability standards. TE has also partnered with other NGOs with major stakes in related industries—primarily fashion and textile manufacturing—to amplify the impact of the TE standards. By partnering with organizations that promote sustainability in consumer facing industries, TE has created a sustainable network from the growers through the end-users.

V. Conservation Easements

PEG can play an important role in lands managed for commercial resources such as timber and agricultural products, but it is even more significant for land managed for non-commercial purposes. Land trusts are a uniquely American invention. They preserve and enhance valuable open space, recreation, biodiversity habitat, and other services. Land trusts are private nonprofit organizations found in almost every state, from the Central New York Land Trust and the Colorado Headwaters Land Trust to the Central Arizona Land Trust.

As of 2020, these land trusts protected over 61 million acres of land, larger acreage than states such as Utah or Minnesota, and double the area under protection just a decade earlier. Large national land trust organizations, such as The Nature Conservancy (TNC), have been involved in protecting about three fifths of this land. Although the number of land trusts has leveled off, the amount of land they protect continues to grow.

While land trusts often own large amounts of land in fee simple (meaning outright full ownership), they hold conservation easements—a more limited property right—to far more land. In fact, conservation easements are the principal tool that land trusts use to preserve habitat and open space. A type of property servitude, conservation easements benefit from their ease of creation and flexibility of design. Equally important, easements restricting use cost much less than purchasing full title to the land and can provide significant financial benefit to the landowners.

A conservation easement looks and operates much like a contract. Following negotiation, the landowner and the conservation easement holder sign an agreement detailing restrictions on particular types of uses and activities—what can and cannot occur on the land. The easement is held by a third party, not the landowner. Thus the restrictions stay in place even when ownership of the underlying land parcel changes. State and federal laws regarding conservation easements generally require the holder of the conservation easement benefit to be either a nonprofit organization or a government entity. The easement holder has the right to enforce the easement against the current owner of the land if its terms are violated.

A property owner, for example, could grant TNC an easement preventing all future development of her property. The property owner would still own the land and be able to use the property for fishing, hiking, or just contemplation. TNC, though, owns the right to stop any proposed development on the land.

Alternatively, a conservation easement might allow the underlying property owner to develop the land in limited fashion, but prevent a wide variety of activities that might harm the environmental, aesthetic, historical, or recreational amenities of the land. The easement, for example, might prohibit subdivisions, commercial use, surface mining, or clear-cutting. This mechanism is cost-effective, since land trusts can protect habitat without needing to purchase land outright. Indeed, a number of land trusts are explicitly designed to support agriculture because agriculture maintains open space in a working landscape. The motto of the Texas Agricultural Land Trust for example, is "Keeping Texas Big, Wide and Open."

When a landowner donates a conservation easement, tax savings are often a major incentive. Section 170(h) of the Internal Revenue Code sets out the requirements for conservation easements to qualify for charitable income, gift, and estate tax deductions. The tax savings from donated easements can be significant if the donors have large tax bills. Generally, the value of a conservation easement is the difference between the fair market value of the land before the conservation easement is in place and the land encumbered with the conservation easement. Donors can deduct up to 50% of their income, with certain donors able to deduct 100%, for up to sixteen years. There are additional deductions related to estate and gift taxes, not to mention state income tax deductions and reduced property taxes.

To qualify for federal tax deductions, the easement must:

- Be donated to a qualifying organization (either a nonprofit organization or governmental entity);
- Be perpetual; and
- Have a qualifying conservation purpose.

In practice, the requirement for a qualifying conservation purpose spans a wide breadth, including "the preservation of land areas for outdoor recreation by, or the education of, the general public, the protection of a relatively natural habitat of fish, wildlife, or plants, or similar ecosystem, the preservation of open space (including farmland and forest land) where such preservation is for the scenic enjoyment of the general public. . .or the preservation of a historically important land area or a certified historic structure."[12]

American law has long disfavored perpetual land restrictions because it is impossible to know how future generations will want to utilize land. The Uniform Conservation Easement Act (UCEA), which forms the basis for most state laws regarding such easements, however, presumes that conservation easements are perpetual unless stated otherwise. Under the federal tax code, property owners can obtain tax benefits only if they create perpetual conservation easements.

QUESTIONS AND DISCUSSION

1. The FSC and SFI systems compete to regulate forests around the world. We tend to assume that private competition leads to improved performance.

[12] Internal Revenue Code 170(h).

Do you think competition among certification providers works this way, too? Is it likely to result in more stringent or less stringent standards? Why?

2. What aspects of the agriculture sector make it so difficult for governments to regulate? Why are some PEG systems able to bypass these difficulties? Could they potentially prove more effective than public governance?

3. To what extent do the administrative procedures of certification and standards systems such as MSC and FSC parallel the administrative procedures that federal agencies are required to follow by the Administrative Procedure Act? Why would private systems adopt these procedural standards? Do these private standards include procedures not required by the Administrative Procedure Act? Why?

4. Visit the website for the LEAF Coalition at leafcoalition.org and examine the Resources section. What steps have the coalition partners taken to address the concerns with offsets described in the text? Do you think these will ensure credibility?

5. Why do agricultural commodities pose difficult problems for public and private regulators? Why can't retail grocers rely on supply chain contract provisions with farmers? What aspects of the commodities roundtables for palm oil and cotton address these problems?

6. Government environmental regulatory programs typically target industrial polluters, and they focus on air or water pollution or reducing risks from toxic chemicals or hazardous wastes. The USGBC LEED standards focus on buildings. Do parallel national, state, or local regulatory standards exist for buildings? What are the advantages and disadvantages of shifting the target of governance from industrial polluters to buildings? What are the advantages and disadvantages of focusing on the demand for pollution-emitting products rather than on the emissions generated from supplying the products?

7. The significant amount of land trust conservation in America arises in large part from the federal tax deductions granted to landowners who donate conservation easements to land trusts. In effect, the federal government is using public funds to support the decisions of private individuals and organizations regarding which lands to protect and how to protect them. Is this appropriate? If the government wants to protect private lands from development, would it be better if the government did so directly, in a systematic and planned manner? Is it feasible for governments to do so?

Chapter 12

WATER RESOURCES

A recent issue of *Reader's Digest* features a picture of a glass of water with a question superimposed in bold type: "**How Safe Is Our Water?**" To make sure the interested reader is left with no doubt, an arrow connects a product warning in bright red type to the glass, saying, "MAY CONTAIN: ROCKET FUEL, BIRTH CONTROL PILLS, ARSENIC, AND MORE SHOCKING INGREDIENTS." The same month's cover of the trendy magazine *Fast Company* features a head shot of the movie star Matt Damon. No mention is made of his current starring role or love life. Instead, the attention-grabbing title reads, "Matt Damon and His Global War for Water."

There is likely little overlap in the audiences of *Reader's Digest* and *Fast Company* (indeed, it would be hard to come up with two titles less likely to be bought by the same person), but editors of both clearly think that their readers care about water. And they're right. Few human actions and conditions are truly universal. Some people choose to eat red meat; some eat only fish; some eat no meat at all. But everyone drinks water.

And just as water is central to the well-being of people so, too, is it central to the viability of many private organizations. Start with water quality. Consider for a moment how the beverage giants Coca Cola and Coors Brewing depend on clean water for their products. The entire bottled water market was threatened in the late 1980s when benzene was found in Perrier bottled water. Water quantity is central to industries' business models, as well. Hydropower utilities cannot produce electricity without a reliable source of water held in their reservoirs. Farmers must fallow their fields when water is scarce. And environmental groups understand well that the birds, fish, and plants in natural systems all depend on water.

Governments are equally aware of the dual necessities for provision of adequate water quality and quantity. It is no coincidence that comprehensive and complex laws have been passed to govern water management and treatment. For the past fifty years, the Clean Water Act has prohibited the discharge of pollutants from pipes into navigable waters without a permit. When one of this book's co-authors capsized in a boat in the Charles River of Boston in the 1970s, the fetid waters caused rashes. Today, people happily play in the same waters with no worries at all.

Despite this significant progress, challenges to water quality still remain. Roughly one-third of assessed waterbodies remain out of compliance with water quality standards. Water quality remains an even greater challenge in poorer countries with less investment in infrastructure. Our water laws also generally fail to provide significant protection of water sources. Preventing contamination and development of watersheds requires land use regulation. This is politically difficult and weakly addressed in both the Clean Water Act and the Safe Drinking Water Act. Hence the need for private water governance in both the United States and abroad.

This chapter focuses on two of the policy instruments in the PEG toolkit: Payments and Prescription.

I. Payments

A. The Manhattan Company

We tend to assume that government must be central to providing drinking water but that is a fairly recent development. For much of European history, water was provided by private actors. This was equally true in the early days of New York. At the time of European settlement, residents relied for water on a pond known as the "Collect" (the anglicized pronunciation of the original Dutch name, Kalch-Hook). Over time, the Collect, once the best source of drinking water on Manhattan, had become polluted by the tanneries and slaughterhouses on its banks. Peter Kalm, a Swedish botanist visiting New York in 1748, observed that the well water was so terrible horses from out of town refused to drink it.

To those with an entrepreneurial spirit, the poor maintenance of the public wells and the increasingly disgusting state of the Collect posed not a problem but a business opportunity. People with means began to purchase water from springs outside of town and from deeper wells. The best known of these wells, located near the main settlement, became a popular source of water for tea and other kitchen uses. Water sold from the pump and other sources became generically known as Tea Water. "Tea Water Men" purchased water directly from pump owners and carted it throughout the city for sale in buckets and barrels at a healthy profit. By the middle of the eighteenth century, sale of Tea Water had become the best and dominant source of New York drinking water. It was only available to the wealthy, however, and useless in fighting fires.

New York had been badly hit by yellow fever in 1795, and many blamed the disease on the city's foul water and fouler streets. The state legislature decided to take action. In Albany, Assemblyman Aaron Burr teamed with Alexander Hamilton, recently retired as the nation's first Secretary of the Treasury (and an unlikely Broadway musical star two centuries later) to transform the city's request for public financing powers into a private project. This is the same Aaron

Burr who, nine years later as vice president, shot and killed Hamilton in a duel over insults supposedly made by Hamilton about Burr's candidacy for governor in New York.

In an argument that would echo two centuries later through privatization around the world, Hamilton persuaded the New York state legislature that privatization was preferable to public financing because the service provider would be able to raise the necessary capital and save the city the politically difficult task of raising money through loans and taxes. Nor was this an unreasonable argument. Through the eighteenth and early nineteenth century, urban water projects were generally provided by private enterprise. Municipal authorities were often politically weak and, daunted by the high capital costs and maintenance expenses, city councils were much more comfortable relying on private capital to provide a public service. The corporation's shareholders might reap the profit, but they also bore the risk.

Burr hurried a bill through in just three days. Authorized by the New York state legislature, the Manhattan Company, as the new organization would be called, was limited to $2 million in capital but granted broad-ranging powers. With the power of eminent domain, it was free to select whatever land it thought necessary for construction and any waters it deemed appropriate. The only constraint was that, within ten years of its creation, the Manhattan Company shall "furnish and continue a supply of pure and wholesome water sufficient for the use of all such citizens dwelling in the said city as shall agree to take it on the terms to be demanded by the said company." If this condition were not met, the company would lose its charter.

This was a sweeping range of powers for a water company, but Aaron Burr had more than water supply on his mind. Near the end of the company's charter, a short paragraph gave the Company authority to spend its surplus capital as it saw fit.

Burr didn't care about providing water. He wanted a bank charter, and one with far fewer constraints than other banks of the day. In short order, the company directed only 10% of the Manhattan Company's $2 million toward investments in waterworks. The other money was profitably invested in the banking business. The bank could not ignore water completely, for its existence depended upon satisfying the charter's requirement to furnish and supply "pure and wholesome water." Just how pure and wholesome, though, was a matter of dispute.

Rather than piping in water from more distant but cleaner sources, the Manhattan Company waterworks drew most of its water from the closer, cheaper, more revolting Collect. Doing the bare minimum to maintain its charter, the company laid only twenty-three miles of pipe in its first thirty-two years.

A letter in the New York Commercial Advertiser described the company as "the most outrageous insult ever offended to an afflicted city." Despite unhappy water customers, the company defended its monopoly power over water provision and helped drive Tea Water pumps out of business.

Over time, this water company gave up all pretense and developed into the powerful Chase Manhattan Bank (now known as JP Morgan Chase), undoubtedly the first commercial bank that owes its origins to drinking water. In homage to its origins, the corporate logo of Chase Manhattan is a stylized cross section of a wooden water pipe. Ironically, Burr, the mastermind of the enterprise, ran into financial difficulties, sold his stock in the company, and was forced off the board in 1802.

Only after a large fire caused extensive property damage in 1828 and soon after a severe cholera epidemic killed 3,500 people did the New York City Council step in and take over water management. A permanent Board of Water Commissioners was created and authorized to raise infrastructure capital and condemn land in order to supply water to the city.

The New York story, then, provides an early case where PEG failed and government intervention became necessary. It's a shame this story never made its way into the Broadway musical.

B. Vittel

Waters from the town of Vittel, in the northeast of France, have been celebrated since Roman times, and perhaps earlier.[1] The local geology forces waters from the aquifer 250 feet below the surface to springs where they can be drunk or bathed in. The local minerals dissolved in the waters are reputed to be effective in curing kidney ailments. In the 1880s, a bottling plant allowed waters with the Vittel label to be sold in distant markets and within a decade sales exceeded one million bottles annually. A century later, sales exceeded one billion bottles annually in 70 countries.

France has strong regulations for brands marketed as natural mineral waters. Well-known brands such as Perrier, Evian, and Vittel must be bottled onsite above an identified underground source and composition of the water must remain stable. For Vittel, this meant not more than 4.5mg of nitrates per litre (compared to 50mg

---

1 Case adapted from Daniele Perrot-Maitre, *The Vittel Payments for Ecosystem Services: A "Perfect" PES Case?*, IIED (Sept. 2006).

for tap water) and, of course, no trace of pesticides or other pollutants. Monitoring is rigorous, with over 300 tests conducted daily.

Public confidence in the water's purity is central to brand success. In the late 1980s, traces of benzene were found in Perrier bottles, prompting a global recall. The recall cost the company over $260 million and tumbling market share. Vittel therefore paid very close attention when its scientists warned that the land use in the Vittel catchment area was changing.

Local farmers had traditionally raised hay for free range cattle feed. Intensified agriculture was leading to farmers planting corn crops instead of hay and managing greater density of cattle. This had serious impacts on water quality, with increased pesticide use and nitrates leaching from fertilizer for corn as and cow manure. While not yet a direct threat to the Vittel waters, it seemed only a matter of time before the nitrates and pesticides changed the chemistry of the aquifer.

There was no public governance option available. The farmers were complying with the laws (indeed their intensified agriculture was a direct result of laws seeking to increase yields). Moving to a less threatened region would mean losing the Vittel brand name. Nor, even if they could afford it, would buying the land work. French law strictly controls the sale of farmland for non-agricultural purposes. The only tool left was payment—creating an incentive structure for farmers to change their practices and protect water quality.

In the early 1990s, Vittel partnered with the local agricultural institute in a four year program to understand the impacts of current farming practices on water quality, identify practices that would improve water quality, and examine incentive structures that would change farmers' behavior. Researchers concluded that farmers basically needed to return to their earlier practices—raising hay instead of corn, low density cattle (essentially free range), and stop using chemical fertilizers and pesticides. In short, Vittel needed to persuade farmers to return to the labor-intensive practice they had recently rejected in favor of more capital-intensive agriculture.

Working closely with the farming community, Vittel developed a payment scheme with the following key features:

- Predictability of payments through long-term contracts (18 or 30 years)
- Guaranteed income per hectare for five years
- Subsidies to pay for new farm equipment
- Free labor to apply manure

- Free technical assistance

The program proved effective, with all the farms enrolling and 92% of the sub-basin protected.

The Vittel story presents a clear example of a strategy known as Payments for Ecosystem Services (PES). Landowners are paid for changes in land management that provide valuable ecosystem services to the paying beneficiaries. In this case, farmers were paid to change their crops and methods in order to maintain water quality in the aquifer. Importantly, payments were based not on performance (i.e., whether the water quality actually improved) but on practice (putting in place the required actions). This reflects the negotiation over risk allocation. Vittel bears the risk that their modeling is correct. If the farmers do everything they were asked to do and the water quality worsens, they still get paid.

PES has become an increasingly important policy instrument and often involves purely private actors. The carbon offsets described in Chapter 8 are a growing current example, where companies seeking to offset their greenhouse gas emissions pay for forest conservation or tree planting somewhere else. PES programs operate all over the world. A 2018 study found over 550 programs with annual transactions up to $54 billion.

The next case of water funds provides another example of a growing PES model.

C. Water Funds

Ask most people where their water comes from and you will likely be met with a blank stare. Water comes from the tap, of course, but how it got there is a mystery. In many cities, the reliable source of the clean water lies in the upper watershed, often rural areas distant from the city. As in the Vittel case, development in the watershed can degrade the quality of water. Public governance to address this concern is limited because often the development complies with local land use rules.

Most of the examples in this book are drawn from the United States, but private environmental governance in the form of payments for ecosystem services is an important strategy around the globe, and most certainly in South America. We turn, then, to Quito, Ecuador.[2]

Quito is the largest city in Ecuador. The watershed providing water for Quito is located high above the city in the Andes. The area consists of four different communities in a habitat known as *paramo*,

---

[2] Adapted from Lisa Mandle et al., Green Growth That Works 118 (2019)

a high-altitude region of forests, plains and wetlands dominated by grazing and agriculture.

The water utility for Quito, EMAAP, had long been concerned over the impacts of more intensive agriculture and fire used for agricultural management on water quality, particularly from increased sediments and nutrient pollution. The Nature Conservancy (TNC) was equally concerned about protecting endangered species in the paramo such as the condor, jaguar, and spectacled bear.

In 1997, the two groups founded The Fund for the Protection of Water (FONAG). They donated funds into an endowment that would support FONAG's efforts going forward. In the next few years, other donors joined to address their own concerns and contributed to the fund. A beer company, bottled water company, and Coca Cola joined in order to ensure water quality—their key product ingredient. The electric utility joined out of concern over erosion and sediments filling the reservoir for its hydroelectric facility. The irrigation district contributed to help ensure regular flow of water throughout the year. In a short period of time, the endowment grew from $22,000 to over $12 million.

FONAG invests in the upper watershed, but does not pay landowners directly. Instead, it funds projects that promote the ecosystem services of water purification and erosion control. Fences have been built to keep cattle out of sensitive areas. Funding has been made available to support switching from raising cattle to the less destructive alpaca, to provide seeds for revegetation, and to pay for fire control training, among many others. Landowners agree on the specific investments and sign conservation agreements detailing the in-kind payments.

In all, FONAG has protected and restored over 25,000 hectares in the upper watershed, working with 400 local families in environmental outreach efforts. The board directing FONAG is intentionally diverse, with members from local communities, NGOs, and government.

The Quito model has spurred many other water funds around the globe. Each has a somewhat different governance structure, depending on the local parties and geography, but they all share the basic structure of an endowment funding mechanism managed by a joint governance body and a dedicated group carrying out conservation and management on the ground. Some funds mandate contributions by the local water utility, usually a regular tariff on the water bill, while others are purely voluntary.

TNC reported in 2020 that it had created 43 water funds by working with over 600 partners in 13 countries.[3] The funds are most common in South America but may be found across 4 continents, ranging from the Upper Tana water fund in Nairobi and the Qiandao Lake water fund in China to the Monterrey water fund in Mexico, among many others.

D. BirdReturns

For thousands of years and likely much longer, the Pacific Flyway has provided the route for millions of birds migrating north and south along the West coast. Following the seasons, up to the Arctic for summer breeding and down to warmer climes for the winter, birds would stop during their long trek in marshes and lakes to rest and feed. Many of these stops were in the Central Valley of California. This area used to be full of wet places thanks to the annual runoff from the Sierra Nevada snowpack. Over the last decades, though, the number of birds has declined as has most of the available habitat. Indeed, over 90% of the Central Valley's wetlands have been lost, developed into rich farmland or cities. Yet the remaining birds still need to stop on their routes to rest and feed.

TNC, the same organization that developed water funds in Ecuador and around the world, has played a role in protecting bird habitat in the Central Valley as well. TNC, which is the country's largest non-governmental land trust organization, has long been concerned with the loss of habitat in the Central Valley. National and state wildlife refuges—the public governance option—are critically important but limited in size and not likely to grow. TNC purchasing land seems the obvious answer but that would be too expensive. TNC could only afford to buy a small percentage of the habitat needed to make a real difference across the 4 million acre region.

A little over a decade ago, TNC staff had two brilliant insights. The first is that the birds don't need access to stopover habitat for the entire year. They just need a few weeks when they are migrating. If TNC purchased land, it would not actually be useful to the birds for most of the time. Second, Central Valley rice farmers routinely flood their fields following harvest. This softens the rice straw so it more easily decomposes into the field, providing more fertile soil for the next crop.

Combining these insights, what if TNC were able to negotiate with the farmers, paying them to flood the fields (or keep them flooded) when they were needed? This would provide TNC access to potentially a large area when needed for a fraction of the price were

[3] You can read the details of different water funds in TNC's Water Funds Toolbox at waterfundstoolbox.org.

they to purchase the land. As a *New York Times* article put it, TNC was "using the Airbnb model to protect the environment." The result was BirdReturns and this is how it works.

TNC and its partner non-profit scientific groups determine which areas of land are likely to be suitable for stopover habitat during migration seasons. TNC staff approach farmers and ask if they would be willing to agree to flood some of their fields, if needed. Using a simple app, farmers provide information on the number of acres they are willing to flood, the location, and the periods these would be available. Crucially, they also state how much they are willing to accept to provide this service.

This bidding structure is known as a "reverse auction." Unlike a regular auction where people compete by bidding the price higher and higher to obtain the contested item, whether a painting or a car, in a reverse auction the bids are secret and the price is driven *down* as bidders reveal their lowest willingness to accept.

Once migration season has commenced, TNC relies on data from eBird, an iPhone crowdsourcing platform that collects millions of reports from amateur birdwatchers in the field. This allows the scientists to model where and when the largest groups of birds will likely need to rest during their migration. Combining this with the location and timing offered by the farmers, TNC can identify those locations offering the "biggest bird habitat bang for the buck" and accept those bids. The net result is "pop-up wetlands"—fields flooded just before arriving birds need them and then drained once they have left.

The program has been effective, with reports of pop-up wetlands having 20 times greater density of birds than control fields. Farmers are content because they get paid for a small change in behavior, as well as the satisfaction of helping bird migrations. TNC gains because it can significantly increase the available stopover habitat in a targeted manner and at low cost.

II. Prescription

Prescriptive requirements—thou shalt do this, thou shalt not do that—is the backbone of most public environmental law. While non-state actors cannot impose requirements backed by the power of the state, they can use contractual obligations to achieve a similar effect. We have seen this strategy of supply chain management effectively used in the climate change and toxics contexts, and it can be equally important addressing water pollution.

A. Supply Chain Management

An increasing number of companies now have standard terms in their supplier contracts requiring compliance with applicable law. The hardware chain, Lowe's, has supply chain contract terms that "Vendors must comply with all national and local environmental laws applicable to air emissions, waste handling and disposal, water use, wastewater discharges, and hazardous and toxic substances." The car company, Nissan, similarly requires that its suppliers "Comply with current laws and try to anticipate changes or trends in law in each country or region of operation regarding the prevention of air, water and soil pollution."

On its face, this may not seem much. One would hope that businesses and their suppliers are law-abiding. But these contractual obligations provide an extra layer of enforcement of public law that can become particularly important. Consider, for example, a merger and acquisition situation where a company seeks to purchase or invest in a company that is a supplier to Lowe's. The company will hire lawyers to conduct due diligence and review the inspection and compliance records. Breached supply chain contract covenants to comply with environmental laws can affect the relationship of the supplier with a key buyer, and thus affect the price paid for the supplier.

Such environmental law compliance terms are now common for major companies' supply contracts. The extent to which these actually provide leverage in private negotiations to put pressure on companies to comply with environmental law in regard to water is uncertain and an important area of research.

Some companies go beyond the broad requirement for legal compliance and impose supplier contract terms with additional mandates beyond existing legal rules. The computer hardware firm, Hewlett Packard, for example, includes the following terms in its Supplier Code of Conduct:

> Participant shall implement a water management program that documents, characterizes, and monitors water sources, use and discharge; seeks opportunities to conserve water; and controls channels of contamination. All wastewater is to be characterized, monitored, controlled, and treated as required prior to discharge or disposal. Participant shall conduct routine monitoring of the performance of its wastewater treatment and containment systems to ensure optimal performance and regulatory compliance.

This is a far different type of obligation than simply complying with relevant law. This detailed set of prescriptive requirements necessitates additional investments to business as usual and can be verified by an inspection. It is important to note that this text comes directly from the Responsible Business Alliance Code of Conduct—an international set of social, environmental and ethical industry standards.

Founded in 2004 by leading electronic companies, the Responsible Business Alliance is the world's largest industry coalition dedicated to responsible business conduct in global supply chains in the electronics, retail, auto and toy sectors. It now has more than 500 members with combined annual revenues of greater than $7.7 trillion, directly employing over 21.5 million people, with products manufactured in more than 120 countries. Other members include Amazon, Ford Motor Company, and Samsung.

B. Other Commercial Contracts

Supply chain contracts are not the only types of commercial transactions that have the potential to play important governance roles for water pollution and wetlands protection. Environmental lawyers and managers work on many thousands of commercial transactions every year involving billions of dollars in assets. These transactions range from merger and acquisition and asset purchase agreements, to commercial loans, to commercial real estate sales and leases, to project finance agreements, insurance agreements, and many others.

These agreements also enable environmental advocates to use the existence of environmental reports and other documents generated during commercial transactions in advocacy campaigns and litigation, and to use the contractual requirements between private parties to pressure companies to address water pollution and other environmental issues. Although private contracts are not typically available to the public, the Securities and Exchange Commission requires publicly traded companies to file certain types of material agreements and makes them available in its EDGAR database. This free database is a valuable source of data for environmental lawyers, managers, and advocates.

Each type of commercial transaction has its own core features and documents, but several common aspects play an important role in the way PEG affects water pollution. At the outset of transactions, due diligence seeks to uncover information about the risks associated with the transaction, including environmental risks. Thus agreements often include representations, warranties, and covenants that require disclosure of environmental information.

For instance, in a transaction in which one party is acquiring a factory, a representation states that the "Seller has made available to Buyer copies of all Environmental Reports that are in the possession or within the reasonable control of Seller." The representations in these transactions disclose information about the environmental status of a facility or company, and representations are often accompanied by warranties that provide the counterparty with the opportunity to sue if it later learns that the representations were untrue.

Agreements in commercial transactions also often require a party to provide access to its facilities, documents, and employees for environmental investigations. These inspections often include the Phase I and Phase II investigations we discussed in Chapter 9, but many environmental investigations also include water and air pollution issues that are beyond the scope of typical Phase I and II investigations.

The private disclosures and investigations that occur during commercial transactions differ from government document requests and inspections. The private party can exert economic pressure to access facilities and documents, but it cannot obtain a search warrant or subpoena and cannot impose civil or criminal penalties if the counterparty fails to provide access or disclose information. In addition, the risks that arise from a government investigation include civil and criminal penalties, but in a commercial transaction the principal risks are economic: a party can withdraw from the transaction, demand a price reduction, or in some cases bring a civil suit for breach of contract. Yet these economic incentives can be influential, and in states that have limited environmental enforcement capacity private investigations may be more common and more extensive than government inspections.

Environmental investigations and disclosures are just the first aspect of commercial transactions that can create incentives to reduce water pollution. Commercial agreements often include additional covenants that require ongoing compliance with public and private environmental standards, provisions for monitoring, and requirements to disclose and remediate problems. Many also include provisions that require one party to indemnify the other in the event environmental issues arise in the future, an arrangement that puts one private party in the position of enforcing environmental contractual requirements against the other.

An example involving a commercial lease for a factory demonstrates why commercial transactions can affect water pollution control. At the outset, a landlord that owns a factory and is preparing to lease it to a manufacturing company can anticipate that the new tenant will want to conduct an environmental investigation to ensure that the manufacturing company will not incur liability under government environmental statutes or tort law or suffer financial or reputational harm from discharges of pollutants to waterbodies. The prospective landlord may conduct an environmental study in advance to enable it to manage the issue before the tenant is involved, or the landlord may wait for the tenant to conduct its own investigation.

In addition to environmental investigations, leases and other commercial transactions also often include contract provisions that play a prescriptive or regulatory role. These provisions create incentives for companies to comply with government water pollution requirements and, in some cases, to reduce water pollution even if government requirements do not apply. An example from an agreement available in the EDGAR database is a commercial lease entered into in 2021 by U.S. Data Tech (the tenant) and the owner of a commercial property (the landlord) which includes provisions that regulate not only water pollution that violates government regulatory requirements, but also pollution that the Landlord determines may affect human health, welfare or safety:

> Tenant shall not intentionally or unintentionally discharge, Release or emit, or permit to be discharged, Released or emitted, any material into the atmosphere, ground, sewer system or any body of water, if such material (as reasonably determined by Landlord or any governmental authority) does or may pollute or contaminate the same, or may adversely affect the health, welfare, or safety of persons, whether located on the Demised Premises or elsewhere.

These lease terms put the landlord in the position of a regulator of the tenant's environmental actions. The landlord may have incentives to take an active role if pollution will reduce the value of the property, affect the landlord's reputation, affect the landlord's relationship with its investors or lenders, or trigger government enforcement actions against the tenant or the landlord. The overall result of the lease is that the tenant has incentives to investigate in advance the status of water pollution at the facility and the facilities' pollution control systems, and to reduce water pollution during the term of the lease. In turn, the landlord has the legal authority and incentive to play an enforcement role—to monitor the tenant's behavior and to enforce the lease's requirement for the tenant not only to remain in compliance with government requirements, but also to avoid pollution that may harm human health.

In addition to commercial real estate leases for factories, many other types of transactions—including mergers and acquisition and asset purchase agreements, commercial loans, commercial real estate sales, project finance agreements, insurance, and others—

create the legal authority and incentives for investigating, monitoring, and controlling water pollution. As with commercial leases, these transactions often complement the work of government environmental agencies by placing private parties in monitoring and enforcement roles for government environmental requirements. In many cases the language of these agreements and the incentives of the parties that enter into them extend well beyond simple compliance, resulting in the creation and enforcement of private environmental standards.

These agreements do not always increase incentives for environmental protection, of course. For instance, an asset sale agreement may transfer a polluting factory to a company that has less visibility, less oversight, or less resources to pay for compliance. Or a commercial loan may increase financial pressure on factory managers to reduce investments in environmental compliance. The key lesson is that environmental lawyers, managers, and advocates should be aware of the role that commercial transactions play in affecting the environmental incentives of companies and account for these forms of PEG when thinking about water pollution and other important environmental issues.

QUESTIONS AND DISCUSSION

1. Imagine that your law firm has been hired to conduct due diligence reviews for Hewlett Packard's corporate procurement department. How would you conduct the review for the company's five most important suppliers? When you show up at a facility in Thailand or Mexico, what information do you ask for? Whom do you seek to meet? How would you verify whether the supplier has sought "opportunities to conserve water"?

What do you think happens (or should happen) if the supplier cannot demonstrate it is satisfying these requirements? Should the audit results be made public so that the corporate commitments can be publicly confirmed?

2. Perhaps surprisingly, the bottled water market is fairly recent. A century ago, bottled water was mainly sold in pharmacies for medical purchases. When Perrier burst on the U.S. market in the late 1970s, there was very little relevant regulation and none by the EPA (it was lightly regulated as a drink by the Food and Drug Administration). Realizing that the purity of bottled water was central to its brand, companies urged their trade association, the International Bottled Water Association (IBWA) to create voluntary standards.

These were published in 1982 as the Code of Practice and followed by all the major companies. IBWA actively lobbied state and federal regulators to use the Code of Practice as the basis for their own bottled water regulations. This proved so effective that the Code of Practice was effectively made unnecessary because of laws that were modeled on the Code of Practice.

It seems unusual for a company or trade association to push the government to adopt *more stringent* standards. A common strategy of PEG is to use voluntary standards to forestall regulation. Why do you think IBWA and its member companies welcomed regulation? What risks were they trying to address by shifting from PEG to public environmental governance? Can you think of other sectors where this has occurred?

3. CDP (formerly called The Carbon Disclosure Project) was created in 2000 to develop a common reporting standard for companies to disclose their climate impact at the request of their investors. Over the past two decades, it has become a global leader in corporate disclosure and has expanded its mission to reporting on deforestation and water management. Indeed, it changed its name to CDP in order to demonstrate its coverage beyond climate. Nonetheless, climate concerns drive much of its activities. In what specific ways do you think climate change is related to water security?

CDP has developed an extensive web-based Water Security Questionnaire for companies broken down by sector and subsector (e.g., agriculture and cocoa production). You can review the questionnaire by doing an internet search for "CDP Water Security Questionnaire." Are you surprised at the level of detail required? Do you think most companies would be able to provide the answers?

4. The strategy of payments for ecosystem services (PES) worked well for TNC with water funds and Vittel for ensuring water quality. In each case, landowners were paid to manage their environment for improved service provision. It proved a better investment for the beneficiaries to pay for "green infrastructure" than for "grey infrastructure" such as water treatment plants. What do you think are the most important factors to ensure successful watershed PES? Can you think of situations where PES would likely be an ineffective strategy?

5. What does the history of New York City's drinking water tell us about today? Tea Water and the Manhattan Company were some of America's earliest private providers of drinking water and their brief lives showed clearly the limits of early private governance.

What do you think about private management of water infrastructure today? Several Senators have proposed legislation making it more difficult for companies to own water utilities. What dangers might private ownership pose?

Can you think of reasons why private management might actually be preferable to public ownership? What forms of governance might be imposed on top of private ownership to ensure responsible governance?

6. Research by political scientists in 2015 provided an unexpected insight into one potential benefit of private over public ownership of water infrastructure.[4] The study looked at compliance by both public and private utilities under the Clean Air Act and Clean Water Act. They found that government owned utilities were *more likely* to violate environmental laws

---

[4] David M. Konisky and Manuel P. Toedoro, *When Governments Regulate Governments*, 60 AMERICAN JOURNAL OF POLITICAL SCIENCE 559 (July 2016).

than privately owned utilities and *less likely* to be punished for their noncompliance. Public water utilities committed 14% more Safe Drinking Water Act health violations and were 29% more likely to commit monitoring violations than privately owned water utilities.

How can you explain this finding? Why might it be more difficult to enforce environmental laws against public rather than private water utilities?

7. Why would a company that sells chicken to a retail grocery chain insist on water pollution restrictions in its supply chain contracts? Should environmental advocacy groups encourage the use of these provisions in supply chain contracts? How can they ensure that companies enforce these provisions?

SUPPLEMENTAL READING

Kenneth W. Abbott & Duncan Snidal, *Hard and Soft Law in International Governance*, 54 INTERNATIONAL ORGANIZATION 421 (2000)

Graeme Auld et al., *The New Corporate Social Responsibility*, 33 ANNUAL REVIEW OF ENVIRONMENT & RESOURCES 413 (2008)

Stephen M. Bainbridge, *Making Sense of the Business Roundtable's Reversal on Corporate Purpose*, 46 JOURNAL OF CORPORATION LAW 285 (2020)

David P. Baron, *Corporate Social Responsibility and Social Entrepreneurship*, 16 JOURNAL OF ECONOMICS & MANAGEMENT STRATEGY 683 (2007)

David P. Baron, Private Politics, *Corporate Social Responsibility and Integrated Strategy*, 10 JOURNAL OF ECONOMICS & MANAGEMENT STRATEGY 7 (2001)

Tim Bartley, *Institutional Emergence in an Era of Globalization: The Rise of Transnational Private Regulation of Labor and Environmental Conditions*, 113 AMERICAN JOURNAL OF SOCIOLOGY 297 (2007)

Steven Bernstein & Benjamin Cashore, *Can Non-State Global Governance Be Legitimate? An Analytical Framework*, 1 REGULATION & GOVERNANce 347 (2007)

John C. Coffee Jr., *The Future of Disclosure: ESG, Common Ownership, and Systematic Risk*, 2021 COLUMBIA BUSINESS LAW REVIEW 602

Cary Coglianese, *Policies to Promote Systematic Environmental Management*, *in* REGULATING FROM THE INSIDE: CAN ENVIRONMENTAL MANAGEMENT SYSTEMS ACHIEVE POLICY GOALS? 181 (Cary Coglianese & Jennifer Nash eds., 2001)

Mark A. Cohen & Michael P. Vandenbergh, *The Potential Role of Carbon Labeling in a Green Economy*, 34 ENERGY ECONOMICS S53 (2012)

Madison Condon, *Externalities and the Common Owner*, 95 WASHINGTON LAW REVIEW 1 (2020)

Quinn Curtis, Jill Fisch & Adriana Z. Robertson, *Do ESG Funds Deliver on Their Promises?*, 120 MICHIGAN LAW REVIEW 393 (2021)

Jason Czarnezki, Joshua Ulan Galperin & Brianna M. Grimes, *Sustainable Business Law & The Role of ESG Lawyers*, 32 NYU ENVIRONMENTAL LAW J. ___ (2023)

Jason Czarnezki & Colin Myers, *Sustainable Business Law? The Key Role of Corporate Governance and Finance*, 51 ENVIRONMENTAL LAW 991 (2022)

Jason Czarnezki, Katrina Fischer Kuh & K. Ingemar Jönsson, *Crafting Next Generation Eco-Label Policy in Environmental Law*, 48 ENVIRONMENTAL LAW 409 (2018)

David A. Dana & Janice Nadler, *Regulation, Public Attitudes, and Private Governance*, 16 JOURNAL OF EMPIRICAL LEGAL STUDIES 69 (2019)

DATU RESEARCH, SHARED VALUE: HOW SMITHFIELD FOODS CREATES ENVIRONMENTAL AND BUSINESS BENEFITS THROUGH SUPPLY CHAIN PARTNERSHIPS, ENV. DEF. FUND (2018)

DANIEL DIERMEIER, REPUTATION ANALYTICS: PUBLIC OPINION FOR COMPANIES (Univ. of Chicago Press, 2023)

JOHN C. DERNBACH, MATTHEW BOGOSHIAN & IRMA RUSSELL, SUSTAINABILITY ESSENTIALS: A LEADERSHIP GUIDE FOR LAWYERS (ABA Press, 2022)

THOMAS DIETZ, DECISIONS FOR SUSTAINABILITY: FACTS AND VALUES (Cambridge Univ. Press, 2023)

Einer Elhauge, *Sacrificing Corporate Profits in the Public Interest*, 80 N.Y.U. LAW REVIEW 733 (2005)

Daniel C. Esty & Nathan de Arriba-Sellier, *Zeroing in on Net-Zero: From Soft Law to Hard Law in Corporate Climate Pledges*, 94 UNIVERSITY OF COLORADO LAW REVIEW 635 (2023)

Daniel C. Esty & Quentin Karpilow, *Harnessing Investor Interest in Sustainability: The Next Frontier in Environmental Information Regulation*, 36 YALE JOURNAL ON REGULATION 625 (2019)

Daniel C. Esty, *Environmental Protection in the Information Age*, 79 NYU LAW REVIEW 115 (2004)

Milton Friedman, *The Social Responsibility of Business Is to Increase Its Profits*, THE NEW YORK TIMES MAGAZINE (Sept. 13, 1970)

Joshua U. Galperin, *Environmental Governance at the Edge of Democracy*, 39 VIRGINIA ENVIRONMENTAL LAW Journal 70 (2021)

Joshua U. Galperin, *Board Rooms and Jail Cells: Assessing NGO Approaches to Private Environmental Governance*, 70 ARKANSAS LAW REVIEW 403 (2019)

Jonathan M. Gilligan & Michael P. Vandenbergh, *A Framework for Assessing the Impact of Private Climate Governance*, 60 ENERGY RESEARCH & SOCIAL SCIENCE 101400 (2020)

Ash Gillis, Michael P. Vandenbergh, Kaitlin Toner Raimi, Alex Maki & Ken Wallston, *Convincing Conservatives: Private Sector Action Can Bolster Support for Climate Change Mitigation in the United States,* 73 ENERGY RESEARCH & SOCIAL SCIENCE 101947 (2021)

Neil Gunningham, Robert A. Kagan & Dorothy Thornton, *Social License and Environmental Protection: Why Businesses Go Beyond Compliance*, 29 LAW & SOCIAL INQUIRY 307 (2004)

JAMES HANSEN, SABINE MARX & ELKE WEBER, THE ROLE OF CLIMATE PERCEPTIONS, EXPECTATIONS, AND FORECASTS IN FARMER DECISION MAKING: THE ARGENTINE PAMPAS AND SOUTH FLORIDA. INTERNATIONAL RESEARCH INSTITUTE FOR CLIMATE PREDICTION (IRI), PALISADES, NY: TECHNICAL REPORT 04–01 (2004)

Virginia E. Harper Ho, *"Enlightened Shareholder Value": Corporate Governance Beyond the Shareholder-Stakeholder Divide*, 36 JOURNAL OF CORPORATION LAW 59 (2010)

Oliver Hart & Luigi Zingales, *Companies Should Maximize Shareholder Welfare Not Market Value*, 2 JOURNAL OF LAW, FINANCE, AND ACCOUNTING 247 (2017)

MICHAEL A. HELLER & JAMES SALZMAN, MINE! HOW THE HIDDEN RULES OF OWNERSHIP CONTROL OUR LIVES (DOUBLEDAY 2021)

Dennis D. Hirsch, *A Holistic Policy Agenda to Promote Green Business: Reflexive Law Fills the Gap*, 42 ENVIRONMENTAL LAW REPORTER 10228 (2012)

Dennis D. Hirsch, *Green Business and the Importance of Reflexive Law: What Michael Porter Didn't Say*, 62 ADMINISTRATIVE LAW REVIEW 1063 (2010)

Heather Hughes, *Enabling Investment in Environmental Sustainability*, 85 INDIANA LAW JOURNAL 597 (2010)

THE INVESTMENT INTEGRATION PROJECT (TIIP), *APPROACHING THE TIPPING POINT: RECOMMENDATIONS FOR BUILDING THE MARKETPLACE FOR SYSTEM-LEVEL INVESTING* (2022)

Robert B. Jackson, Jessica Owley & James E. Salzman, *Mineral Estate Conservation Easements: a New Policy Instrument to Address Hydraulic Fracturing and Resource Extraction,* 47 ENVIRONMENTAL LAW REPORTER 10112 (2017)

Brayden G. King & Sarah A. Soule, *Social Movements as Extra-Institutional Entrepreneurs: The Effect of Protest on Stock Price Returns*, 52 ADMINISTRATIVE SCIENCE QUARTERLY 413 (2007)

Hajin Kim, Joshua Macey & Kristen Underhill, *Does ESG Crowd Out Support for Public Regulation?*, SSRN working paper available at https://papers.ssrn.com/sol3/papers.cfm?abstract_id=4521781

Markus Kitzmueller & Jay Shimshack, *Economic Perspectives on Corporate Social Responsibility*, 50 JOURNAL OF ECONOMIC LITERATURE 51 (2012)

Carolyn Kousky & Sarah E. Light, *Insuring Nature*, 69 DUKE LAW JOURNAL 323 (2019)

Louis G. Leonard, *Under the Radar: A Coherent System of Climate Governance, Driven by Business*, 50 ENVIRONMENTAL LAW REPORTER 10547 (2020)

SANFORD LEWIS & DIANE HENKELS, GOOD NEIGHBOR AGREEMENTS: A TOOL FOR ENVIRONMENTAL AND SOCIAL JUSTICE (1996)

Sarah E. Light & Christina P. Skinner, *Banks and Climate Governance*, 121 COLUMBIA LAW REVIEW 1895 (2021)

Sarah E. Light, *The Law of the Corporation as Environmental Law*, 71 STANFORD LAW REVIEW 137 (2019)

Sarah E. Light & Michael P. Vandenbergh, *Private Environmental Governance in* ENVIRONMENTAL DECISION MAKING, ENCYCLOPEDIA OF ENVIRONMENTAL LAW 253 (Robert Glicksman & LeRoy Paddock eds., 2016)

Sarah E. Light, *The New Insider Trading: Environmental Markets within the Firm*, 34 STANFORD ENVIRONMENTAL LAW JOURNAL 3 (2015)

Sarah E. Light & Eric W. Orts, *Parallels in Public and Private Environmental Governance*, 5 MICHIGAN JOURNAL OF ENVIRONMENTAL & ADMINISTRATIVE LAW 1 (2015)

Jonathan Lipson, *Promising Justice: Contract (as) Social Responsibility*, 2019 WISCONSIN LAW REVIEW 1109

Thomas P. Lyon & A. Wren Montgomery, *The Means and End of Greenwash*, 28 ORGANIZATION & MANAGEMENT 223 (2015)

Thomas P. Lyon & John W. Maxwell, *Corporate Social Responsibility and the Environment: A Theoretical Perspective*, 1 REVIEW OF ENVIRONMENTAL ECONOMICS & POLICY 1 (2008)

TIMOTHY D. LYTTON, KOSHER: PRIVATE REGULATION IN THE AGE OF INDUSTRIAL FOOD (2013)

Alex Maki, Emmett McKinney, Michael P. Vandenbergh, Mark A. Cohen, & Jonathan M. Gilligan, *Employee Energy Benefits: What Are They and What Effect Might They Have on Employees?* 12 ENERGY EFFICIENCY 1065–1083 (2019).

Errol Meidinger, *Private Import Safety Regulation and Transnational New Governance*, *in* IMPORT SAFETY: REGULATORY GOVERNANCE IN THE GLOBAL ECONOMY 233 (Cary Coglianese, Adam M. Finkel & David Zaring eds., 2009)

Eric W. Orts, *Climate Contracts*, 29 VIRGINIA ENVIRONMENTAL LAW JOURNAL 197, 228–31 (2011)

ALAN R. PALMITER, CAPITALISM HEAL THYSELF 1 (2021), available at https://papers.ssrn.com/sol3/papers.cfm?abstract_id=3940395

Michael E. Porter and Mark R. Kramer, *Creating Shared Value*, HARVARD BUSINESS REVIEW (Jan.–Feb. 2011)

Matthew Potoski & Aseem Prakash, *Green Clubs and Voluntary Governance: ISO 14001 and Firms' Regulatory Compliance*, 49 AMERICAN JOURNAL OF POLITICAL SCIENCE 235 (2005)

PRINCIPLES FOR RESPONSIBLE INVESTING, UNIVERSAL OWNERSHIP: WHY ENVIRONMENTAL EXTERNALITIES MATTER TO INSTITUTIONAL INVESTORS (2011)

Tracey M. Roberts, *The Rise of Rule Four Institutions: Voluntary Standards, Certification and Labeling Systems*, 40 ECOLOGY LAW QUARTERLY 107 (2013)

CHARLES F. SABEL & DAVID G. VICTOR, FIXING THE CLIMATE: STRATEGIES FOR AN UNCERTAIN WORLD 693 (Princeton Univ. Press, 2022).

JAMES SALZMAN & BARTON THOMPSON, JR, CONCEPTS AND INSIGHTS IN ENVIRONMENTAL LAW, (Foundation Press, 2018, 5th ed.)

JAMES SALZMAN, DRINKING WATER: A HISTORY (Overlook Press, 2017, 2nd ed.)

James Salzman, *Teaching Policy Instrument Choice in Environmental Law: The Five P's*, 23 DUKE ENVIRONMENTAL LAW AND POLICY FORUM 363 (2013)

James Salzman, *Creating Markets for Ecosystem Services: Notes from the Field*, 80 NYU LAW REVIEW 870 (2005)

James Salzman, *Informing the Green Consumer: The Debate Over the Use and Abuse of Environmental Labels*, JOURNAL OF INDUSTRIAL ECOLOGY (Summer 1997)

William Savitt & Aneil Kovvali, *On the Promise of Stakeholder Governance*, 106 CORNELL LAW REVIEW 1881 (2021)

Amanda Shanor & Sarah E. Light, *Greenwashing and the First Amendment*, 122 COLUMBIA LAW REVIEW 2033 (2022)

THE SHAREHOLDER COMMONS, CLOSING THE ENGAGEMENT GAP: TWO NEW CASE STUDIES ON CLIMATE CHANGE & AMR (2022)

Judd F. Sneirson, *The Sustainable Corporation and Shareholder Profits*, 46 WAKE FOREST LAW REVIEW 541 (2011)

ARAME TALL ET AL., ENABLING PRIVATE INVESTMENT IN CLIMATE ADAPTATION AND RESILIENCE: CURRENT STATUS, BARRIERS TO INVESTMENT AND BLUEPRINT FOR ACTION, WORLD BANK REPORT (2021)

Khan M.R. Taufique, Kristian S. Nielsen, Thomas Dietz, Rachael Shwom, Paul C. Stern & Michael P. Vandenbergh, *Revisiting the Promise of Carbon Labeling*, 12 NATURE CLIMATE CHANGE 132 (2022)

Unilever (2019). Unilever Issues First Ever Green Sustainability Bond. Available online at: https://www.unilever.com/news/press-releases/2014/14-03-19-Unilever-issues-first-ever-green-sustainability-bond.html

U.S. ENVIRONMENTAL PROTECTION AGENCY, 2021 BIENNIAL REPORT SUMMARY RESULTS: 2021 (2021)

U.S. ENVIRONMENTAL PROTECTION AGENCY, ATTACK ON HAZARDOUS WASTE THE CHALLENGE OF THE 1980'S, *National Service Center for Environmental Publications* (1980)

Michael P. Vandenbergh et al., *Model Environmental Supply Chain Contracts* in CONTRACTS FOR RESPONSIBLE AND SUSTAINABLE SUPPLY CHAINS: MODEL CLAUSES, LEGAL ANALYSIS, AND PRACTICAL DISCUSSION (American Bar Association, David Snyder & Susan Maslow, eds., 2023)

Michael P. Vandenbergh, *Disclosure of Private Environmental Governance Risks,* 63 WILLIAM & MARY LAW REVIEW 1695 (2022)

Michael P. Vandenbergh & Patricia Moore, *Environmental Governance by Contract: The Growth of Environmental Supply Chain Contracting*, 12 MICHIGAN JOURNAL OF ENVIRONMENTAL & ADMINISTRATIVE LAW 1 (2022)

Michael P. Vandenbergh & Bruce Johnson, *The Role of Private Environmental Governance in Climate Adaptation*, 3 FRONTIERS IN CLIMATE 715368 (Sept. 2021)

Michael P. Vandenbergh & Benjamin Raker, *Private Environmental Governance and the New Private Advocacy,* 32 NATURAL RESOURCES & ENVIRONMENT 45 (Fall 2017)

MICHAEL P. VANDENBERGH & JONATHAN M. GILLIGAN, BEYOND POLITICS: THE PRIVATE GOVERNANCE RESPONSE TO CLIMATE CHANGE (2017)

Michael P. Vandenbergh, *Private Environmental Governance,* 99 CORNELL LAW REVIEW 129 (2013)

Michael P. Vandenbergh, *The New Wal-Mart Effect: The Role of Private Contracting in Global Governance,* 54 UCLA LAW REVIEW 913 (2007)

Michael P. Vandenbergh, *The Private Life of Public Law,* 105 COLUMBIA LAW REVIEW 2029–2076 (2005)

David Vogel, *The Private Regulation of Global Corporate Conduct: Achievements and Limitations,* 49 BUSINESS & SOCIETY 68 (2010)

Andrew Winston, Elizabeth Doty & Thomas Lyon, *The Importance of Corporate Political Responsibility,* MIT SLOAN MANAGEMENT REVIEW (Oct. 24, 2022)

Alan Wiseman, *Information and Political Institutions,* 25 JOURNAL OF THEORETICAL POLITICS 301 (2013)

TABLE OF CASES